Skateboarding and Religion

"Paul O'Connor's *Skateboarding and Religion* is an exhilarating book; it is simultaneously a challenge to all mainstream ideas about religion and religious experience, and a rich and nuanced study of the religious dimensions of skateboarding. O'Connor interrogates the origin myths of the sport, sketches portraits of the saints and mystics of the skateboarding world, profiles a diverse group of skaters from different geographical and religious contexts and offers a sophisticated reading of the aesthetics and symbolism used by skateboarders. The sacred spaces of the sport, the impulse for pilgrims to visit and engage with these sites, and the ritual dimensions of their activities are chronicled, and the text is enriched by images that make the phenomena discussed comprehensible for the reader. This original and joyous study is a major contribution to the study of contemporary religious and spiritual trends."

—Carole M. Cusack, *Professor of Religious Studies,*
University of Sydney, Australia

"Through a sociologist's nuanced analysis and a skateboarder's commitment to the daring, Paul O'Connor makes clear the often surprising religiosity that underpins skateboarding's culture, industry, and even the act itself. This groundbreaking book will convince even the most stubbornly secular reader that skateboarding is something especially sacred in the modern world."

—Christian N. Kerr, *Writer and Editor at Jenkem Magazine*

"At once insightful, questioning and provocative, Paul O'Connor's *Skateboarding and Religion* takes two seemingly disconnected phenomena and shows how they are intrinsically inter-related. This massively original study will be of interest to anyone concerned with the sociology of skateboarding and other youthful practices. Very highly recommended."

—Iain Borden, *Professor of Architecture and Urban Culture,*
University College London, UK

Paul O'Connor

Skateboarding and Religion

palgrave
macmillan

Paul O'Connor
Lingnan University
Tuen Mun, Hong Kong

ISBN 978-3-030-24856-7   ISBN 978-3-030-24857-4   (eBook)
https://doi.org/10.1007/978-3-030-24857-4

Cover illustration: © Zered Bassett by Ryan Allan Design © Fatima Jamadar

This Palgrave Macmillan imprint is published by the registered company Springer Nature Switzerland AG.
The registered company address is: Gewerbestrasse 11, 6330 Cham, Switzerland

For the Pious

Acknowledgements

I originally hatched the plan to write a book about religion and skateboarding at the age of 14. In the 30 years since that time, the seed of that nascent idea has been tended and nurtured by more people than I can possibly recall. I have learnt from skateboarders and academics alike, I have observed, and I have discussed with the help of so many.

One early exploration in this topic was previously published as an article on sacred places in skateboarding. Chapter 7 is derived in part from an article published in *Sport in Society* (2017) copyright Taylor & Francis, available online: http://www.tandfonline.com/10.1080/17430437.2017.1390567.

The book also draws on research funded by a faculty seed grant from Lingnan University, and a Social Sciences faculty research grant on ethnicity and gender in Hong Kong skateboarding.

My first thanks must go to my academic skateboard peers: chiefly Professor Iain Borden who has always generously encouraged and supported my work and has become a terrific friend along the way. Iain's work is a touchstone for all skateboard academia, and I am humbled and honoured to have had his help throughout. Professor Brian Glenney has also been an enthusiastic supporter and inspiration as well as cherished friend. I recall fondly thrashing out ideas for this text as we skated in the summer of 2018 through the streets of London. Valuable encouragement and expert advice have come from Dr Sander Hölsgens, another trusted friend and exemplary colleague. We spoke at length throughout this project, either while skateboarding in Hong Kong or chatting over Skype.

I am also grateful to my academic peers at Lingnan University where the bulk of this manuscript was written. My colleagues Roman David, Annie Chan, David Phillips, Ray Forrest, Chen Hon Fai, and Stefan Kühner have all been generous with their time and support. Special thanks go to Peter Baehr whose intellectual rigour has always inspired me, Grace Wong whose care and attention to detail have been tremendously valuable, and Esra Burak Ho who more than any other provided a sympathetic ear to both my frustration and elation throughout the project. I must also thank Gordon Mathews and Joseph Bosco in Anthropology at the Chinese University of Hong Kong where my research agenda on skateboarding initially began.

My enduring thanks go to the production staff at Palgrave. I am indebted to Sharla Plant for taking a chance on what, to many publishers, appeared a bizarre academic exercise in suturing skateboarding and religion together. Her support and polished expertise has been deeply appreciated. Similarly the production guidance I have received from Poppy Hull has been impeccable, with clear guidance and sensitivity for my demands about the exceptionalism of publishing work on skateboarding.

The bulk of what is addressed in the following pages is a direct result of conversations and contributions from the following people; their help has been instrumental in piecing this ambitious work together and I am deeply grateful to them all: Ajiem, Anthony Tafuro, Barry Peak, Becky Beal, Candy Jacobs, Chris Bird Culotta, Chris Giamarino, Chris Grosso, Chris Lawton, Chris Magee, Chris Sedition, Christian Cooper, Christian Greiffenhagen, Clara Fok, Clifton Evers, Dani Abulhawa, David Thornton, David Chu Kin Tung, Depth Leviathan Dweller, Dinia Sahana, Gavin Farley, Glen Wood, Gregory Snyder, Guru Khalsa, Haadii, J. Grant Brittain, Jake Johnson, James Callahan, Jeff Grosso, Jud Heald, Kristin Ebeling, Kyle Beachy, Lantian D., Luke Cianciotto, Marc McKee, Marcus Hartopp, Matt Huddleson, Mike Hill, Neftalie Williams, Patrik Wallner, Ryan Allan, Scott Laderman, Shari White, Shaun Hover, Sonal Chandra, Sophie Friedel, Tara Jespen, Ted Barrow, Thom Callan, Tim Ruck, Yusef Alahmad, and Zered Bassett.

Special thanks to Hong Kong's superb skateboarding scene, which is vibrant, welcoming, and loving. I have been fortunate to have had the help and friendship of so many skateboarders in Hong Kong and have always been grateful to have this second family. To mention just a few who have helped out along the way, Alex Abagian, Calvin Tong, Chris Bradley, Chun Chai, Dani Bautista, Kit Lau, Margielyn Didal, Mat Morgan, Mike Gallogly, Mouse Shingyang Tong, Neris Magar, Owen Yu, Piet Guilfoyle, Tat Tat, Ting, Tristan Modena, and many more. Especially important in the Hong Kong input of writing this book was support from Anthony Claravall, Brian Siswojo, and Warren Stuart.

Too many wonderful conversations along the way, but in addition to the names mentioned, I must express thanks to Tim Sedo who importantly asked 'so what?,' to Carole Cusack who generously provided feedback on my writing, to Daniel Grano for his superb comments on the manuscript, and to James Jarvis who was always able to provide thoughtful inspiration.

Lastly it is my family who require the most thanks and who know most about the marathon process of writing this book. Hours spent watching H-Street videos with Mark Russell helped form the foundation for this book decades ago. I am grateful to my sister Mickey for indirectly introducing me to Powell Peralta. I must also thank my parents Mike and Di for always supporting my passion for skateboarding, and for somehow always knowing just how important it was to me. My three wonderful sons Sennen, Perec, and Liran have provided love and inspiration throughout. Hanging out with these lively and fascinating children has been a welcome distraction throughout the project. Lastly, my wife Sarah has been a valuable sounding board whilst writing and I am dearly grateful for her support and skateboard knowledge. My love and thanks to you all.

O'Connor, P. (2017). Handrails, Steps and Curbs: Sacred Places and Secular Pilgrimage in Skateboarding. *Sport in Society, 21*(11), 1651–1668. https://doi.org/10.1080/17430437.2017.1390567

Contents

List of Figures

List of Tables

1

Introduction

Several years ago, I attended the funeral of one of my skateboarding friends. Along with other middle-aged skateboarders we would gather on weekends at a local skatepark. There he would chat about newly released skateboard videos, music, and very often shoes. He enjoyed documenting his tricks on video and was comically self-deprecating about his ability on his board. Like me he was originally from the UK, but he had also lived in Japan for many years where he met his wife and worked as a teacher before coming to Hong Kong. He was in his forties and his death was sudden and unexpected. His funeral was a Daoist ceremony where I sat with fellow skateboarders and we sombrely paid our respects while monks chanted for more than two hours. As we arrived, we lit incense and approached an altar where a photo of our departed friend was on display. Alongside his picture were two of his skateboards and some cans of his favourite Japanese beer. Many local skateboarders came to pay their respects along with his school pupils and friends of both him and his wife. Some days later I learned from his wife that after the cremation she had scattered his ashes in the garden area overlooking the local skatepark. Skateboarding was an important part of his life and this was signified in the ritualised way his death was commemorated.

© The Author(s) 2020
P. O'Connor, *Skateboarding and Religion*,
https://doi.org/10.1007/978-3-030-24857-4_1

With hardly anyone noticing, skateboarding has become one of the most religious sports in the world. In this book I present skateboarding as a religion, as a central and meaningful motif in the lives of countless individuals who have committed years and sometimes decades to this demanding, difficult, and sometimes dangerous pastime. Skateboarding often contributes to the well-being, health, creativity, sociality, and even livelihood of its practitioners. In recent years the phrase 'skateboard culture' has emerged largely without contestation and is seen to denote the *lifeworld* of the activity. Skateboarding is recognised as having its own lifestyle, practices, and history that unite millions across the globe. Skateboarding is now a distinct element of our broader global popular culture, influential in street fashion, and debuting as an Olympic sport in 2020. Skateboarding is also in flux, celebrated and contested by both those inside and outside the subculture. This book, like other recent tomes (Atencio, Beal, Wright, & ZáNean, 2018; Borden, 2019; Butz & Peters, 2018; Snyder, 2017), is an attempt to make sense of the impact of these changes and to understand skateboarding as a meaningful part of people's lives. This is a timely sociological task because skateboarding, despite its increasingly mainstream and commercial success, has long been a heterodox activity drawing in and including a host of disparate practices and individuals.

It is also significant that skateboarding has a preoccupation with religion. A cursory survey of skateboard magazines reveals board art (termed graphics) with religious imagery both holy and satanic. The same magazines interview professional skateboarders who at times use evocative spiritual language to talk about their exploits. These professionals are often regarded as legends by devoted fans who study and recall their tricks like scripture. Skateboard photographs and videos capture banal urban spaces and elevate some locations to the status of hallowed ground where history has unfolded, and myth can be sought. These sites are visited by both local and globetrotting pilgrims sometimes purely to gaze at a marble ledge or handrail in an office plaza, and on other occasions to perform their own acts of skateboarding worship, devotion, or penance through arcane physical feats that they find meaningful.

Beyond these elements skateboarding has developed distinct connections to organised religion, either in the confessional religious status of some famous skateboarders or in the union between religious organisations and skateboarding facilities. Churches, youth clubs, and even the famous non-governmental organisation (NGO) Skateistan, fuse a combination of skateboarding and organised religion. Less obvious are the various philanthropic endeavours that seek to enrich lives through skateboarding, such as the *A-Skate Foundation, Board Rescue, Skate for Change*, and the *Tony Hawk Foundation*. Devout Muslim skateboarders in Malaysia skate before they break their fast during the holy month of Ramadan, observe modesty laws by covering their arms in the heat, and adopt a militant attitude that fuses the discipline of skateboarding with the orthopraxy of their faith.

Some religious elements are incontestable, from professional skateboarder Paul Rodriguez saying prayers before performing tricks in the globetrotting Street League Skateboarding competitions to the religious iconography associated with the skateboards of professional, or pro, skater Jamie Thomas. However, there is little discussion on how skateboarding is actually part of the spiritual lives of skateboarders. Skateboarding is often connected to organised religion, but like other sports, it can be a religious activity in itself including holy people, sacred places, and ritual processes. Some skateboarders have as a result sought to create skateboard cults or religions that can be likened to the consciously fictive new religious movements of the *Church of All Worlds, Discordianism*, and *Jediism* (Cusack, 2010). This text addresses such movements and frames them in the broader topic of skateboarding and religion. I argue that nascent forms of religious identification can and do act as a form of resistance to the increasing institutional control being exerted over skateboarding. I also see skateboarding as a kin to religion in that it is plural, *sui generis*, and difficult to define (Glenney & Mull, 2018).

Yet to many the association between religion and skateboarding is not just unpopular but also controversial. One of my informants told me he ardently believes in the separation of 'Church and Skate.' Within the culture of skateboarding many are suspicious of religion as a force seeking to co-opt or control the activity. Others are hostile because they see religion as representing forms of institutionalisation and regulation that drove them away from mainstream sport and attracted them to skateboarding in the first place. For those outside of the culture looking in, the notion of skateboarding and religion may equally seem absurd, knowing little more of the activity than a rebellious and sometimes illegal youth culture. Skateboarding is loud, dirty, and physically demanding; arguing that it is religious is, perhaps, a futile endeavour.

In the introduction to Tait Colberg's book *The Skateboarding Art*, he confesses that he has little patience with those who describe skateboarding as transcendental or mystical. He justifies this by claiming that the embodied process of skateboarding is too brutal, concrete, and painful to equate with 'delusions of disembodied spiritual soaring' (Colberg, 2012, p. 15). To an extent I agree, and to many people skateboarding is anything but religious, philosophical, and spiritual. But this point trivialises the embodied experiences that people engage in for transcendental purposes. Take religious flagellation as an example, a recognised rite of affliction. The *Magdarame* in the Philippines perform voluntary crucifixions to commemorate Christ, and the practice of *Tatbir*, hitting oneself with a knife, is performed by some Shia Muslims to remember Husayn's martyrdom on the Day of Ashura. More contemporary practices of piercing and tattooing, and even forms of cosmetic surgery have been associated with embodied forms of transcendence and *modern primitivism*. Skateboarding involves pain and all skateboarders fall. Yet some skateboarders find an attraction to the pain they encounter describing it as 'life-affirming' and 'addictive' (The Nine Club, 2017). A point also sustained in the realm of sports is that pain and violence can be understood as a catharsis and part of a broader spiritual struggle (Bain-Selbo, 2012). Of even greater consequence to the study of religion and sport is the way that skateboarding destabilises the binaries of the sacred and the profane, frequently recasting them in hybrid and dynamic ways.

There are countless instances where the relevance of religion in skateboarding can be both refuted and asserted. The aim of this book is not simply to provide examples of religious relevance in skateboard culture; these are numerous. The task of this text is threefold: to highlight how religion is observable in skateboarding, how it is performed, and how it is organised. In the process I offer the reader an alternative insight to skateboard culture at the end of the second decade of the twenty-first century. I also provide an additional narrative to complement discussions of both religion and popular culture, and religion and sport. Skateboarding as both a communal and ritual activity need not be recognised as a religion in order for it to function as religion. This is not a simple and prosaic point; it connects to the more central question of the role and identity of religion in the modern world. I recognise skateboarding as religion in the lives of many of my participants even while they do not acknowledge it themselves. This does not discredit my thesis though; as Bourdieu notes, 'it is because subjects do not, strictly speaking, know what they are doing that what they do has more meaning than they know' (1977, p. 79). At the same time, I address conscious and distinct examples in which religion is invoked and used by skateboarders with intention and purpose.

Religion: A Working Definition

Before religion is explored in more depth, it is of chief importance to provide a brief working definition. For the purpose of this study I adopt a polythetic approach to religion, meaning that I recognise a number of salient features to be indicative of religion, but none to be essential. While belief in a god may be a key tenet of Christianity, it is absent in Buddhism. Similarly, most religions are characterised by a founder or prophet, yet this is untrue of Hinduism. Contingent in my polythetic approach is the understanding that religion is a cultural system, in itself a subset of culture. Influential in this understanding is the cultural definition of religion applied by Clifford Geertz (1973, p. 90) which I adopt as a framework. I believe that religion cannot and does not exist outside of culture, that it is a human way to process, understand, and communicate spirit, transcendence, and community. This does not exclude spirituality, but instead underscores that some choose to express a spiritual understanding through the cultural field of skateboarding. This discussion builds on work related to religion and popular culture. I propose that skateboarding can be understood as a lifestyle religion, borrowing from both Belinda Wheaton's (2004, 2013) notion of 'lifestyle sports' and Conrad Ostwalt's (2012, p. 212) identification of 'lifestyle Christianity.' This recognises the powerful sense of communitas derived from and facilitated by the heterodox activity. Communitas is a sense of communal joy where the individual is 'gifted with an immediate and genuine sense of the other, the plural of beings' (Turner, 2012, p. 6). I turn to the topic of religion in more depth in the following chapter; I must proceed here by foregrounding an understanding of skateboarding and what it has become in recent years.

Skateboarding: A Wooden Plank with Four Wheels

Describing skateboarding is problematic. Various attempts at a definition have acknowledged some ambiguity. Is it a sport, a subculture, an art form, or a political act? Brian Glenney and Steve Mull tackle this quandary and assert that skateboarding is both a mystery and a paradox (2018). Over the last two decades skateboarding has transformed, multiplied, and fragmented in an astounding variety of ways. It has become big business with the industry variously estimated to be worth US$5 billion, while commanding the interests of a powerful youth demographic worth hundreds of billions of dollars for sports drinks, computer games, and fashion brands (Borden, 2019). Skateboarding has also changed our cities, with thousands of skateparks being constructed since the turn of the century and transforming the recreation of young people and families throughout the world (Atencio et al., 2018; Howell, 2008). This book represents some of the transformations taking place and connects them back to the putative origins of skateboarding enshrined in do-it-yourself (DIY) experimentation.

Myth has it that Californian surfers in the late 1950s began to affix wheels to small planks of wood to ride along the beach front when there was no surf. They quickly saw a commercial edge to this activity and began manufacturing boards. In truth, various experimentations with boards were conducted throughout the USA and Europe from at least the late 1890s before skateboarding arrived in mass appeal in the early 1960s (Borden, 2019; Emery, 2015; The New York Times, 1893). The simplicity of the wooden board with two metal axles and four small wheels belies the fact that in just over 60 years a robust industry and culture have emerged surrounding it. This simple toy has influenced fashion, altered youth culture, entered the Olympics, and changed the world.

In skateboarding the simplicity of the object appears to translate into its versatility. Skateboarding is not a game with rules and an objective. You do not play skateboarding, you *do* skateboarding. However, it has emerged as an increasingly organised sport with elaborate international competitions. Still, unlike many sports there is no discrete objective and while there is much to achieve and conform to, skateboarders privilege freedom, individuality, and creativity (Beal, 1995; Beal & Weidman, 2003; Wheaton & Beal, 2003). I believe that the simplicity and versatility of the skateboard ensure that it is not a closed-off system with one singular purpose. If anything essential resonates about skateboarding it is that its origins as a democratic DIY exercise in creativity continue to be distinct in its contemporary performance. I cannot answer why the football or tennis racket has not been treated with same ingenuity, but I can attest to the fact that skateboarding's origins resonate in its practice. To be explicit on this point, skateboarding emerged as experimentation and this is precisely what it continues to be, while trailing six decades of history along with it.

However, in its global growth in popularity there are many more claims about what skateboarding is. There are numerous voices bemoaning the sportification of skateboarding, arguing that skateboard coaching, skateboard celebrities, and corporate endorsements go against the core of skateboard culture (Wharton, 2015). In opposition, a tide of skateboarders have welcomed the inclusion of skateboarding in the Olympics as a further step in the path to the legitimation of their sport, and a way to increase public participation, enhance facilities, and improve remuneration and healthcare for athletes (Lombard, 2010).

Professor of architectural history Iain Borden (2001) wrote the first academic monograph on skateboarding applying a spatial analysis through the critical theory of Henri Lefebvre. Borden's work is intellectually highbrow and meticulously referenced. He has repeatedly confirmed that skateboarding is notoriously difficult to write about, and simply 'not amenable to words' (Gilligan, 2014, p. 11). Over 20 years of academic study has enabled Borden to eloquently express the diversity of skateboarding. In a revised text *Skateboarding and the City* (2019) he highlights that skateboarding is plural, malleable, and open-ended. Borden explores the subcultural world of skateboarding, which includes all ages, various ethnicities, religions, classes, genders, sexualities, geographies, and disabilities. Another seminal skateboard academic Becky Beal, in her most recent book with colleagues (Atencio et al., 2018), also charts transformations in skateboarding. She recognises how the subculture she initially studied 25 years ago is now understood by many as a healthy positive family activity promoted and encouraged by parents, local government, and corporations.

In recent years a collection of excellent work in the field of lifestyle and action sports has been instrumental in exploring how a group of activities such as skateboarding, surfing, snowboarding, BMX, and parkour all exhibit numerous similarities in their unstructured practice, their ethics of individuality and creativity, and often their middle-class, white, and male practitioners. Belinda Wheaton's work has promoted the term lifestyle sports, arguing that these activities form part of the lifestyle and identity of the practitioners. This typology frames these sports as historically recent activities, distinct in requiring considerable commitment in time and resources, whilst also being subcultural and consumerist. Skateboarding, like other lifestyle sports, deviates from this typology in various ways. Most distinctly skateboarders largely reject the white middle-class label, pointing to countless examples of multi-ethnic professional skateboarders back into the 1970s. Indeed, Yochim's (2010) study commits to the notion of the whiteness of skateboarding while Snyder (2017) advocates an understanding that is fundamentally multi-ethnic. The difference in these studies is in part due to the timing of the research, but is also much more contingent in the location the research takes place: for Yochim it is Michigan and for Snyder Los Angeles. Seeing skateboarding as a nominally white activity resonates with my childhood in the rural confines of the English county of Devon, but finds less purchase for my own experiences living, working, and skateboarding in Hong Kong for the last 18 years.

As skateboards are comparatively inexpensive and riding them requires little more beyond concrete and tarmac, skateboarders have always emerged from all types of class backgrounds. Top skateboarders like Paul Rodriguez and Riley Hawk hail from wealthy backgrounds and have made it to the top of the professional ranks. Yet others like 2018 Asian Games gold medallist Margielyn Didal from the Philippines ascend in the sport from the most humble of positions. Didal, for example, grew up in a large family in the shantytown district of Cebu. As a female, Asian, gay, skateboarder, she comes from a marginal position and yet has become a national role model to millions. On the issue of gender, Wheaton and her peers have been correct. Male skateboarders have dominated since the 1980s and it has only been in the last decade that considerable changes have emerged in the gender dynamics of skateboarding. Along with these changes have come greater recognition of the historic, exclusive, heteronormative, and misogynistic norms of the skateboarding subculture. Skateboarding is increasingly promoted as an inclusive culture open not just to those who are committed white heterosexual males, but to a plethora of varying gender, ethnic, and sexual identities. The popular ascent of skateboarding to a politically correct inclusive activity is perhaps a little misleading. Skateboarding is also exclusive, values the quest of proving oneself, and continues to attract those who feel outside of the mainstream, whatever their political persuasion. One frontier that remains largely overlooked and ambiguous is that of religion. Religious skateboarders are frequently criticised, as are some religious athletes (Feezell, 2013), and are treated with suspicion and in turn marginalised by the industry.

Skateboarding as a Culture

My definition of skateboarding is one that is similarly inclusive of the varying perspectives shared by skateboarders and academics. I recognise that skateboarding is a sport, that it is also a lifestyle, a subculture, a philosophy, and an art form. As a qualitative ethnographer and sociologist I find it simplest to define and explain skateboarding as a culture. In practising skateboarding one embodies a particular way of viewing the world and engaging with it. Skateboarding becomes a part of human software, a field of communication, understanding, and symbolism. It is no longer helpful to discuss skateboarding simply as a subculture because, as Butz (2018, p. 89) notes, subculture denotes a separation from mainstream society, and this division has been mostly eroded in skateboarding. Snyder (2017) also highlights that the skateboard industry challenges many of the assumptions of early subcultural theory through what he identifies as the prominence of the subcultural career in skateboard culture. Skateboarding is now a global culture and it is recognised and understood as a legitimate pastime (even with certain constraints), a career, and an Olympic sport. It is not class-, culture-, or ethnic-specific and is increasingly becoming more inclusive of gender and sexual orientation. Yet at the same time skateboarding has also become infused with new populist notions of social justice, championing the rhetoric of inclusion while actively seeking to exclude by purging racist, misogynistic, and homophobic attitudes both past and present.

There is now significant popular acknowledgement of skateboarding as a culture with its own history and practices. The success of the heritage campaign Long Live Southbank (Blayney, 2014; Borden, 2015), the preservation and reconstruction of the Bro Bowl (Pratt, 2015; Skateboarding Heritage Foundation, 2016), and the listed status of the Rom skatepark in London (Brown, 2014), all point to the recognition of skateboarding's cultural rights. As Gilchrist and Wheaton (2017, pp. 4–5) highlight, skateboarding is now so widely understood as prosocial that the veneer of subversion and antisocial behaviour has largely been removed. In short, social changes and transformations in skateboarding over the last 20 years have seen skateboarding grow from a subculture to a culture. As we shall see, the growth in acknowledgement of ethnic, religious, and social diversity, particularly in Western multicultural nations, has also contributed to a social climate sensitive to alternative identities and has in part facilitated the recognition of skateboarding as a lifestyle. In turn, skateboarders have become self-aware of the cultural elements of their pastime, and many have sought methods to preserve them.

The notion of the culture of skateboarding is so well recognised by skateboarders, it is even used reflexively and sometimes derisively in discussions. For example, an increasingly common refrain is 'for the culture' and is used to encourage and motivate skateboarders in their efforts to perform tricks, document their activities, and to host and participate in events. While this phrase emerges from hip-hop it has been adopted in skateboard culture as a reflexive trope recognising the heritage and lifeworld of skateboarding.

Skateboard culture is influenced at its core by the skateboard industry, which manufactures and sells skateboards, clothing, and media. Boards and clothes employ designs, motifs, and artwork, which are both branded and replete with symbolism that resonate the values and aesthetics of skateboarders. Skateboard graphics have a long history of being subversive and satirical, emphasising in various ways the fact that skateboarders enjoy a different lifestyle to the mainstream. Skateboard companies have teams of professional skateboarders who are chiefly involved in promoting the brand by performing innovative tricks for documentation in magazines and videos, and/or participating in competitions. Skateboarders particularly scrutinise the activities of professional skateboarders, following their changing sponsors, and the media they are included in. Videos in particular are regarded as important landmarks for companies and their skateboarders, demonstrating new levels of progression and innovation while communicating the values and aesthetics of skateboarding to the broader community. Skateboarders are not uncritical of this content and negotiate the value and contribution of professionals in various forms of approval and commercial endorsement. As Snyder highlights, professional skateboarding can be a precarious entrepreneurial activity requiring skateboarders to push the boundaries of their physical capabilities while remaining free from injury. Beyond these feats professional skateboarding is also a popularity contest where culturally appropriate behaviour is policed and negotiated within the industry and outside of it by skateboard consumers. As Yochim (2010, p. 88) notes, 'skateboarders frequently communicate to instruct one another in skateboarding's core principles and values' and hold enormous power as consumers to decide the fate of companies and their riders. Complicating this matter further is the focus on videos and photographs documenting skateboarding in new or iconic locations. These locations, termed 'spots,' are typically banal and functional urban apparatus, sets of steps, handrails, and all manner of street architecture. Despite the mainstream popularity of skateboarding and its Olympic inclusion it is paradoxical that celebrity millionaire athletes still have to fight for the legitimacy to use public space to document their tricks, frequently being criminalised in their activities, chased out of public and private spaces, and fined in the process.

Skateboarders, as I address them in this book, largely conform to the practices of street and park, or transition skateboarding. Various other forms of skateboarding exist and are somewhat marginalised by these dominant practices. Longboarding, downhill racing, street luge, freestyle, motorised boards, Mega Ramp skateboarding, fingerboarding, and palmboarding all represent various forms of skateboarding evolution and particularisation. It may be more apt to see skateboarding as a discursive process where what is understood and accepted as skateboarding is negotiated by various groups of skateboarders. This connects to Yochim's (2010, p. 4) argument that skateboarding is a corresponding culture, negotiated in discussion with the community and the media it produces. Yochim's notion is also useful because it recognises that despite the mainstream popularity and sportification of skateboarding, there remains a strong identification that the practice is both rebellious and marginal. In short, skateboarders believe they have an alternative lifestyle, that they see the world differently, and that they are only truly understood by other skateboarders. This leads Yochim to assert that skateboarding is both inside and outside of mainstream culture, that in various ways it rejects the values, institutions, and beliefs of mainstream society (2010, p. 28). Skateboarding can be understood as heterodox, containing practices and beliefs at odds with conventional ways of life, yet subsumed within them and tolerated, even celebrated as a legitimate form of deviance. This heterodox conclusion indicates once more that skateboarders may be in opposition to the idea of religion and its characteristics of mainstream conformity and institutionalisation. The tendency to be suspicious of religion is distinct, but the fact that skateboarding can be understood as a culture also provides a rich context in which new notions and expressions of religious identification can emerge.

The Study

This work is qualitative and interpretive. It draws heavily from ethnographic research I have conducted with a variety of skateboarders in Hong Kong, and 65 qualitative interviews performed with an international cohort of individuals both in person and online via Skype between

2015 and 2019. Of these 65 audio-recorded and transcribed interviews, 15 were women aged 18–50 and 50 were men aged 20–55. The cohort included a mix of ethnicities, sexual orientations, and two individuals with physical disabilities. In addition to these semi-structured interviews, I spoke more informally with dozens of skateboarders in my multisite fieldwork and liberally spread the knowledge of my research focus in order to recruit and involve more participants.

The research began with a focus on the experiences of middle-aged skateboarders. During interviews I was surprised by how much religious language was used by my informants and I began to explore these themes in greater detail. I have supplemented my research with fieldwork visits to North America, Europe, and throughout East and South East Asia. I have spoken to professional skateboarders, skateboard artists, videographers, numerous academics in the niche world of skateboard academia, and also sociologists of religion. Much of my data came from informal discussions on skateboarding, at skate parks, or skateboarding events where I would reveal my research to people and solicit participation. I would follow these discussions by taking notes, and at other times record a brief interview on my phone. Unlike other research projects with a distinct focus, I was interested in capturing a range of religious, spiritual, and emotional reflections on skateboarding. I found many individuals with fascinating stories by chance, and I was directed to others by a host of sympathetic friends and colleagues along the way. Social media provided me with depth of access to this topic unimaginable a decade ago. I have been able to follow and analyse social media content to contrast with my interviews and fieldwork. On several occasions I was able to interview people I had initially found online, either hosting blogs or posting religious content on their social media accounts. As such this is also a work that corresponds richly with skateboard media, which, as scholars have highlighted (Borden, 2019; Snyder, 2017; Yochim, 2010), is a central element of the culture of skateboarding. This media is essential in understanding skateboarders as it communicates so much of their shared knowledge, aesthetics, and values. Indeed, when skateboarders talk, they are often talking amidst media, referencing tricks, locations, and significant events that have been captured and shared. Snyder argues that the community does not exist in a 'physical space' but is more rightly understood as facilitated by 'media' (2017, p. 54).

In combination with these elements this book has also been a personal meditation for many years. I began skateboarding at the age of 11, and while I stopped for a few years in my late teens, I began skateboarding again at the age of 20 and have continued ever since. My academic studies, research, and raising a family have slowed down my skateboarding, but not dampened my passion for it. At the same time my academic interests in religion extend back to my teens. I recall being passionate about skateboarding when I was 14, spending as much as possible of my spare time on my board, and even sleeping with it, but also retreating to study the Bhagavad Gita and political Islam in my bedroom. It took me many years to learn that this was a peculiar mix of interests for a teenager. Skateboarding enabled me to develop the skills and endurance required to be an academic, and skateboarding continues to provide a release from both the bureaucracy and pomp of the academy (not to downplay the significant amount of pomp in skateboarding).

So, this book is partly an academic treatise and partly a personal exorcism: an attempt to make sense of an activity that has been an important preoccupation in my life. It is a product of a fortuitous combination of a lifetime of skateboarding and an equally long preoccupation with the sociology of religion. I have always been curious about how religious practice informs peoples' everyday lives, and I came to understand that skateboarding has been one of the most meaningful activities in my own life. Skateboarding has provided me with a physical and spiritual outlet, ritual processes, text, and community. I am obviously not alone. In the ethnographic research I performed with middle-aged skateboarders I was privy to touching accounts of how skateboarding had become deeply meaningful, if not central, in the biographies and narratives of so many lives. It is this depth of feeling that I hope to be able to explore in this book.

The Book

The book is organised around three themes: observation, performance, and organisation. I lay forth the groundwork for this structure in the following chapter, crafting it from my polythetic and cultural understanding of religion. These perspectives provide different examples of how skateboarding and religion intersect. I have already stated that skateboarding has a preoccupation with religion. This is arguably superficial; it is notable in skateboard graphics, or the likening of professionals to saints and gurus. In the first part of the book (Chaps. 3, 4 and 5) I focus on some of these manifestations, simple observations of how religion appears in skateboard culture. My discussions revolve around the origin myth of how California has emerged as a holy land in skateboarding, how some professionals have earned the moniker of *Skate Gods*, and how religious iconography has been used in skateboard graphics. In these observations I lay the groundwork that there is an attraction and fascination with religion in skateboard culture and that it does extend beyond tokenism. I also use the frame of observation to highlight that our religious understanding of a phenomenon includes some fundamental clauses. In this first part of the book I take the premise that, for an activity to be understood as religious, we must address the ways in which it engages with religion, be that in myth, veneration, or iconography. In this first part I propose that skateboarding can be understood as a lifestyle religion on the basis that such a concept would provide space for religious identification and symbolism even if in a very shallow or superficial way.

In the second part of the book (Chaps. 6, 7 and 8) I look at how religion is performed. This borrows from John Lyden's (2003) approach to religion and film in which he proposes that film in some circumstances acts as religion. In performance I turn my scrutiny to examples which can be seen as nascent forms of religious expression, or activities fecund for religious imagination. Similarly, through the perspective of performance I etch out examples in which skateboarding acts as a religion, providing communion, transcendence, and ritual. These are my observations and while I argue that they are religious in content, it does not mean that they are understood in this way by the people involved in these activities. The first of these chapters looks at the idea of journey as expressed in two skateboard videos. These provide a narrative about the meaning and purpose of skateboarding and show some historic consistency about the worldview of skateboarding as it is expressed through skateboard media. My focus in this chapter is to highlight how media is instrumental in building communitas. I then present the notion of pilgrimage as a vibrant example of how skateboarders engage with an emerging spirituality attached to place. This connects with the practice by which skateboarders see mundane functional architecture as infused with a special energy. Stairs and handrails are venerated for the activities that have been performed on them much like a football stadium is regarded as hallowed ground by sports fans. The final chapter addressing performance looks at the rich and varied ways skateboarders engage in ritual practice. This relates to how skateboarders prepare for tricks, mark rites of passage, perform sacrifice, and engage in festivity. I argue more broadly that skateboarding is in itself an urban ritual of play, subtly critiquing the status quo and infusing the city with magic. These chapters on performance build to suggest that skateboarding in some instances can be seen to be religious, only devoid of name and formal structure. It is here that the notion of lifestyle religion becomes helpful once more giving generous room not to theology and dogma, but ritual process, lived religion, and community.

The final part of the book (Chaps. 9, 10 and 11) looks at how skateboarding and religion are organised, addressing more formal and established bonds with organised religion, invented religion, spirituality, and philanthropy. In organisation I present some very different examples of how skateboarding and religion have been fused together, and indeed how skateboarding can be conceived as a lifestyle religion. The first chapter in this part explores skateboard ministry, a Christian evangelical practice which seeks to bring Christ to skateboarders. I show how skateboard ministry is a large and well-connected movement including churches, skateparks, NGOs, and skateboard companies. Through interviews with skateboard ministers we learn of some Christian attitudes towards skateboard culture and the obstacles for Christian skateboarders in the skateboard industry. I conclude this exploration by looking at forms of Islamic skateboard dawah and show that for many religious people, skateboarding is a vehicle for faith. Chapter 10 is an enquiry into DIY skateboard religions and observes examples in which skateboarders have consciously made efforts to curate a skateboard religion or cult. The chapter includes an exploration of the Barrier Kult, but also addresses individual expressions of skateboard religiosity. The final chapter takes on the issue of skateboarding as self-help and looks at some manifestations in which skateboarding has become part of a new age movement of well-being and spirituality. I connect this theme to skateboard charities and NGOs involved in philanthropy, and while acknowledging the tremendous good that these groups do, I ask if they are ultimately just self-help for skateboarding, projecting a moral code, and promoting skateboarding fallaciously as a tool for peace, healing, and social change.

In the concluding chapter of the book I review and summarise the arguments I have made relating to observation, performance, and organisation. I suggest that nascent forms of religious expression can be understood as part of a broader cultural politics invested in maintaining and preserving values which some see as inherent in skateboarding. While I see no dramatic change in the way religion is regarded with suspicion within the skateboard industry, I do see continuing efforts to sacralise parts of skateboarding culture, be this the legacy of professionals, the veneration of iconic spots, or through philanthropic movements that reify the inclusive ethics of skateboard culture. I also argue that these elements must be addressed in the cultural politics of other lifestyle sports, and that they are in no way separate from the broader transformations of religious life in the twenty-first century. I explore once more the features of lifestyle religion and propose how they can be explored beyond skateboarding.

References

Atencio, M., Beal, B., Wright, M. E., & ZáNean, M. (2018). *Moving Boarders: Skateboarding and the Changing Landscape of Urban Youth Sports*. Fayetteville, AR: University of Arkansas Press.

Bain-Selbo, E. (2012). On the Sacred Power of Violence in Popular Culture. In T. R. Clark & D. W. Clanton Jr. (Eds.), *Understanding Religion and Popular Culture: Theories, Themes, Products and Practices* (pp. 72–88). London: Routledge.

Beal, B. (1995). Disqualifying the Official: An Exploration of Social Resistance through the Subculture of Skateboarding. *Sociology of Sport Journal, 12*(3), 252–267.

Beal, B., & Weidman, L. (2003). Authenticity in the Skateboarding World. In R. E. Rinehart & C. Sydnor (Eds.), *To the Extreme: Alternative Sports, Inside and Out* (pp. 337–352). New York: States University of New York Press.

Blayney, S. (2014). *Long Live South Bank*. London: Long Live Southbank.

Borden, I. (2001). *Skateboarding, Space and the City*. Oxford: Berg.

Borden, I. (2015). Southbank Skateboarding, London and Urban Culture: The Undercroft, Hungerford Bridge and House of Vans. In K. J. Lombard (Ed.), *Skateboarding: Subculture, Sites and Shifts* (pp. 91–107). London: Routledge.

Borden, I. (2019). *Skateboarding and the City: A Complete History*. London: Bloomsbury Visual Arts.

Bourdieu, P. (1977). *Outline of a Theory of Practice* (R. Nice, Trans.). Cambridge: Cambridge University Press.

Brown, M. (2014, October 29). The Rom, Hornchurch, Becomes First Skatepark in Europe to Get Listed Status. *The Guardian*. Retrieved from https://www.theguardian.com/culture/2014/oct/29/the-rom-hornchurch-first-skatepark-europe-listed-status

Butz, K. (2018). Backyard Drifters: Mobility and Skate Punk in Suburban Southern California. In K. Butz & C. Peters (Eds.), *Skateboard Studies* (pp. 88–105). London: Koenig Books.

Butz, K., & Peters, C. (2018). *Skateboard Studies*. London: Koenig Books.

Colberg, T. (2012). *The Skateboarding Art*. Morrisville, NC: Lulu Press.

Cusack, C. M. (2010). *Invented Religions: Imagination, Fiction and Faith*. Farnham, UK: Ashgate.

Emery, B. (2015). The Prehistoric Skateboard? *Jenkem Magazine*. Retrieved from http://www.jenkemmag.com/home/2015/02/11/the-prehistoric-skateboard/

Feezell, R. (2013). Sport, Religious Belief, and Religious Diversity. *Journal of the Philosophy of Sport, 40*(1), 135–162. https://doi.org/10.1080/00948705.2013.785423

Geertz, C. (1973). *The Interpretation of Cultures: Selected Essays*. New York: Basic Books.

Gilchrist, P., & Wheaton, B. (2017). The Social Benefits of Informal and Lifestyle Sports: A Research Agenda. *International Journal of Sport Policy and Politics, 9*(1), 1–10. https://doi.org/10.1080/19406940.2017.1293132

Gilligan, R. (2014). *DIY/Underground Skateparks*. Munich: Prestel Verlag.

Glenney, B., & Mull, S. (2018). Skateboarding and the Ecology of Urban Space. *Journal of Sport and Social Issues*. https://doi.org/10.1177/0193723518800525.

Howell, O. (2008). Skatepark as Neoliberal Playground: Urban Governance, Recreation Space, and the Cultivation of Personal Responsibility. *Space and Culture, 11*(4), 475–496. https://doi.org/10.1177/1206331208320488

Lombard, K.-J. (2010). Skate and Create/Skate and Destroy: The Commercial and Governmental Incorporation of Skateboarding. *Continuum, 24*(4), 475–488. https://doi.org/10.1080/10304310903294713

Lyden, J. C. (2003). *Film as Religion*. New York: New York University Press.

Ostwalt, C. (2012). *Secular Steeples: Popular Culture and the Religious Imagination* (2nd ed.). London: Bloomsbury.

Pratt, D. (2015, June 16). Demolition of Historic Bro Bowl Skateboard Park Begins. *Tampa Bay Times*. Retrieved from http://www.tbo.com/news/politics/demolition-of-historic-bro-bowl-begins-in-downtown-tampa-20150616/

Skateboarding Heritage Foundation. (2016, March). Save the Bro Bowl. *Skateboarding Heritage Foundation*. Retrieved from http://www.skateboardingheritage.org/programsmenu/brobowl/

Snyder, G. (2017). *Skateboarding La: Inside Professional Street Skateboarding*. New York: New York University Press.

The New York Times. (1893, May 21). Dangerous Sport in Brooklyn, News. *The New York Times*. Retrieved from http://query.nytimes.com/mem/archive-free/pdf?res=9A0CE7DA1431E033A25752C2A9639C94629ED7CF

The Nine Club. (2017). Nora Vasconcellos | *The Nine Club* with Chris Roberts—Episode 33. *YouTube Video*. Retrieved from https://youtu.be/FnRUzjxnO4s

Turner, E. (2012). *Communitas: The Anthropology of Collective Joy*. New York: Palgrave Macmillan.

Wharton, D. (2015, October 12). Some Skateboarders Want No Part of the Olympics. *Los Angeles Times*. Retrieved from http://www.latimes.com/sports/sportsnow/la-sp-sn-skateboarders-no-olympics-20151012-story.html

Wheaton, B. (2004). *Understanding Lifestyle Sport: Consumption, Identity, and Difference*. London: Routledge.

Wheaton, B. (2013). *The Cultural Politics of Lifestyle Sports*. New York: Routledge.

Wheaton, B., & Beal, B. (2003). 'Keeping It Real': Subcultural Media and the Discourses of Authenticity in Alternative Sport. *International Review for the Sociology of Sport, 38*(2), 155–176.

Yochim, E. C. (2010). *Skate Life: Re-imagining White Masculinity*. San Francisco: University of Michigan Press.

2

Skateboarding, Religion, and Lifestyle Sports

In 2013, artist James Callahan was commissioned to produce a painting of the Hindu deity Shiva the destroyer. The brief was to depict Shiva skateboarding. The customer wanted to display the finished work in their home above their skateboard mini ramp. Shiva was selected because the customer wanted to draw on their own Hindu heritage and also fuse this spiritual orientation with skateboarding. The art that Callahan produced (Fig. 2.1) was inspired by the diverse ways in which Shiva had been represented in Indian culture, as a god, a comic book hero, and a popular culture icon. Callahan, a skateboarder himself, immersed himself in the project in which he was given free reign. The finished painting depicts Shiva deep in the cosmos skateboarding in a giant canyon, grinding the edge with his rear truck (axle). The picture helps to orient the way in which religion is discussed throughout the rest of this text. In part it relates to existing traditions; more frequently though we see that religion is a part of an individualised and creative expression. We see people invoking religious sentiments in combination with the things they find meaningful. We see people seeking out religion in their own lifestyles, our focus being skateboarding.

© The Author(s) 2020
P. O'Connor, *Skateboarding and Religion*,
https://doi.org/10.1007/978-3-030-24857-4_2

Fig. 2.1 Shiva the Destroyer, James Callahan

The previous chapter touched briefly on the issue of religion and fore-grounded an understanding of lifestyle sports. It is here that I unpack these elements in more detail providing a definition of religion and pro-posing a concept of lifestyle religion. While I see this book as essentially an academic work on skateboarding, it is also a contribution to the litera-ture on the sociology of religion, and the study of lifestyle sports. This chapter lays the groundwork for theoretical arguments that build through-out the rest of the book. I observe increasing religious identification in skateboarding and I understand this to be a product of the growth in popularity of the sport. In part this sacralisation of skateboarding emerges from veterans who seek to emphasise the meaning of their one-time sub-culture in the face of increased institutionalisation and sportification. However, the popularity of skateboarding has also made it an attractive vehicle for outreach from religious organisations and philanthropic NGOs. Skateboarding and religion is a topic with several tentacles. To render this in conversation with existing debates, I have explored a web of fascinating research that discusses religion with reference to sport and popular culture. While I recognise that many of my readers will be famil-iar with skateboarding, they may well be less conversant with these broader fields of study. Likewise, readers who come from a religious or sports perspective will find this chapter helpful in orienting this study in a field of existing work.

Firstly, I will begin by elaborating on the definition of religion I pro-vided in the opening chapter. This polythetic perspective is explored alongside a variety of foundational texts on the study of religion, and more contemporary accounts of religion and spirituality in the modern world. In clarifying my definition of religion as polythetic and culturally premised, I return to the three modes of analysis used to discuss skate-boarding and religion throughout the book. These encompass observa-tion, performance, and organisation. Secondly, I touch briefly on the vast and established study of sport and religion and highlight from the outset that lifestyle sports such as skateboarding, surfing, and snow-boarding include a very different orientation to other forms of sport and thus need to be addressed from a somewhat different approach. Debate on sport and religion has focused almost exclusively on competitive mediated commercial sport and in most cases team sports. Here I find work on religion and popular culture more accessible to the commercial-ism, symbolism, and performance of lifestyle sports. Building on the research of Wheaton (2004, 2013), I argue that more work must be done to understand and chart the way in which lifestyle sports are increasingly a focus of Christian ministry (Abraham, 2017) and the need for research-ers to explore the religious and spiritual worlds of lifestyle sports practi-tioners. Thirdly, I propose lifestyle religion as a frame by which to recognise and understand religion in skateboarding. I foreground the notion that community and individualism are two primary concerns regarding modern society and the transformations of religious life. Importantly, it is these two components that skateboard culture fuses. Skateboarding, like other lifestyle sports, is an individual activity that builds communities around its practice. I conclude the chapter by arguing that skateboarding and religion is not only a curious topic of investigation, but one that is of growing relevance and tied directly to the growth in popularity of the sport itself.

Defining Religion

Alike skateboarding, the term religion has proven to be a problematic and contested word. No agreed definition exists and yet religion is one of the most powerful and enduring elements of human experience and culture. It is commonly regarded as *sui generis*, unique and unlike other human phenomena. Yet, despite this quality, definitions have repeatedly fallen short in either clarity or efficacy. One very important reason for the contested notion of religion relates to the Western bias of the term which has emerged privileging the notion of Christianity as an archetype or blueprint for all other belief systems to be verified against. I have already identified a definition of religion that is polythetic. In the following sections I refer to several different approaches and unpack how the polythetic approach is applied in order to capture and analyse the religious data of this study.

Anthropological Approaches

Many of the belief systems of pre-industrial peoples encountered and colonised by Western nations from the fifteenth century onwards were so alien to Europeans that they were not initially recognised as religious. As Mary Douglas highlights, 'where religion is concerned there is no theory comparing dogmas that does not take its own position for dogma' (2003, p. xii). Anthropology has a special role here, providing rich exploration of the diversity of religious life around the globe. One of the earliest and simplest academic definitions of religion comes from anthropologist Edward B. Tylor's writing in the nineteenth century. He asserts that religion is the 'belief in spiritual beings' (1871, p. 384). This is a broad categorisation that addresses animist practices. Melford E. Spiro goes further and suggests that 'religion is an institution consisting of culturally patterned interaction with culturally postulated superhuman beings' (Livingstone, 2005, p. 5). This definition even has room to accommodate ghosts and characters from the Marvel Cinematic Universe but does not attend to various traditions regarded as religious such as Buddhism and Daoism.

Anthropologists investigate the role of religion in a culture, its function and performance. They are not necessarily interested in the metaphysics of belief and theology. Mary Douglas (1984, 2003) has provided powerful contributions in recognising the role of religion in social order and the importance of the body as a natural symbol in such a worldview. Bronislaw Malinowski has been influential in exposing the function of myth (2013), Victor Turner in deconstructing pilgrimage (1977). One of the most influential anthropological perspectives on religion comes from Clifford Geertz, who argues that religion is a cultural system. He understands religion as a set of symbols that generates affect which in turn builds an understanding of the order of the world and stimulates a recognition of truth or reality (1973). Famously, his definition is explicit in highlighting five constitutive elements, clarifying that religion is

(1) a system of symbols which acts to (2) establish powerful, pervasive, and long-lasting moods and motivations in men by (3) formulating conceptions of a general order of existence and (4) clothing these conceptions with such an aura of factuality that (5) the moods and motivations seem uniquely realistic. (Geertz, 1973, p. 90)

This cultural definition is appealing and reaches beyond functionalism to address the emotional content of religion. He addresses both the symbolism inherent in religion and the fact that a worldview extends from religion regarding the order of the universe. However, Geertz is a particularist and in his exegesis of religion he stops short of exploring worldviews or mythology in depth (Munson, 1986). He also appears to dismiss the idea of religion in popular culture through an example of sport. Geertz argues that 'a man can indeed be said to be "religious" about golf,' thus being both committed and passionate, but golf could only be seen to be religious if it were 'symbolic of some transcendent truth' (1973, p. 98). Here I disagree and recognise that religion need not always involve transcendent experience, or faith; for some people it is simply order and function. Or alternatively it could be argued that golf, or any other activity, is symbolic of some transcendent truth. Geertz emphasises the ritual element of religion and sees that ritual is most importantly believed to be significant. One could similarly argue that golfing contains rituals that, to golfers, strike at the heart of all that is meaningful in the cosmos. Nevertheless, Geertz's definition is powerful, especially if it can be rendered more malleable. I shall return to this issue later.

Sociological Approaches

While anthropologists are interested in the role of religion in human culture, sociologists have traditionally been focal on the social world of religion in modern industrial society. The sociological perspective is thus ripe for the exploration of skateboarding, itself a product of the contemporary city. The forefathers of sociology, Marx, Weber, and Durkheim, all have distinct conceptions of religion. Marx (2009) sees religion as infantile, and a distraction to class struggle. Weber (1995) famously proposes that ascetic, self-denying Protestantism was a catalyst for the capitalist world system. The sociological perspective of Durkheim is typically simplified to the notion of society worshipping itself, and recognises a division between the sacred and the profane. This division is popular with some sports sociologists who see sport as a portal to move from the profane world and enter sacred space and time (Higgs, 1995; Novak, 1993; Prebish, 1993). This binary treatment of religion in sports is one that has recently been critiqued by some scholars (Grano, 2017; McCloud, 2003) and is further challenged in this text. As Lynch (2007, p. 136) argues, 'this binary is unhelpful because it creates a false distinction between mundane everyday life, and the realm of the transcendent mediated through specific spaces, rituals and personnel.' However, the relevance of religion as a model for society is still compelling and a longstanding contribution from sociology to our understanding of religion. As Mark Cladis writes in the introduction to Durkhiem's classic book *The Elementary Forms of Religion*, '[r]eligion, then, is a set of beliefs and practices by which society represents itself to itself … divinity and society are one' (Durkheim, 2001, p. xx). Thus, a society that is patriarchal will manifest a religious system in which men hold the dominant power. Moreover, in most nations of the world, members of the establishment are also members or followers of the dominant religion in that society. Thus, society and religion act as mirrors sharing values which affirm the order and hierarchy of each system. This functional definition continues to be influential today, but at the same time is prosaic. Arguably it is self-evident that religion would mirror or mimic the social and cultural context in which it is practised. If religion were to be stripped of social symbolism, it may simply be so alien to humans that it would be incomprehensible and void of meaning. So, in any cultural setting religion in some ways mirrors or represents elements of the social hierarchy, and, in turn, can be seen to legitimise them. This sociological perspective complements the worldview notion provided by Geertz and the symbolism of Douglas. However, all these conceptions marginalise or overlook the emotional power and force of religion.

Religious Studies

In the field of religious studies there has also been considerable effort to devise a working definition that captures a more precise understanding of religion. Significant contributions have fashioned new understandings of the transcendent notions of sacred, holy, and god(s). Recognising that much of religious experience is ineffable has seen concerted work devise a new language by which to describe the experience. Rudolf Otto (1959, pp. 16–17) argues that the ineffable can still be known and can be expressed rationally. His focus has been on explaining the experience of the holy beyond the confines of Christianity, recognising the experience as universal in all religion. He presents the term *numinous* to describe the powerful force individuals feel as an expansive experience that is 'objective and outside the self' (1959, p. 24). Livingstone (2005, p. 43) elaborates on Otto's idea of the numinous, seeing the experience of it as 'positively attractive, fascinating, and even intoxicating.' For Otto, enmeshed with this idea of the numinous is the fact that those who experience it also feel dependence and self-deprecation, even fear and awe. He classifies this experience of the numinous as *mysterium tremendum*, an awesome mystery, and *mysterium fascinans*, a fascinating mystery. As both theologian and historian of religion, Otto provides varied examples in which such religious experience is manifest in religion. Directly influenced by his work, Mircea Eliade (1959, 1963) developed further notions of holy, myth, and ritual, describing the numinous as *hierophany*, becoming manifest in both objects and places, hence in sacred religious artefacts and sacred spaces. Religious studies, like skateboarding, have accordingly developed a specialised language to deal with its *sui generis* nature. The previous phrases are ones that I call upon occasionally throughout the text. I especially adopt the term numinous as it moves beyond notions of god and monotheism, more readily associated with the term holy. Such caution and reflexivity about religious terms are a hallmark of contemporary debate, where religion is often discussed in terms of spirituality, energy, and individualism. Thus, discussions on religion and religious experience do not exist in a vacuum. As they have developed, the role of religion in our societies has also been in flux. I refer to Eliade throughout the text and have found his ideas helpful as have many sociologists; however, I do not adopt his assumptions that the sacred and profane are ontologically separate spaces.

Contemporary Challenges

While traditional and pre-industrial communities have historically posed a challenge to Western definitions of religion, a contemporary complaint can be found in the need to address new forms of religious practice. These are related to social change, spiritual activities, new-age beliefs, and the increasing diversity of religion in modern urban multicultural and secular communities familiar with global media and the norms of individualism and mass consumption. A litany of work on religion and popular culture has sought to revise definitions of religion. Contrary to popular sociological thought towards the end of the twenty-first century, religion is not disappearing in the secular societies of the West (Berger, 1990); it is simply transforming. This process has seen a rise since the 1970s in alternative spiritual practices in the West such as Yoga, Tai Chi, aromatherapy, meditation, and the Alexander Technique, which some have suggested constitute a form of spiritual revolution. In fact, traditional religion in the UK and the USA has not been eclipsed by such new practices, but there is evidence that a steady transformation is at play (Heelas, Woodhead, Seal, Szerszynski, & Tusting, 2005). Part of this transformation is an increased interest in personal choice rather than institutionalised religion. This personal religious organisation, or 'religious individualism' (Bellah, Madsen, Sullivan, Swidler, & Tipton, 2008), is often termed spirituality and equated with self-cultivation rather than engagement in a religious community. While it is simple to think that religions have a spiritual component, it may also be fair to consider that religion is not an intrinsic part of spirituality. Stuart Rose (2001) helps qualify the ambiguity surrounding the term 'spirituality' in research with various representatives of multiple faiths. He finds consensus on the notion that

> [s]pirituality can be experienced in the wonder of nature, in joy in the arts, in humanism, football, the funeral of Princes Diana, mutual tolerance for all living things, in acts of complete selflessness, and in service. Overall, membership of, or belief in, a particular religion was not thought to be a prerequisite for the experience of the spiritual. (Rose, 2001, p. 202)

His research identified three criteria that appear to be central in the notion of a spiritual life: the experience of an ongoing reverential relationship, some maintained effort or commitment, and some form of love, altruism, or benevolent kindness. With such open criteria, the development of spirituality removed from traditional religious forms becomes an obvious consideration. If people can experience the spiritual, or numinous, in broadly different contexts, there is no reason to suggest that religion is not malleable enough to also take on all manner of cultural forms. For example, there is increasing openness in deriving religious significance from popular entertainment such as film, music, and television.

Popular Culture

Terry Ray Clark (2012) suggests that religion continues to be of central importance in the products of our contemporary popular culture. While comic books, horror movies, and Coca-Cola might not be regarded as religion, they too have religious implications, motifs, and lessons for us, and these are perhaps a powerful part of their mass appeal. For Clark, religion 'refers to those practices of any society that are attentive to what is believed to be a sacred, unique, or extraordinary element or quality of human experience' (2012, p. 3). Such a definition dispenses with institutionalised creeds, texts, and sacred buildings, and provides a stronger focus on a broad subjective notion of belief. In Clark's discussion there is great sympathy for the sacred and the mundane as fluid concepts used differently throughout history, across cultures, and of course by individuals. Similarly John C. Lyden (2003) argues that film can operate as religion by employing the theoretical perspective of Geertz. He makes the case that film can be religion through both the ritual and the emotional content it contains and seeks to evoke. Yet his work, which is richly theoretical and beautifully explored, stops short of developing a method that can be operationalised to explore his arguments. While he does address the need for more qualitative research on film-going rituals, this could also be the area to test the empirics necessary to ground his argument.

Further exploration of religion and popular culture is performed by Conrad Ostwalt (2012), who seeks examples of religious (typically Christian) motifs in literature, architecture, film, and communities. His focus is on the dualism of the sacred and secular, which are at times opposed and more frequently enmeshed. If we take Durkhiem's argument as instructive, religion not only replicates society but also its institutions and organisations, thus becoming worldly and practical. Ostwalt sees religion becoming more secular as it concedes to scientific reason and modern bureaucracy, while secular life becomes increasingly religious, enchanted with popular culture myth and symbolism as points of shared meaning. Ostwalt (2012, pp. 218–223) shows how the interplay between the sacred and the secular is a central motif in American life. He argues that individualism and freedom are understood as virtues in the USA, and lifestyles that reproduce these values take on new forms of sacralisation. He refers to religious motorcycle groups and argues that the motorcycle is itself a freedom machine that signals power and independence. He also recognises that risky activities like motorcycle riding and snake handling are powerful ways to build community bonds. In the confusion surrounding the boundaries of religion in contemporary society, Ostwalt (2012, pp. 244–245) highlights the importance of community as both a motivation for religion and an acceptance of the secular. While providing a rich discussion on religious transformation, Ostwalt focuses almost exclusively on Christianity's interplay with popular culture and secularisation. What is absent in Ostwalt's working is the relevance of new forms of religious imagination that take popular culture as inspiration.

Invented Religions

Entirely new forms of religion born out of film or literature have been termed 'invented religions' by Carole Cusack. She explores *Discordianism*, *The Church of all Worlds*, and *Jediism* amongst other invented religions. These new groupings reject the need to make a myth surrounding their origin as a path to legitimisation. Instead they revel in the play and creativity of their faith. In acknowledging that their religion is human they made many adherents see that they are only being honest and recognise that all religions are in some form the product of human creation. Addressing the validity of these invented religions, Cusack adopts a definition of religion that is non-essentialist, and thus sees religion as polythetic, being contingent to no single necessary feature while sharing 'family' features which identify it as alike others (2010, p. 20). This is influenced by the work of Robert McDermott (1970), who uses Wittgenstein's language games to circumvent the problematic essentialism of a definition. Wittgenstein showed how words could have multiple meanings that can be mutually exclusive; similarly, so can religion. McDermott states that 'a range of things called religious may have no common essence in the strict sense of the term, but they may have family resemblances or all of these religious particulars as part of the religion family' (1970, p. 392). This is an appealing approach to religion for those who are comfortable with plurality and hybridity, but frustrating to essentialists who wish for clear boundaries and divisions.

I have great sympathy for Cusack's definition, yet it is challenged by the powerful arguments made by Teemu Taira (2010, 2013). Influenced by Zygmunt Bauman's prolific work (2003, 2005, 2006, 2012), he proposes a notion of 'liquid religion,' unsettled by the processes of modernity, and like other once concrete notions (family, gender, culture, nationality) he argues that religion has become an amorphous untethered classification. As a result of these transformations, religion is seen as a discursive category, where what matters is not how to define a religion, but what is recognised as religion. Taira (2013) argues that religion has become a resource for establishing and accessing rights. In reference to the example of a British man excluded from a job centre because of his refusal to lower his hood, Taira shows how the claiming of religious identity (in this case Jediism) provides individuals and communities with leverage. Thus religion, for Taira also, has no essential meaning. More importantly, definitions of religion are based on power and not reason. In critique of Cusack's invented religions, Taira argues that there is no need to define them as different to other religions as this panders to the need for religion to be legitimised and ultimately negotiated in terms of access rights. Refraining from defining religion corresponds with Taira's thesis on 'liquid religion,' asserting that as a free-floating category what is important is how it is discussed rather than what it is. However, in reference to the work of Heelas et al. (2005), despite significant change in the spiritual landscape of the West, religion continues to be an important focus on how many people organise their lives. Taira's argument begins to close off the cultural importance of religion as community, a field of communication and sharing between people. His focus on power is significant but begins to eclipse other meaningful elements of religion. Religion as a social fact is important for our social needs of communitas, to experience the spiritual in company, to feel equality, to communicate and be understood. Cusack's notion of invented religion is thus helpful because it acknowledges a post-rational embracing of a recognised fiction, disregarding seemingly inauthentic origins while prioritising the authentic numinous. Moreover, this polythetic notion of religion corresponds with my intellectual disposition to challenge essentialism and work with the messiness of hybridity.

Observation, Performance, Organisation

I adopt a polythetic definition that recognises religion as a sociological process that, in turn, mirrors our cultural practices and institutions. For these reasons the label of religion, despite Taira's compelling argument, remains important for the negotiation of recognition and rights in spite of its increasing liquidity. One challenge posed by the polythetic approach is that it is inherently nebulous, a wonderful tool for dealing with plurality, but potentially problematic in clarifying what exactly the data on religion should be. In response, I set forth a schema that structures the analysis within this book. Here the definition provided by Geertz (1973) is helpful to return to as it delineates culture, experience, and structure. I reformulate his five points into the categories of observation, performance, and organisation. My purpose in doing so is to provide modes of analysis that represent religion in categories that can overlap or be considered mutually exclusive. I want to be able to address religious symbolism as a religious component, one of a family of ideas, while not constraining it exclusively within an essentialist rubric that ties it to the ritual process, or an institution. Thus, I adopt Geertz's notion that religion includes symbolism, and moods and motivations (points 1 & 2). Accordingly, I believe a fundamental way for us to observe religion is to see how symbolism is used and the moods it creates. Secondly, I take Geertz's points (4 and 5) that religion appears as a realistic fact that gives way to the numinous, as an affirmation that people see truth in religion and that it affects them emotionally and viscerally. I understand this to also mean that religion is something that is not just experienced but performed or practised. Thirdly, Geertz's definition speaks of an 'order of existence' (point 3), which I understand as encompassing both a worldview or cosmology and the bureaucratic features of institutional (secular) organisation. Thus, I commit to a pluralistic definition of religion, but I order these three

Table 2.1 Polythetic notion of religion

Mode of analysis	Geertz's definition	Family of ideas
Observation	Points 1 and 2	Symbolism, Language, Myth, the Numinous, Artefacts
Performance	Points 4 and 5	Ritual, Worship, Factual Motivations, Pilgrimage, Communitas
Organisation	Point 3	Worldview, Institutions, Ideology, Collective Action

criteria as modes of analysis, or 'family characteristics' of religion as it manifests in skateboard culture (Table 2.1).

Sport and Religion

Conceptually, this book contributes to the sociology of religion, pursuing a largely new theme in the connection between religion and a particular type of sport. Religion and spirituality are, however, established areas of academic enquiry into sport. The most simple examples tend to trace and map similarities between religious phenomena—rituals, saints, churches—and corresponding elements of sports—rules, athletes, stadiums (Magdalinski & Chandler, 2002). The more ambitious explorations, as this text strives to portray, move beyond these binary comparisons and seek to explain other processes. However, research has tended to focus almost exclusively on traditional sports and also has a bias towards institutionalised religion (Baker, 2007; Hoffman, 1992; Parry, Watson, & Nesti, 2010). Little work has been done in the field of lifestyle sports and religion. I propose that this is in part because these sports tend to be historically new, and that as a result they are still maturing in establishing their cultural politics. The contribution that this work offers is to extend some arguments about the porous boundary between the profane and sacred that research on religion and popular culture has identified and to show how they are relevant to sport, unsettling the binaries that have dominated much scholarship. Some academics have, however, begun to foreground the notion of religion in connection to some lifestyle sports, recognising that they can be regarded as having their own ethics and rituals that permeate daily life in a similar manner to religion (Atkinson, 2008, p. 419).

Surfing, arguably more than any other lifestyle sport, has a distinct and authentic spiritual association (B. Taylor, 2007). This is best expressed in roots that reach back to around 500 CE and ritualised pantheism in Hawaii (Ford & Brown, 2006, p. 30), where surfing was an elite and aristocratic pursuit (Weyland, 2002, p. 12). Like many religions, surfing is regarded as having a homeland, a mythology, and distinct ritual practices. Laderman (2014, p. 14) shows how the influence of Christian missionaries in Hawaii in the nineteenth century contributed to the rapid decline of indigenous surfing. Riding waves became Americanised, and in the process aligned with new forms of spiritual practice such as the 'Soul Surfer' movement of the 1960s (Booth, 1994). Some surfers sought self-realisation and practised yoga as part of the lifestyle (Evers, 2010, p. 27), echoing many of the new-age subjective spiritual practices of the present. The spiritual association with surfing is suggested by Ford and Brown (2006, p. 15) to now be entwined with its closeness to nature, and a bodily aesthetic of freedom demonstrated in liberated attitudes to clothing and exposed skin. Taylor (2007) sees media as being instrumental in developing a broader spiritual identification, communicating the ethics of surf culture, and curating forms of pilgrimage to iconic beaches made sacred by surfing prophets. These associations are being extended through social media and in turn highlight new forms of spiritual practice. Indeed, networked technology and new media provide an important form of human presentation and outreach to express identity, emotion, and community (Duffy, 2017; Humphreys, 2018; Lupton, 2016; Miller, 2011; Miller & Sinanan, 2017). For example, 'paddle outs' are a collective ritual that surfers perform as a memorial for their dead brethren (Thorpe, 2014, p. 100). The impact of such activities should not be underestimated, as Thorpe details that one YouTube video of the Andy Irons paddle out has been viewed over 100,000 times. Thus, these activities are not only performed, they are recorded, memorialised, and revisited. Mirroring many of the comments I have gathered with regard to skateboarding, some surfers are concerned with the commercialisation of their lifestyle into a competitive sport and see it as a sign of 'spiritual pollution' (Evers, 2010, p. 28), while others see the 'defiling act' of such commodification as ultimately unable to 'obviate' surfing's 'spiritual power' (B. Taylor, 2007, p. 925). A further development is the way in which surfing has been promoted as a force of good, tackling not spiritual but environmental pollution. A wide variety of surfing NGOs have chosen to adopt a socially responsible attitude towards places where surfing is performed (Thorpe & Rinehart, 2013), seeking to protect communities, empower women (A. Taylor, 2016), and protect wildlife and the physical environment.

Some works have approached spirituality and religion in lifestyle sports with considerable scepticism. There are important questions such as 'why can't surfing be a religion?' (Melekian in Taylor, 2007, p. 924) and concerns that spirituality is simply mistaken psychological exhilaration or, worse, absurd and self-absorbed. Yet, at the same time, there is an acknowledgement that participants earnestly feel religious significance in their sports and feel spiritually enhanced by participating in them (Allman, Mittelstaedt, Martin, & Goldenberg, 2009, p. 241; Higgs & Braswell, 2004, p. 195; Poulson, 2016, p. 34). Wheaton highlights that one of the defining attributes of lifestyle sports is the identification of the 'buzz' of participation, and the danger that through negotiation can elicit feelings of transcendence (2013, p. 29). Indeed, a common feature of work that has looked at a tie between religion and lifestyle sports (Abraham, 2017; Friedel, 2015; B. Taylor, 2007; Watson & Parker, 2014) is the identification of Csikszentmihalyi's (1975, 1997) notion of flow. The experience of flow is achieved when one is performing an activity in which one is totally engaged. In flow, temporal states are disrupted and sensations are heightened, providing intense focus and feelings of elation and even transcendence. The association of the 'highs' of lifestyle sports has accordingly been marketed as exhilarating, extreme, and edgy. In Steven Kotler's *West of Jesus* (2006), the author provides a biographical journey into the heart of surfing and spirituality, a treatise on death, and the psychology of flow.

Bringing both play and flow together is Stephen Lyng's (1990, 2005) concept of edgework, or voluntary risk-taking. Developed initially in reference to skydiving, edgework recognises that people who are involved in risky sports are actually deeply focused and draw on years of trained experience to negotiate their exhilarating feats. A clear connection can be made between the notions of flow and edgework and the experience of religious awe and terror: for example, the *Mysterium Tremendum* and

Mysterium Fascinans that Otto (1959) describes, and the fear and trembling touched upon by Kierkegaard (1968). Edgework corresponds with what Sophie Friedel (2015) describes as part of the 'gifts' of skateboarding, where practitioners pursue the experience of 'stoke,' which is analogous to the feeling of flow. Alternatively, edgework can also be read as a political practice, a commentary on society and its alienation. Ferrell (2005) argues that the edgework of skateboarding a handrail may well be the only possible adventure left in a society that controls and commodifies every experience. In edgework, people enact a form of anarchy, rejecting the conventions of everyday life and transcending in mind, body, and politics. This leads us to identify that the bond between religion and lifestyle sports can also be connected to social change.

Our discussion must similarly address the popular interest in spirituality as an alternative to traditional religions (Rose, 2001; Tacey, 2004). Research in the sociology of religion has identified a weakening and transformation in religious practice in Europe and North America. These changes have noted a 'decline in some forms of the sacred and the rise of others' (Heelas et al., 2005, p. 2). Charles Taylor speaks of a 'massive subjective turn of modern culture, a new form of inwardness, in which we come to think of ourselves as beings with inner depths' (1991, p. 26). Influenced by Taylor's argument, Heelas et al. (2005, p. 3) describe a turn away from proscribed social roles to a 'subjective life' where we are reflexive, concerned with our own experiences and feelings. They note in the UK a growing tendency for individuals to search for the sacred in activities and pastimes that are disconnected from traditional, national, cultural, and religious institutions. New forms of spirituality have been developed in New-Age philosophies such as healing, Tai Chi, and Yoga. It is the physical elements of these practices which can be seen as analogous to skateboarding. Indeed, the bond between sport and religion rests on the fact that the body is a primary symbol in religion and the principle tool of ritual (Douglas, 1984). In terms of sport, the primacy of the body may also be understood as a reason for its apparent anti-intellectualism. Bodily knowledge is difficult to translate into language, but this in no way trivialises its importance (Bourdieu, 1990, p. 166).

Skateboarders speak in nuanced terms about a religious connection to skateboarding itself. A number of male youths in the research of Emily

Chivers Yochim (2010, pp. 93–94) declare forms of spiritual engagement with skateboarding. One informant states that 'some people do meditation, some people do yoga, I skateboard,' while others explain it as 'orgasmic,' 'almost like meditation,' and 'super relaxing.' Two of my women informants compared skateboarding to yoga in terms of it being a physical activity that is both exercise and spiritual. In a different approach, sociologist Gregory Snyder (2017, p. 197) speaks of skateboarders as having a 'quasi-spiritual' relationship with the banal urban spaces they use. Thus, framing the topic of skateboarding and religion allows us to explore both these nascent expressions of spiritual identification and more distinct forms of organisation and integration with established world religions.

Skateboarding as a Lifestyle Religion

The fact that skateboarding and religion have become connected suggests something intriguing about our contemporary moment. This may be a concern about the individualism of modern societies and the erosion of communal practices of politics, religion, and more broadly social capital. As Robert Putnam (2000) has famously observed, there has been a sharp decline in the communal affiliations of American public life, typified in the falling number of bowling leagues and the rise in the number of people 'bowling alone.' For Charles Taylor (1991), this is part of a larger concern with modernity and the rise in notions of personal morality and authenticity. He argues that we are now reliant on our own feelings and the need to be true to ourselves rather than committed to an external notion of authority. The consequence of this effect is fragmentation and atomism in modern society which entrench division. Taylor sees that in the American context a preference for judicial review creates the setting of a win or lose outcome that only further entrenches fragmentation and removes opportunity for debate. These arguments relate broadly to the work of sociologists who have seen modernity unsettle trust, intimacy, and identity (Beck, 2013; Anthony Giddens, 1991, 2002), and who recognise modern society as insecure, unmoored, and liquid (Bauman, 2004, 2005, 2012). These are processes long at work as evidenced in

Marx and Engels (1985, p. 83) *Communist Manifesto*, where they declare that 'all that is solid melts into air, all that is holy is profaned.'

Individualism is both a cause and effect of modernity, and one that religion problematically explores. While we may seek greater intimacy and community, it is apparent that the majority of us stay committed to our individualism. This has been argued as part of the draw towards new age and alternative spiritual practices which are often highly subjective in contrast to traditional institutionalised religion which imposes a reality of a life dictated to us (Heelas et al., 2005). What we see with forms of communal association that have grown is that they continue to emphasise subjective well-being and individuality (Bellah et al., 2008, p. xxiii). No better example of this exists than the prominence of social media, which, while clearly social to a degree, has been manufactured to play on our impulses and self-interests, and may well be better termed narcissistic media. In short, we are facing a paradox, the need for community premised on individualism.

This, however, is precisely what skateboarding is—a communal activity and an individualised one. As Yochim (2010, p. 179) states in the closing paragraph of her book, 'you do it together, and everyone just does it their own way.' Recognising this flexibility and with it an ability to accommodate all sorts of people, Borden argues that 'diversity is not a weakness for skateboarding, but conversely its very strength' (2019, p. 3). Indeed, its capacity to be both a valorised individual pursuit and a culture with its own community makes skateboarding an exemplarily modern pursuit. Skateboarding has risen to be a celebrated activity because it is seen to remedy some of the maladies of modern life. Bellah et al., (2008, p. xxiv-xxv) argues that it is desperately difficult for individuals seeking to be civically engaged to transcend the confines of their class and ethnic communities; yet in skateboarding this is quite evidently not the case. Ritual elements in skateboarding are able to unsettle social hierarchies and facilitate communitas. Consciously or not, people are finding solace in skateboarding because of the community and inclusion it offers. It therefore seems only natural that it has emerged, and I argue that it will continue to develop along with other lifestyle sports, as a lifestyle religion, an activity from which individuals can derive communitas, spirituality, and religious significance—structured not around a dogma, but a way of life.

I propose a concept of lifestyle religion that can be rendered in reference to the earlier arguments. Building on Wheaton's (2013) concept of lifestyle sports, we can recognise the importance of new forms of physical expression that are subcultural, consumptive, and individualised. Similarly, Ostwalt's (2012) work identifies a trend in secular activities becoming recognised as sacred, echoing the fact that religion is more palatable when presented in accessible popular tropes. Conversely, the mundane features of everyday life become more meaningful when enchanted with sacred representation. Heelas et al. (2005) complement these arguments promoting an emphasis on feelings and subjective experience provided by Charles Taylor (1991), demonstrating how religious experience can relate to new-age practices, and in the case of Cusack's (2010) work, entirely fictional and invented beliefs. Accordingly, lifestyle religion can encompass new articulations of world religion such as 'lifestyle Christianity,' drawing on and appropriating popular culture motifs as channels to demonstrate a reimagining of faith that is as youthful, heterodox, individualised, and consumptive as Ostwalt (2012, p. 202) suggests. With our polythetic definition of religion, lifestyle religion is a malleable concept that has room to accommodate spiritual expressions of flow, ritual practice without theology, sacred symbolism, and indeed secular humanism itself. I propose that skateboarding can demonstrate a form of lifestyle religion precisely because it is able to generate the feelings, community, and optics of religion while being free of orthodox strictures and dogma. This is significant because contemporary culture in the global north is marked by concerns about the weakening of human bonds and the absence of community (Ostwalt, 2012, p. 206), and activities such as skateboarding, motorbike gangs, yoga groups, cosplay meetups, film clubs, and veganism provide access, community, and belonging. The exploration of how this can be observed, how it is practised and organised, is the task of the remainder of this book.

References

Abraham, I. (2017). *Evangelical Youth Culture: Alternative Music and Extreme Sports Subcultures*. London: Bloomsbury.

Allman, T. L., Mittelstaedt, R. D., Martin, B., & Goldenberg, M. (2009). Exploring the Motivations of Base Jumpers: Extreme Sport Enthusiasts. *Journal of Sport & Tourism, 14*(4), 229–247. https://doi.org/10.1080/14775080903453740

Atkinson, M. (2008). *Battleground: Sports*. London: Greenwood Press.

Baker, W. (2007). *Playing with God*. London: Harvard University Press.

Bauman, Z. (2003). *Liquid Love: On the Frailty of Human Bonds*. Cambridge: Polity Press.

Bauman, Z. (2004). *Wasted Lives: Modernity and Its Outcasts*. Cambridge: Polity Press.

Bauman, Z. (2005). *Liquid Life*. Cambridge: Polity.

Bauman, Z. (2006). *Liquid Fear*. Cambridge: Polity Press.

Bauman, Z. (2012). *Liquid Modernity*. Cambridge: Polity Press.

Beck, U. (2013). *Risk Society: Towards a New Modernity*. London: Sage.

Bellah, R. N., Madsen, R., Sullivan, W. M., Swidler, A., & Tipton, S. M. (2008). *Habits of the Heart: Individualism and Commitment in American Life*. Los Angeles: University of California Press.

Berger, P. L. (1990). *The Sacred Canopy: Elements of a Sociological Theory of Religion*. New York: Anchor Books.

Booth, D. (1994). Surfing '60s: A Case Study in the History of Pleasure and Discipline*. *Australian Historical Studies, 26*(103), 262–279.

Borden, I. (2019). *Skateboarding and the City: A Complete History*. London: Bloomsbury Visual Arts.

Bourdieu, P. (1990). *Other Words: Essays Towards a Reflexive Sociology*. Cambridge: Polity Press.

Clark, T. R. (2012). Introduction: What Is Religion? What Is Popular Culture? How Are They Related? In T. R. Clark & D. W. Clanton Jr. (Eds.), *Understanding Religion and Popular Culture: Theories, Themes, Products and Practices* (pp. 1–12). London: Routledge.

Csikszentmihalyi, M. (1975). *Beyond Boredom and Anxiety*. San Francisco: Jossey-Bass Publishers.

Csikszentmihalyi, M. (1997). *Creativity: Flow and the Psychology of Discovery and Invention*. New York: Harper Perennial.

Cusack, C. M. (2010). *Invented Religions: Imagination, Fiction and Faith*. Farnham, UK: Ashgate.

Douglas, M. (1984). *Purity and Danger: An Analysis of the Concepts of Pollution and Taboo*. London: Ark.

Douglas, M. (2003). *Natural Symbols*. London: Routledge.

Duffy, B. E. (2017). *(Not) Getting Paid to Do What You Love: Gender, Social Media, and Aspirational Work.* New Haven, CT: Yale University Press.

Durkheim, É. (2001). *The Elementary Forms of Religious Life.* Oxford and New York: Oxford University Press.

Eliade, M. (1959). *The Sacred and the Profane.* New York: Harcourt.

Eliade, M. (1963). *Myth and Reality.* New York: Harper & Row.

Evers, C. (2010). *Notes for a Young Surfer.* Melbourne: Melbourne University Press.

Ferrell, J. (2005). The Only Possible Adventure: Edgework and Anarchy. In S. Lyng (Ed.), *Edgework: The Sociology of Risk Taking* (pp. 75–88). New York: Routledge.

Ford, N., & Brown, D. (2006). *Surfing and Social Theory: Experience, Embodiment and Narrative of the Dream Glide.* London: Taylor & Francis.

Friedel, S. (2015). *The Art of Living Sideways: Skateboarding, Peace and Elicitive Conflict Transformation.* Wiesbaden: Springer.

Geertz, C. (1973). *The Interpretation of Cultures: Selected Essays.* New York: Basic Books.

Giddens, A. (1991). *The Consequences of Modernity.* Cambridge: Polity.

Giddens, A. (2002). *Runaway World: How Globalisation Is Reshaping Our Lives.* London: Profile Books.

Grano, D. A. (2017). *The Eternal Present of Sport: Rethinking Sport and Religion.* Temple University Press.

Heelas, P., Woodhead, L., Seal, B., Szerszynski, B., & Tusting, K. (2005). *The Spiritual Revolution: Why Religion Is Giving Way to Spirituality.* Oxford: Blackwell.

Higgs, R. J. (1995). *God in the Stadium: Sports and Religion in America.* Lexington: University Press of Kentucky.

Higgs, R. J., & Braswell, M. C. (2004). *An Unholy Alliance: The Sacred and Modern Sports.* Macon, GA: Mercer University Press.

Hoffman, S. (1992). *Sport and Religion.* Champaign, IL: Human Kinetics.

Humphreys, L. (2018). *The Qualified Self: Social Media and the Accounting of Everyday Life.* Cambridge, MA: MIT Press.

Kierkegaard, S. (1968). *Fear and Trembling, and the Sickness Unto Death.* Princeton, NJ: Princeton University Press.

Kotler, S. (2006). *West of Jesus: Surfing, Science and the Origins of Beliefs.* New York: Bloomsbury.

Laderman, S. (2014). *Empire in Waves: A Political History of Surfing.* Los Angeles: University of California Press.

Livingstone, J. C. (2005). *Anatomy of the Sacred.* Upper Saddle River, NJ: Pearson/Prentice Hall.

Lupton, D. (2016). *The Quantified Self*. Cambridge: Polity Press.

Lyden, J. C. (2003). *Film as Religion*. New York: New York University Press.

Lynch, G. (2007). What is this "Religion" in the Study of Religion and Popular Culture? In G. Lynch (Ed.), *Between Sacred and Profane: Researching Religion and Popular Culture* (pp. 125–142). London: I.B. Tauris.

Lyng, S. (1990). Edgework: A Social Psychological Analysis of Voluntary Risk Taking. *American Journal of Sociology, 95*(4), 851–886.

Lyng, S. (2005). *Edgework: The Sociology of Risk-Taking*. New York: Routledge.

Magdalinski, T., & Chandler, T. J. L. (2002). With God on Their Side: An Introduction. In T. Magdalinski & T. J. L. Chandler (Eds.), *With God on Their Side: Sport in the Service of Religion* (pp. 1–19). London: Routledge.

Malinowski, B. (2013). *Myth in Primitive Psychology*. Alcester, UK: Read Books.

Marx, K. (2009). *Critique of Hegel's Philosophy of Right*. Cambridge: Cambridge University Press.

Marx, K., & Engels, F. (1985). *The Communist Manifesto*. London: Penguin Classics.

McCloud, S. (2003). Popular Culture Fandoms, the Boundaries of Religious Studies, and the Project of the Self. *Culture and Religion, 4*(2), 187–206. https://doi.org/10.1080/01438830032000135674

McDermott, R. (1970). The Religion Game: Some Family Resemblances. *Journal of the American Academy of Religion, 38*(4), 390–400.

Miller, D. (2011). *Tales from Facebook*. Cambridge: Polity Press.

Miller, D., & Sinanan, J. (2017). *Visualising-Facebook*. London: UCL Press.

Munson, H. (1986). Geertz on Religion: The Theory and the Practice. *Religion, 16*(1), 19–32. https://doi.org/10.1016/0048-721x(86)90003-5

Novak, M. (1993). *Joy of Sports, Revised: Endzones, Bases, Baskets, Balls, and the Consecration of the American Spirit*. Madison Books.

Ostwalt, C. (2012). *Secular Steeples: Popular Culture and the Religious Imagination* (2nd ed.). London: Bloomsbury.

Otto, R. (1959). *The Idea of the Holy* (J. W. Harvey, Trans.). Harmondsworth: Penguin.

Parry, J., Nest, M., & Watson, B. (2010). *Theology, Ethics and Transcendence in Sports* (J. Parry, M. Nest, & B. Watson, Eds.). Routledge.

Poulson, S. C. (2016). *Why Would Anyone Do That? Lifestyle Sport in the Twenty-First Century*. New Brunswick, NJ: Rutgers University Press.

Prebish, C. S. (1993). *Religion and Sport: The Meeting of Sacred and Profane*. Westport, CT: Greenwood Press.

Putnam, R. D. (2000). *Bowling Alone: The Collapse and Revival of American Community*. New York: Simon & Schuster.

Rose, S. (2001). Is the Term 'Spirituality' a Word That Everyone Uses, But Nobody Knows What Anyone Means by It? *Journal of Contemporary Religion, 16*(2), 193–207.

Snyder, G. (2017). *Skateboarding La: Inside Professional Street Skateboarding*. New York: New York University Press.

Tacey, D. (2004). *The Spirituality Revolution: The Emergence of Contemporary Spirituality*. New York: Brunner-Routledge.

Taira, T. (2010). Religion as a Discursive Technique: The Politics of Classifying Wicca. *Journal of Contemporary Religion, 25*(3), 379–394. https://doi.org/10.1080/13537903.2010.516546

Taira, T. (2013). The Category of 'Invented Religion': A New Opportunity for Studying Discourses on 'Religion'. *Culture and Religion, 14*(4), 477–493. https://doi.org/10.1080/14755610.2013.838799

Taylor, A. (2016). From Ireland to Iran, Easkey Britton Is Connecting the World through Surfing. *Huck Magazine*. Retrieved from https://www.huckmag.com/outdoor/surf/easkey-britton-huck-50-full/

Taylor, B. (2007). Surfing into Spirituality and a New, Aquatic Nature Religion. *Journal of the American Academy of Religion, 75*(4), 923–951. https://doi.org/10.1093/jaarel/lfm067

Taylor, C. (1991). *The Malaise of Modernity*. Concord, ON: Anansi.

Thorpe, H. (2014). *Transnational Mobilities in Action Sport Cultures*. New York: Palgrave Macmillan.

Thorpe, H., & Rinehart, R. (2013). Action Sport NGOs in a Neo-Liberal Context: The Cases of Skateistan and Surf Aid International. *Journal of Sport & Social Issues, 37*(2), 115–141. https://doi.org/10.1177/0193723512455923

Turner, V. (1977). *The Ritual Process: Structure and Anti-structure*. Ithaca, NY: Cornell University Press.

Tylor, E. B. (1871). *Primitive Culture*. London: Bradbury Evans and Co.

Watson, N. J., & Parker, A. (2014). *Sport and the Christian Religion: A Systematic Review of Literature*. Newcastle upon Tyne: Cambridge Scholars Publishing.

Weber, M. (1995). *The Protestant Ethic and the Spirit of Capitalism*. London: Routledge.

Weyland, J. (2002). *The Answer Is Never: A Skateboarder's History of the World*. New York: Grove Press.

Wheaton, B. (2004). *Understanding Lifestyle Sport: Consumption, Identity, and Difference*. London: Routledge.

Wheaton, B. (2013). *The Cultural Politics of Lifestyle Sports*. New York: Routledge.

Yochim, E. C. (2010). *Skate Life: Re-imagining White Masculinity*. San Francisco: University of Michigan Press.

Part I

Observation

3

Origin Myth

Haadii is a skateboarder and a former student of the Islamic school in the Malaysian city of Kota Bharu. He has been skateboarding for 16 years and at the time of our conversation was working on finishing a video documenting the tie between skateboarding and his faith. Haadii is also a conscientious Muslim and enjoys visiting Kota Bharu because of its rich heritage and strong Islamic culture. A part of the Kelantan district, the city is governed by the Pan-Malaysian Islamic Party (PAS). This is a religiously conservative part of the country where the state government employs morality police to ensure people dress modestly and refrain from immoral acts. Even though the city has a population of nearly 400,000 people, it has not had a cinema since 1990. One reason for this is that Kelantan district has strict rules for cinemas that require them to show films with bright lighting in the theatre and to shut down entirely during the month of Ramadan. Cinemas in Kota Bharu are not profitable. One eye-catching feature of the city is the vibrant urban art near the street Jalan Dato Pati. Numerous walls are adorned with paintings featuring scenes from across the Islamic world. Some of the murals depict the struggles of Palestinians in the Middle East, showing scenes of war with tanks, flags, and helicopters. Others feature the Dome of the Rock

© The Author(s) 2020
P. O'Connor, *Skateboarding and Religion*,
https://doi.org/10.1007/978-3-030-24857-4_3

mosque in Jerusalem, women preforming the Dabke Arab folk dance, regional foods, and the Malaysian martial art Melayu Silat.

Haadii does not idolise any skateboarder, preferring to see all as equals. Yet, he holds one local religious leader, Tok Guru, in high esteem. Tok Guru, whose full name is Nik Abdul Aziz, died in 2015 and is regarded as the spiritual leader of PAS. He is known throughout Malaysia for his hard-line conservative views. Fusing his two passions, Haadii asked his friend Ajiem, a renowned Malaysian skateboard photographer, to document him performing a trick at the famous Tok Guru wall which features a commemorative mural. The photograph (Fig. 3.1) is evocative and includes a quote from Tok Guru. The text on the wall behind Haadii translates as a motivation for good work and piety stating that 'while the reward is not visible, we keep that money in the afterlife.' I read this image as an illustration of how some Malay skateboarders take pride in their dedication and commitment to skateboarding, and see it as a metaphor for spiritual struggle and piety. What is even more fascinating is that Haadii, like skateboarders all across the

Fig. 3.1   Haadii at Tok Guru wall in Kota Bharu. (Photo: Mohd Azim Nong)

globe, has a recognition and understanding that skateboarding emerges from a wholly different context. The craft that he has given Islamic meaning to began on the beach sidewalks of California some 60 years ago. Just like Haadii's faith of Islam, skateboarding has an origin myth and it has become one that is universally recognised by skateboarders across the globe. Haadii confesses that he does not know much about the history of skateboarding but he is certain that the sport is tied to California and emerges from surfing. California resonates in the actions and dress of Haadii as he flips his skateboard in the streets of Malaysia's conservative Eastern province. He wears Vans Era Pro shoes, jeans, and a light floral shirt.

Mircea Eliade states that 'every myth shows how a reality came into existence' (1959, p. 97). For skateboarders that reality is tied to California and as such this place recurs throughout the following chapters as an important focus. It represents a putative homeland to skateboarding and also a quasi-holy land, a territory full of sacred sites and cultural heroes. In this chapter I provide an example of how skateboarding and religion interact in terms of an origin myth. This is not solely focused on how the Californian narrative emerged, but also upon how skateboard media, and academic enquiry into skateboarding has reified a cultural world from which skateboarding is seen to emerge. Firstly, every text on skateboarding speaks of a history of skateboarding originating from California and in the process contributes to the myth-building process. Take, for example, the most important and authoritative scholarly works by Borden (2001, 2019), Beal (2013), Yochim (2010), Butz (2012), and Snyder (2017). In one recent work it is San Francisco that is pinpointed as the skate capital of the world (Atencio, Beal, Wright, & ZáNean, 2018, p. 34). Of more popular relevance are the cultural products of skateboarding—magazines, videos, and the proliferation of sources available on blogs and social media—which continue to orient to California in both overt and tacit ways. These represent the values, aesthetics, and language of skateboarding which are again connected to this legacy. Skateboarding has not only a native land, but an origin myth, a dense and evolving historiography that has been documented through the written word, photography, art, and video. It also, like religion, possesses an elaborate language that is at once functional and esoteric. These all combine to signal a cultural movement with values and ethics that influence skateboarders globally from the past to the present.

This chapter serves a dual purpose: I not only observe an origin myth, but I also introduce the fundamentals of skateboarding necessary to navigate the rest of this text. I unpack the vernacular of skateboarding for readers uninitiated in this cultural world. I also reproduce the origin myth and show how it has been intellectually challenged, and emotionally embraced. In sum, this first chapter applying the trope of observation looks at how skateboarding and religion interact in the fundamentals of the activity. It observes what skateboarding is, how it is communicated, and where it comes from. Relating this chapter back to Geertz's (1973, p. 90) definition of religion, our mode of analysis focuses on his first and second points, that religion can operate as a system of symbols that establish powerful motivations and moods amongst people. It also connects to the family of ideas that includes symbolism, language, and myth. As a feature of lifestyle religion, contemporary myth appears both sacred and plausible providing a necessary narrative to those without religion, and similarly providing context to a heterodox identity to the faithful like Haadii who are committed to more traditional beliefs.

The Myth

Far removed from Malaysia, California is the holy land of skateboarding. While much significance in the world of skateboarding is found entirely beyond this singular state in the USA, it is beyond question the place most closely associated with skateboarding both past and present. All cultures, like nations and religions, have some narrative that forms an origin story. Skateboarding's origin story has been contested (C. B. Snyder, 2015; The New York Times, 1893), yet it is almost universally associated with California. Arguably the history became widely recognised in popular culture following the commercial and critical success of Stacy Peralta's documentary *Dogtown and Z Boys* (Peralta, 2001). The film provides a narrative of the origins of street skateboarding through the creative and rebellious activities of 1970s Californian youth who sought out empty backyard pools as places to develop new styles of skateboarding. Following this early history, Yochim (2010) argues that skateboarding represents a mythic quality about the American maverick, typified as adventurous, entrepreneurial, and male. For many people the association with California as the primary home of skateboarding is matched not only in its popularity in the state, but also with the imagining of California as a place of freedom, creativity, and openness. In exploring a mythology of skateboard history Butz (2012, p. 53) identifies that almost all academic and non-academic sources on skateboarding's origins make reference to surfing and its cultural influence. He explores the fusion of surfing's exotic Polynesian origins with Southern Californian beaches and urban sprawl, highlighting the enduring connection that skateboarding has to the region. Professional skateboarder Rodney Mullen relays accounts of early visits to California to participate in competitions during this era. He refers to California as a 'Skateboard Mecca' (Mullen & Mortimer, 2004, p. 49) and curates a shrine of unremarkable items such as bus tickets and other artefacts he brings back from his sojourns (2004, p. 54). It is clear from Mullen's account that there is an essence in California that provides a foundation to an understanding and recognition of skateboarding.

Most religions have some form of an origin story, a narrative that is often steeped in mystery and revelation. A recognised beginning is an integral part of both religion and culture, both old and new. This process of fleshing out a history has been shown to be part of how religions, ethnicities, and nations are constructed (Cusack, 2013; Eriksen, 2010; Hutchinson & Smith, 1996; Woodhead, 2011). Most famously Hugh Trevor-Roper in *The Invention of Tradition* (Hobsbawm & Ranger, 1994) describes how the history of Scottish clan tartan has been revised to fit the needs of a national identity. Thus, while an origin story may be assumed, or widely known, it need not be true or uncontested. Glenney and Mull evocatively argue that 'skateboarding is a mystery: We do not really know when it began or where it is going, or even what it is' (2018, p. 1). This is intellectually correct; however, the wide recognition of the Californian origin serves an important symbolic function. The Californian myth facilitates a worldview, an order of reality in which skateboarders can look towards a genesis and an orientation. In the work of Eliade this is referred to as an *axis mundi*, effectively the centre of the world. More importantly, within the symbol of this centre is the notion of creation and thus an 'archetype of every creative human gesture' (Eliade, 1959, p. 45). Relating this concept to the religion of Islam, Mecca, and specifically the Ka'ba in the Grand Mosque is the *axis mundi* for Muslims. It is to this feature that Muslims orient their prayers five times a day. It is to Mecca that Muslims are obliged to make a pilgrimage once in their lifetime, fulfilling both a religious obligation and mirroring the actions of the prophet Muhammad. So potent is the example of Mecca as an *axis mundi* that it is used as a noun for places of great importance to which people flock. California is thus an undisputed Mecca for skateboarding. This axis or point to which attention is focused also comes to represent an image of the world or *imago mundi* (1959, p. 42). For Eliade this goes even further, we come to understand such sites as schemas for what is sacred and also as models for existence (1959, p. 64). Using Eliade's argument we can suggest that California is not only a homeland and the centre of the world of skateboarding, but also a parable about the values and worldview of skateboarders. A first step in comprehending the validity of such an argument rests in providing a rudimentary overview of skateboarding, its materials, manoeuvres, and language.

The Basics

Skateboarding involves some basic technology. Most typically a board is roughly 8 inches wide and 32 inches long. This is usually made of Canadian hardwood maple, of which seven thin layers of plywood are pressed, glued, and shaped together. These are then decorated with artwork, referred to as graphics. These graphics tend to include the logo and brand name of the board company, and the name of the professional skateboarder whose model it is. These are sold individually at skateshops, retailing for around US$40. Boards are covered on their top side with griptape, effectively sticky black sandpaper, which provides foot grip. The terms board and deck are what skateboarders use to refer to the wooden part of their skateboard, and are terms used interchangeably to refer to the whole of the skateboard. Mounted on the underneath of the board by screwed bolts, are two stainless-steel axles which have rubber bushings placed between the hangar and its base plate to provide manoeuvrability. These axles are referred to as trucks. Hard rubber urethane wheels with precision bearings are placed on the axles and screwed into place. These are the basic components of a skateboard and it is a technology that has changed little over the last 60 years. Skateboards are typically assembled by their owners; this is both a creative and consumerist process where skateboarders choose the brands and paraphernalia that they deem as most cool, authentic, stylish, efficacious, and durable. Even the placement of the griptape on the board can be regarded as a form of self-expression, with skateboarders sometimes making patterns or decorating their griptape with artwork and slogans. Figure 3.2 shows the decorated griptape of one Hong Kong skateboarder in his early twenties on which the cartoon cat character Pusheen is depicted saying 'Hail Satan.' Setting a board up is at once an example of consumption, identity expression, individuality, humour, and DIY self-reliance.

Fig. 3.2 Decorated griptape depicting a creative fusion of Pusheen and Satanism. (Author's photo)

The practice of skateboarding encompasses everything that takes place once an individual mounts their board. While typically boards are stood on, they are also sat upon and used in various ways by people with differing physical abilities, young and old. The skateboard is ridden with its users propelling themselves along. The standard approach to movement is called kicking or pushing, one foot remains constantly on the board while the second foot propels the board by pushing repetitively on the ground. Once the desired speed has been achieved the second (pushing) foot is then placed on the board. Balance is an integral part of skateboarding and is contingent in the basic acquisition of competence in moving on the board. From these fundamentals, skateboarders have developed a variety of novel physical feats that combine the board, physical articulation, and movement. These are manoeuvres that are simply referred to as tricks. One basic trick, and the building block of many others, is the ollie. This is a seemingly paradoxical technique in which the skateboard is propelled into the air with all four wheels simultaneously leaving the ground. This is achieved by the skateboarder explosively banging their rear foot on the back, or tail, of the board while dragging their front foot up the board towards the tip, or nose. The back foot uses the springiness of the wooden board to rise into the air, while the front foot aids the lift and levels the board out flat. The griptape provides additional grip and control for ollies and the many numerous derivations of this technique. Despite the fact that the ollie is regarded as a basic trick, it must be underlined that it still takes considerable practice and determination to achieve, let alone master. For many who skateboard, the process of practising and perfecting new tricks on their board is both a passion and compulsion. As a result, a rich diversity of skateboarding tricks has emerged along with specialised practices. The skateboarding that most people encounter travelling around their home towns and cities is referred to as street skateboarding and involves the performance of tricks in urban spaces. Transition skateboarding refers to ramp, bowl, or half-pipe skateboarding and has increasingly become part of skatepark skateboarding which often includes impressively powerful and high aerial tricks. Downhill luge, longboarding, megaramp, and freestyle skateboarding are further derivatives.

It should already be apparent that skateboarding has its own lexicon. The language of skateboarding reveals in its richness the embodied sensibility of the activity. A sophisticated vernacular is used to describe a technical variety of tricks which enable skateboarders to communicate and imagine physical performances. Most young skateboarders are experts in recognising the degrees of rotational turns and can quickly compute a 180°, 270°, 360°, or 540° spin whilst also being attentive to the orientation of the skateboarder and the direction of the spin. Sociologist Gregory Snyder (2017, pp. 90–91) provides an astute unpacking of the way skateboarders communicate tricks. He recognises that skateboarding terminology is remarkably efficient in describing the ways in which skateboarders move both their bodies and their boards. This terminology is even explicit in describing the orientation of skateboarders to their boards. For example, let us analyse the term *switch frontside flip to 5.0*. Firstly, *switch* means that the skateboarder is riding his/her board in his/her unnatural stance. Skateboarders normally have a preferred way of standing on their board. Left foot front, right foot back is called *regular*, while the opposite is called *goofy*. When a skateboarder switches stance they are riding switch. This is the skateboarding equivalent of handedness—writing with your left hand when you are right-handed. Switch should not be confused with riding backwards, which is called *fakie*. When one ollies fakie they are not changing their stance, just their direction. Immediately it should be apparent that one cannot ride their board switch fakie; this is an oxymoron. *Frontside* refers to the way the trick and the skateboarder move, and without elaboration refers to a 180° turn. Turning frontside involves a turn where you rotate exposing the chest of your body: for a regular-stance rider, an anticlockwise turn, for a goofy rider, a clockwise turn. *Flip* means that the board has been kicked in mid-ollie to spin on its horizontal axis in a 360° rotation. The final part of the trick *to 5.0* refers to a second trick following the first switch frontside flip. A *5.0* is a trick in which the back truck of the board lands on an object and slides, or grinds, along it on the axle. Clearly the brief phrase *switch frontside flip to 5.0* communicates a great deal of information succinctly. Trick terminology in terms of the semiotics of language can be regarded as simply referential, describing action and information. Accompanying these terms is phraseology that describes the feeling and efficacy of tricks. Gnarly refers to something that is rough, difficult, or scary. When a grind is performed on rough concrete the associated feeling of cumbersome friction is a perfect descriptor of the term gnarly. Buttery is another term used to describe the feeling of sliding your board or grinding your trucks on a very smooth surface such as marble. Suffice to say that this scarcely scratches the surface of the extensive repertoire of tricks and their terminology.

Of further significance is the way in which skateboarding has developed internationally and acquired local terms for tricks and manoeuvres. Writing on the emergence of skateboarding in China in the early 1990s, Tim Sedo (2010) recognises that skateboarders developed their own language for tricks. Cut off from the wider world of skateboard media and its corresponding culture, Chinese skateboarders naturally devised their own ways of communicating the complicated physical specificity of skateboarding tricks. In a similar way the students at the world-famous Skateistan NGO programme in Afghanistan have also learnt to skateboard without exposure to skateboard media. As a result they have developed their own associations about skateboarding style, in particular valorising safety equipment (Fitzpatrick, 2012).

Trick names have increasingly become functional, but many reveal a connection to the people who first created them. The ollie, for example, was first performed by Alan 'Ollie' Gelfund, on transition. It was later brought to flat ground by Rodney Mullen and was quickly adopted as part of street skateboarding. The Stalefish, which involves grabbing the board with your back hand, behind your legs and between your feet, refers to the unappetising food at the skate camp Tony Hawk attended when he invented the grab. A more evocative example for the purposes of our study is the trick termed the Christ Air (see Fig. 3.3). This spectacular manoeuvre pioneered by Christian Hosoi involves launching out of a vert ramp and extending both arms (board in one hand) in the symbol of a crucified Christ. Hopefully this will provide those unfamiliar with skateboarding an insight into the compounded nature of the culture. The technology, practice, and language are all tightly entwined. As we shall see time and time again, the simplicity of the skateboard betrays the complex meaning it has been imbued with. Throughout the rest of the text I shall explain new terminology as it is introduced.

Fig. 3.3 Christian Hosoi performs a Christ Air. (Photo: J. Grant Brittain)

Genesis

Two competing narratives exist that serve to chart the origins of skateboarding. There is the surfing origin that is tied to the West Coast of the USA and specifically California. Alternatively, there is the East Coast narrative that emerges from DIY experimentation and technology. Both origin stories serve to tie skateboarding to a holy land, be that the Mecca of California, the Medina of Florida, or the Jerusalem of New York. California reigns supreme as the location most strongly associated with skateboarding both past and present. It is towards California that the global skateboard industry looks, as this is the home of the skateboard industry and remains a place where its most influential companies reside.

Tightly bonded to this Californian homeland is the connection between skateboarding and surfing. The surf narrative is most popularly depicted in the 2001 Stacy Peralta film *Dogtown and Z Boys*. Here we follow the exploits of a group of surfers who created their own style in the spirit of aggressive and innovative street skateboarding. But the bond between surfing and skateboarding extends further back into the 1950s. Konstantin Butz (2012) takes the challenge of skateboarding history in an erudite fashion presenting three paradigms of its origins: *from surf to skate, the Dogtown era*, and the *post-1980s era*. Here, Butz rightly links the fascination of the surfing narrative to a mythology of the spiritual origins of surfing. Skateboarding's association with surfing is often framed as a form of authenticity, reaching to a distant, and spiritual, past. Unlike surfing, which has sustained a spiritual association, skateboarding despite its surfing connection has not been understood as a spiritual practice. Arguably, the urban focus of skateboarding, retreating from the natural setting of the waves and the beach, has framed the practice as spiritually barren. What is established is that by the mid-1960s skateboarding had become a popular preoccupation with its own magazine *Skateboarder* going to press for the first time in 1964. Borden (2001, p. 29) clarifies that the first skateboarders in the 1960s were typically surfers who used their boards when there were no waves. So evident was the association between skateboarding and surfing that it made its way into popular culture in the 1964 song *Sidewalk Surfin* by Jan and Dean. But as both Borden (2019) and Yochim show (2010), the boom of skateboard popularity in the 1960s came from the innovations of childhood recreation. Scooters and roller skates were the technical forbearers to skateboards, as was DIY experimentation.

In an attempt to find the origins of the modern skateboard, Bryan Emery (2015) provides evidence of coaster toys such as the Buffalo Sled dating back to 1910, and Nazis toying with early skateboard devices. Emery also cites a *New York Times* article from 1893 that details the antics of several young boys and girls who are coasting down a steep hill in Brooklyn's Lincoln Place on 'little four-wheeled carts.' The article goes on to state that the 'sport is exciting but it is extremely hazardous, and dangerous' and requires police intervention (The New York Times, 1893).

The early coaster toys document that play and fun have always been at the heart of skateboarding, and that associations of danger and lawlessness accompanied even early experimentations in the sport.

I argue that the relevance of play is a point often obscured in skateboard history. Play is too frequently seen as trivial and inconsequential. However, Henri Lefebvre's (1991, p. 118) argument that 'toys and games are former magical objects and rituals' is an important point. Just as surfing has a spiritual connection in its ritual Hawaiian history, skateboarding has its own playful cosmology. Borden (2001, p. 97) acknowledges this in his analysis of the embodied experience of skateboarding. The skateboard can thus be understood as a ritual tool, a way of relating to the cosmos. In Cusack's (2013) research a focus on invented, intentionally and self-consciously fictive religion is shown to also engage with the importance of joyful play. Johan Huizinga's (1949) influential exploration of play in human cultures asserts that both fun and beauty tend to be dominant aspects of play. He draws many connections between play and religion, noting that 'the concept of play merges quite naturally with that of holiness' (1949, p. 25).

More generally we can identify two strains of ideology in the dominant narrative of skateboarding history. Firstly, skateboarding is born out of surfing; it takes the processes of moving and carving along the waves and transposes them to concrete and asphalt. Secondly, this process was made possible by technological innovation, and DIY creativity. Young children with a curiosity to make their own thrilling vehicles with the tools available to them began to construct their own toy. In both narratives I trace a spiritual component: one that is self-evident in the connection to surfing as a sport embedded in both tradition and nature; the other, the less evident an acknowledged ludic and playful pursuit of fun. A more potent issue is the fact that skateboarding is open to adaptation and interpretation in a way that few other sports are. This is not simply a practical issue but also a philosophical point; skateboarding origins reinforce the notion of experimentation and play. The consequence is that skateboarding has become a system of play open and accessible for practitioners to project their own meaning upon. This can be framed in Bourdieu's (1977, p. 82) notion of habitus, in which a 'system of dispositions ... survives in the present and tends to perpetuate itself.' Thus, Haadii is able to see his skateboarding as an act of piety because skateboarding perpetuates a disposition of versatility. In acknowledging the origins of skateboarding we can recognise that it is diverse enough to accommodate religious identification. Of even greater importance is the fact that we can recognise that in skateboarding's origins there is a signpost to its values and ethics.

The Capturing of History

Not all religious identification is innocent; in various ways religion can be understood as a tool of power and a claim for rights. The writing of history, as de Certeau (1988) notes, is a social construction in itself and origin myths have political and power implications (Foucault, 1978). One way in which this power is exerted is through the control of a narrative. Thus, I have found it particularly interesting to chart the variety of ways in which the history of skateboarding has been reproduced and enshrined. I see this as a response to the increased mainstream popularity of skateboarding, and as attempts to consolidate, control, and reify the culture of skateboarding. This reaches back to early work performed by sports sociologist Becky Beal in which she identified the powerful claim to participant control by skateboarders (Beal, 1995; Beal & Weidman, 2003). Simply put, skateboarders prioritise their control over skateboarding, negotiating the development of the sport and culture, its meaning, and its core values. Yochim (2010) articulates participant control as part of the corresponding culture of skateboarding, and Lombard (2010) recognises that skateboarders have conceded significant control of parts of their industry and culture in a trade for better conditions and remuneration. I argue that as concessions have been made, efforts at participant control have morphed. Non-skateboarders play skateboarding video games, regular journalists report on celebrity skateboarders, and fashion magazines provide editorials on skateboard fashion. No longer are skateboarders solely communicating within the culture, they are also communicating to those on the peripheries, or even outside of the culture. Documentaries, philanthropic NGOs, and a variety of books are now involved in communicating the history and the values of skateboarding.

Let me be clear in stating that skateboarding has an existing text ripe for interpretation. Skateboard magazines and skateboard videos are the fundamental authentic media sources of the culture. However, these emerged as media to document the developments and progression of skateboarding, not as mediums of interpretation and analysis. Early skateboard media was inward-looking, it was subcultural, and it arose out of a necessity that was both commercial and communal. Historically skateboard videos were watched in skateshops and in homes; now they are broadcast on cable channels, available to stream on Netflix, and looped on vast high-definition screens in the athletic apparel stores of Nike and Adidas.

One distinct method to capture and reproduce a narrative of skateboarding comes in book form. The publication of an ever-growing number of coffee table books has been a feature of the last 20 years: for instance, Independent Truck company's *Built to Grind* (Denike, 2004), Vans shoe company 50th anniversary's *Off the Wall* (Palladini, 2016), and Globe footwear's enormous 700-page *Unemployable* (Boulter, 2015); skateboard art histories such as *Disposable* (Cliver, 2004), *Agent Provocateurs* (Carayol, 2014), and *Skate Board Art of Jim Phillips* (Phillips, 2007); magazine anthologies such as *Thrasher* magazine's *Maximum Rad* (Thrasher Magazine, 2012) and *The Big Brother Book* (Cliver, 2016); skateboard photography books such as *Skate the World* (Mehring, 2015), *Skateistan* (Fitzpatrick, 2012), *DIY/Underground Skateparks* (Gilligan, 2014), and *Long Live Southbank* (Blayney, 2014); and a variety of skateboard biographies such as *Hawk: Occupation: Skateboarder* (Hawk & Mortimer, 2001), *The Mutt* (Mullen & Mortimer, 2004), *The Impossible* (Louison, 2011), *The Answer Is Never* (Weyland, 2002), *Nobody* (Thornton, 2016), *Hosoi* (Hosoi & Ahrens, 2012), and *Jay Boy* (Sherwood, 2017). There are also anthologies of skateboard websites such as *Jenkem Vol:1* and *Vol:2* (Michna, 2016, 2018) and *TF at 1: Ten Years of Quartersnacks* (Luckman, 2015). These are just some of the many varied texts that attempt to capture skateboard history. A plethora of skateboard documentaries also do the same from the critically acclaimed *Dogtown and Z Boys* (Peralta, 2001) to *The LA Boys* (Kennedy, 2016). Most recently, and perhaps most surprisingly, skateboarders have embraced a series of podcasts including *The Tim O'Connor Show*, *The Bunt*, *The Shelter Show*, *Vent City*, and arguably the most successful *The Nine Club*, which for skateboarding academics is a remarkable resource of oral history. These are all texts for lifestyle religion, mythologising the past and providing a narrative through which community can be sustained.

My research has also led me to interrogate a collection of texts commissioned and published for young readers. These, I argue, have been the first sources that children will encounter as they seek to find out more about skateboarding. Books purchased by parents or borrowed from the local library are undoubtedly much more accessible for young novices than a skateboard magazine like *Thrasher*. Here in texts like *Skateboarding: Learn to Skate Like a Pro* (Gifford, 2006), *Skateboarding* (Horsley, 2008), *Skateboarding Science* (Becker, 2009), and *No Limits: Skateboarding* (Morgan, 2005), a standard narrative in reproduced. This can be streamlined as the surfing skateboarding connection of the 1960s, Frank Nasworthy's urethane innovation of the 1970s, vert skateboarding and skateparks of the 1980s, and street skateboarding of the 1990s. Reflecting on these sources clarifies how well established the origin myth of skateboarding is.

Kota Bharu

In conclusion I return to Haadii and highlight that skateboarding can be paralleled to his own religious tradition of Islam. Muslims across the world turn to Mecca to perform their prayers. Mecca is the birthplace of the religion of Islam, the home of the prophet Muhammad. It is also a living location for Muslims and one to which they have an obligation to visit once in their life in the form of a pilgrimage. Yet other cities are important in Islam: Medina represents the place where Islam began as a religious community and the Islamic calendar recognises the time Muhammad fled from Mecca to Medina as the start of the religion. As the religion of Islam spread, centres all over the world came to be significant for Muslims, be it Jerusalem, Istanbul, or Córdoba. Skateboarding also has this living relationship with California. Many turn their orientation to it daily, keeping up to date with new tricks performed at a set of steps in Los Angeles or San Francisco. Others seek to visit California and perform their own form of pilgrimage. But multiple other locations have become important to the global world of skateboarding; New York,

Barcelona, Shenzhen, Tokyo, Malmö, and London are all considered important nodes on the skateboarding map. Similarly, the spread of skateboarding has become a rich cultural experiment in which skateboarders of numerous cultures and faiths remake skateboarding as a meaningful activity in their own lives.

Haadii studied at an Islamic college and has learnt to read the Jawi script, which reproduces Malay in the Arabic alphabet. He hopes to one day become a *hafiz*, a person who has committed the entirety of the Qur'an to memory. He describes skateboarding as part of his religious life and sees the example of Tok Guru as instructive. Skateboarding for Haadii is about serving god, about focusing on good works and committed struggle, not the distractions of money and self-interest. In the conservative environment of Kota Bharu, Haadii is free to skateboard. He takes seriously the need to respect people in his community, but as a devout and observant Muslim he feels able and prepared to respond to those who challenge his skateboarding as un-Islamic. Like many skateboarders, he is involved in documenting and filming his tricks. When I spoke with him he was continuing to work on a skateboard video, but confessed that this project was also about religion and his faith. Haadii refused to raise any professional skateboarder up as an idol. Rather, he chose to celebrate each individual and their style in skateboarding as a broader expression of the divine. This, to me, is one of the ways in which Haadii is divergent from many skateboarders. The celebrity side of skateboarding, the adulation heaped upon individuals because of the things they can do on a wooden board with wheels, is very much the engine to the skateboard industry. In our next chapter we observe how some professional skateboarders have been imagined as idols, sages, and quasi-gods and how some have fallen short of such honorifics.

References

Atencio, M., Beal, B., Wright, M. E., & ZáNean, M. (2018). *Moving Boarders: Skateboarding and the Changing Landscape of Urban Youth Sports*. Fayetteville, AR: University of Arkansas Press.

Beal, B. (1995). Disqualifying the Official: An Exploration of Social Resistance through the Subculture of Skateboarding. *Sociology of Sport Journal, 12*(3), 252–267.

Beal, B. (2013). *Skateboarding: The Ultimate Guide.* Santa Barbara, CA: Greenwood.

Beal, B., & Weidman, L. (2003). Authenticity in the Skateboarding World. In R. E. Rinehart & C. Sydnor (Eds.), *To the Extreme: Alternative Sports, Inside and Out* (pp. 337–352). New York: States University of New York Press.

Becker, H. (2009). *Skateboarding Science.* New York: Crabtree Publishing Company.

Blayney, S. (2014). *Long Live South Bank.* London: Long Live Southbank.

Borden, I. (2001). *Skateboarding, Space and the City.* Oxford: Berg.

Borden, I. (2019). *Skateboarding and the City: A Complete History.* London: Bloomsbury Visual Arts.

Boulter, J. (2015). *Unemployable: 30 Years of Hardcore, Skate and Street.* Melbourne, Australia: Thames and Hudson.

Bourdieu, P. (1977). *Outline of a Theory of Practice* (R. Nice, Trans.). Cambridge: Cambridge University Press.

Butz, K. (2012). *Grinding California: Culture and Corporeality in American Skate Punk.* Bielefeld: Transcript-Verlag.

Carayol, S. (2014). *Agents Provocateurs: 100 Subversive Skateboard Graphics.* Gingko Press.

Cliver, S. (2004). *Disposable: A History of Skateboard Art.* Berkeley, CA: Gingko Press.

Cliver, S. (2016). *The Big Brother Book.* Berkeley, CA: Gingko Press.

Cusack, C. M. (2013). Play, Narrative and the Creation of Religion: Extending the Theoretical Base of 'Invented Religions'. *Culture and Religion, 14*(4), 362–377. https://doi.org/10.1080/14755610.2013.838797

de Certeau, M. (1988). *The Writing of History.* New York: Columbia University Press.

Denike, B. (2004). *Built to Grind: 25 Year of Hardcore Skateboarding.* San Francisco: High Speed Publications.

Eliade, M. (1959). *The Sacred and the Profane.* New York: Harcourt.

Emery, B. (2015). The Prehistoric Skateboard? *Jenkem Magazine.* Retrieved from http://www.jenkemmag.com/home/2015/02/11/the-prehistoric-skateboard/

Eriksen, T. H. (2010). *Ethnicity and Nationalism.* London: Pluto Press.

Fitzpatrick, J. (2012). *Skateistan: The Story of Skateboarding in Afghanistan.* Berlin: Skateistan.

Foucault, M. (1978). Nietzsche, Genealogy, History. In J. Richardson & B. Leiter (Eds.), *Nietzsche* (pp. 139–164). Oxford University Press.

Geertz, C. (1973). *The Interpretation of Cultures: Selected Essays*. New York: Basic Books.

Gifford, C. (2006). *Skateboarding: Learn to Skate Like a Pro*. London: DK.

Gilligan, R. (2014). *DIY/Underground Skateparks*. Munich: Prestel Verlag.

Glenney, B., & Mull, S. (2018). Skateboarding and the Ecology of Urban Space. *Journal of Sport and Social Issues*. https://doi.org/10.1177/0193723518800525.

Hawk, T., & Mortimer, S. (2001). *Hawk: Occupation: Skateboarder*. New York: Regan Books.

Hobsbawm, E. J., & Ranger, T. O. (1994). *The Invention of Tradition*. Cambridge: Cambridge University Press.

Horsley, A. (2008). *Skateboarding*. New York: Crabtree Publishing.

Hosoi, C., & Ahrens, C. (2012). *Hosoi: My Life as a Skateboarder Junkie Inmate Pastor*. New York: HarperOne.

Huizinga, J. (1949). *Homo Ludens: A Study of the Play-Element in Culture*. Kettering, OH: Angelico Press.

Hutchinson, J., & Smith, A. D. (1996). *Ethnicity*. Oxford and New York: Oxford University Press.

Kennedy, C. (Writer). (2016). The L.A. Boys. The Berrics.

Lefebvre, H. (1991). *The Production of Space*. Malden, MA: Blackwell.

Lombard, K.-J. (2010). Skate and Create/Skate and Destroy: The Commercial and Governmental Incorporation of Skateboarding. *Continuum, 24*(4), 475–488. https://doi.org/10.1080/10304310903294713

Louison, C. (2011). *The Impossible*. Guilford, CT: Lyons Press.

Luckman, W. (2015). *Tf at 1: Ten Years of Quartersnacks*. New York: power-House Books.

Mehring, J. (2015). *Skate the World*. Washington, DC: National Geographic Society.

Michna, I. (2016). *Jenkem Vol. 1: Skateboarding, Smut, Shenanigans* (I. Michina, Ed., 1st ed.). Brooklyn, NY: Jenkem Magazine.

Michna, I. (2018). *Jenkem Vol. 2: More Skateboarding, Smut, Shenanigans*. Brooklyn, NY: Jenkem Magazine in association with WINS.

Morgan, J. (2005). *No Limits: Skateboarding*. Minnesota, MN: Smart Apple Media.

Mullen, R., & Mortimer, S. (2004). *The Mutt: How to Skateboard and Not Kill Yourself*. New York: Reagan Books.

Palladini, D. (2016). *Vans: Off the Wall (50th Anniversary Edition)*. New York: Abrams.

Peralta, S. (Writer). (2001). Dogtown and Z-Boys [DVD].

Phillips, J. (2007). *Skate Board Art of Jim Phillips*. Pennsylvania, PA: Schiffer Publishing Ltd.

Sedo, T. (2010). Dead-Stock Boards, Blown-out Spots, and the Olympic Games: Global Twists and Local Turns in the Formation of China's Skateboarding Community. In P. Rethmann, I. Szeman, & W. D. Coleman (Eds.), *Cultural Autonomy: Frictions and Connections* (pp. 257–282). Toronto: UBC Press.

Sherwood, K. (2017). *Jay Boy: The Early Days of Jay Adams*. New York: Rizzoli International Publications.

Snyder, C. B. (2015). *The Secret History of the Ollie* (Vol. 1: The 1970s). Cambridge, MA: Black Salt Press.

Snyder, G. (2017). *Skateboarding La: Inside Professional Street Skateboarding*. New York: New York University Press.

The New York Times. (1893, May 21). Dangerous Sport in Brooklyn, News. *The New York Times*. Retrieved from http://query.nytimes.com/mem/archive-free/pdf?res=9A0CE7DA1431E033A25752C2A9639C94629ED7CF

Thornton, D. (2016). *Nobody: Essays from a Lifer Skater*. UK: Amazon.

Thrasher Magazine. (2012). *Maximum Rad: The Iconic Covers of Thrasher Magazine*. New York: Universe.

Weyland, J. (2002). *The Answer Is Never: A Skateboarder's History of the World*. New York: Grove Press.

Woodhead, L. (2011). Five Concepts of Religion. *International Review of Sociology, 21*(1), 121–143. https://doi.org/10.1080/03906701.2011.544192

Yochim, E. C. (2010). *Skate Life: Re-imagining White Masculinity*. San Francisco: University of Michigan Press.

4

Skate Gods

The notion that skateboarding involves some individuals who are valorised, canonised, or even deified is the very crux of this chapter. The career of a professional skateboarder is not simply a way to create material richness through endorsements, it is also a means to consolidate a legacy and a slice of immortality. Iconic skateboarders are those who bear witness to seminal moments in skateboarding history. As Eliade states, 'the persons of the myth are not human beings; they are gods or culture heroes' (1959, p. 95). Skate gods are simply mortal beings who have contributed to skateboarding in such profound ways that they are highly revered. *Thrasher* magazine makes an idol each year by awarding the coveted title of Skater of The Year (SOTY) to a professional skateboarder who has excelled in his/her contributions to skateboarding. There is a long tradition in sports of athletes admired as extraordinary and inspirational figures. Muhammad Ali, Michael Jordan, David Beckham, and Serena Williams have all been described as gifted individuals with unique skill and ability; they have also become celebrities well known and recognised to legions who have little appreciation for their sports. They have been praised for their decorum, morals, and leadership. Indeed, of all my topics in this book, it is this one that connects most readily to the body

© The Author(s) 2020
P. O'Connor, *Skateboarding and Religion*,
https://doi.org/10.1007/978-3-030-24857-4_4

of work on religion and institutionalised sport. The gods I discuss in this chapter are secondary to the 'moods and motivations' they elicit in skateboarders and their symbolic place in a system of skateboard history. I propose that, in the case of lifestyle religion, we choose our own gods.

Throughout this chapter I address some key personalities that are lauded and even praised by skateboarders. Some of them may be regarded as prophets, guides, sages, superhuman, or even holy. Such deference is sometimes apparent in the nicknames professional skateboarders are awarded, Andrew Reynolds is 'The Boss,' Jamie Thomas 'The Chief,' Tony Hawk 'Birdman,' and Christian Hosoi 'Christ.' While interviewing former professional skateboarder Salman Agah, Chris Roberts awards him the title of 'Switch God' (The Nine Club, 2018). This sobriquet is a recognition of Agah's pioneering of ambipedal skateboarding, performing tricks with counter-intuitive foot positioning. In this realm Agah is considered a luminary. At the age of 45, he is no longer at the heights of professional skateboarding, and instead runs a pizza restaurant. However, he declares that his business has been made successful through the continued patronage of skateboarders and the skateboard industry.

All of these various monikers establish a lineage of skateboarders, an eclectic polytheistic universe where each of the personalities is praised for whatever talents they bring, and are thus remembered for their contributions. Andrew Reynolds, for example, is largely regarded as owning the frontside flip, Paul Rodriguez is also praised for his switch abilities, Tony Alva for being the forefather of pool skating, Ray Barbee is inseparable from the no-comply, a trick where the rider takes one foot off the board while using the rear foot to pop the board into the air and catch the board with both feet (@anthonypops, 2018), and Neen Williams is popularly agreed to have the best heelflip, a move where the board is kicked by the heel of the rider's front foot into a horizontal flip rotation during an ollie (Viceland, 2017).

Although dismissive of analogies between religion and skateboarding, Tate Colberg describes his own Pantheon of skateboarding, an imaginary 'hall of fame' where the greatest skateboarders have achieved 'immortality in an historical sense' (2012, p. 215). He includes Rodney Mullen, Mark Gonzales, and Matt Hensley as the greatest street skateboarders of all time, and Tony Hawk, Danny Way, and Bob Burnquist as the greatest vert skaters. His typology, he confesses, is personal, and he acknowledges that each skateboarder is likely to have their own personal favourites that correspond to their taste and experience. More interesting is the way in which Colberg describes the skateboarders as a 'Holy Trinity.' He states: 'Mullen, Gonzales, and Hensley are the Galileo, Newton, and Einstein (or Heisenberg) of street Skating,' or 'Leonardo, Michelangelo, and Raphael,' and again 'Elvis, Beatles, and Rolling Stones' (Colberg, 2012, pp. 265–264). Colberg's admiration for these skateboarders is glowing, devotional, and informed with micro observations of their photographs, manoeuvres, and even the music selection of their video parts. A similar religious comparison is made by Christian Senrud (2018) in an article that likens various skateboarders to saints. His selection includes Mark Gonzales, Fred Gall, Tony Hawk, Heath Kirchart, John Cardiel, and Neil Blender. Each is provided with a personalised treatment—Kirchart is lauded for being quiet but focused, Cardiel for pushing harder than all others. For arguably the world's most famous skateboarder, Tony Hawk, the passage begins thus:

> Praise be to Saint Hawk by being nice to non-skaters and convincing them that the Church of Skateboarding isn't completely composed of degenerate demons. (Senrud, 2018, p. 217)

At the time of writing, a thread on the Slap message board, an online forum for skateboarding, is titled 'If skateboarding were a religion' (Slap Magazine, 2018). Various posts liken professional skateboarders to religious figures. The vast majority of the comments are comical or satirical in intent. The posts on the forum and the writing by both Senrud and Colberg all show a distinct Christian bias with religious terminology such as trinity, saints, and various Biblical characters. They are also all superficial in that they rely on a simple set of comparisons, substituting like for like.

Jeff Grosso's popular YouTube series for Vans called *Loveletters to Skateboarding* explores the meticulous attention paid to the achievements of skateboarders. Grosso often goes into depth discussing the importance of tucking your knee when you do a boneless (a trick where you plant a foot and grab the board and spring into the air), and then lists skaters who have historically done this with style and aplomb. In a similar way, the YouTube series and podcast *The Nine Club* and the Viceland documentary series *Epicly Later'd* have built up an oral history of skateboarding, recording the first-hand accounts of skateboard legends in meticulous detail. These new forms of media build on a long tradition of skateboarders documenting their achievements, and then scrutinising and fashioning their legends. It is media and the DIY origins of skateboard media (skateboarders documenting themselves and their friends) that deified so many of the characters that I discuss in this chapter. A question that this topic raises is: how will the new gods be formed? Does social media, with its speedy reproduction and possibility for universal participation, foreground the reality that legends may be shorter-lived and more quickly forgotten? One only needs mention that Steve Caballero has been a professional skateboarder with Powell since 1980, to highlight that several skateboard legends have had remarkably long careers for athletes. This extended time has afforded the consolidation of a legacy. Yet, in comparison, it is already evident that a younger generation is also making its own gods. An example that needs little elaboration is that of Nyjah Huston, with an imposing competition legacy and a litany of powerful sponsors that have influenced the 'sportification' of skateboarding in the twenty-first century.

Superhuman

My key interest here is to present a variety of examples of how skateboarders have become quasi-gods, or are at least imagined as exceptional. The notion of superhuman is explored by Kotler (2014) in his work on the rise of prodigious human abilities in sport. He speaks of professional skateboarder Danny Way who performed a spectacular stunt jumping the Great Wall of China in 2005. This achievement is portrayed as a superhuman feat. Danny's challenge is not merely ascending the enormous jump ramp that was constructed for the event, but also overcoming a fractured ankle and G-Force beyond that experienced by astronauts during a shuttle takeoff (Kotler, 2014, p. 7). On top of all this, Danny Way had the world watching, and the knowledge that a previous attempt at the stunt on a BMX bike in 2002 resulted in the death of the 30-year-old rider Wang Jiaxiong (Schweikher & Diamond, 2007). The story of the jump dramatically builds up in a 2012 documentary called *Waiting for Lightning*. As the narrative unfolds, Danny overcomes these challenges and jumps the Great Wall not once but twice, performing a 360° rotation on the second attempt. The emphasis that Kotler makes is that Danny has the abilities and strength that position him as an elite; he is able to summon a repertoire of physical skill and mental hardiness that few others can. He is thus, in some way, a superman.

Fashioning Danny Way as some kind of superhero dovetails with another key motif in this book: that the rise in popularity of sports such as skateboarding is connected to other processes regarding identity, individualism, and spiritual transformation. Comic book writer Grant Morrison claims that 'we live in the stories we tell ourselves. In a secular, scientific rational culture lacking in any convincing spiritual leadership, superhero stories speak loudly and bold' (2011, p. xvii). It has been argued that Superman is very much a Christ-like figure (Kozlovic, 2002), and more broadly an archetype of classic hero mythology as popularised by Joseph Campbell (2004). *Waiting for Lightning* shows that Danny Way's story can be articulated to fit quite neatly into Campbell's hero monomyth. As Kotler and Morrison foreground, the notion that skateboarders can be considered gods holds some merit. As an iteration of religion and popular culture, skateboarding icons command a huge amount of scrutiny and attention. Their every action is observed, analysed, rewound, and paused. Their sponsors, tricks, spot selection, and even the hashtags of their Instagram posts are dissected for subtle nuanced clues about industry developments and pending news. This is not just male adulation; in my research with women skateboarders in Hong Kong, numerous respondents praised Brazilian skateboarder Leticia Bufoni for her style, her sponsors, her great body, and her hardiness. One respondent refers to Leticia and Mariah Duran as goddesses, replicating similar devotionals espoused by male skateboarders.

It is therefore apt to highlight the reverence they receive, but also essential to contrast this with the more secular notion of celebrity. Skateboarders are fundamentally athletes who market both their skill and their personality. Gregory Snyder's (2017) exploration of professional skateboarding makes this fact distinctly clear. Being accomplished, or even gifted on a skateboard is not enough to grant you access to professional status. Ultimately, skateboarding is a popularity contest that dictates access in terms of subcultural cool and social capital. Thus, the insights in this chapter correspond also to the cult of celebrity.

However, gods, superheroes, and celebrities are only some of the ways in which these characters are understood. Here, I observe the various ways that the idea of 'skateboard gods' can be conceived. Firstly, I discuss Rodney Mullen, who is imagined as a philosopher-sage in skateboarding. His contribution to both the industry and the culture is immense. Arguably, his footprints are on the manoeuvres that most people recognise and understand as the fundamentals of street skateboarding. He is wholly an individual and, in many ways, set aside from his peers because of his intellect, creativity, and skill. Secondly, Christian Hosoi and Jay Adams represent a different form of reverence; both are key characters in the evolution of skateboarding, and both have had a dramatic fall from grace. Most spectacularly Hosoi has experienced a resurrection, becoming both a born-again Christian and a veteran pro for Vans skateboard shoes. Both Hosoi and Adams represent the prodigal son in skateboarding. They are, like so many other celebrity athletes, flawed and yet idolised at the same time. I also address how by the end of 2018 there was considerable social media debate on the idol worship of professional skateboarders. Controversy surrounding veteran skateboarder Jason Jessee and Nazi paraphernalia, alongside allegations of predatory behaviour and child molestation by veteran vert skateboarder Neal Hendrix, a member of World Skate, the Olympic organising committee for skateboarding, has challenged longstanding protectionist lauding of skateboard idols. As a final part of this discussion I turn to the margins observing the relevance of local heroes, race, gender, and nationhood.

There are many other skateboarders I touch upon who may be regarded as gods, superhumans, and legends in their own right. Indeed, subsequent chapters return to this theme simply because it is potent. As I have already suggested, many of the skateboarders I discuss are middle-aged, and they have had time for their legacies to develop and unfold. There are, however, many younger skateboarders who have the potential to become 'gods' in their own right, such as Ryan Sheckler, Ishod Wair, and

Jamie Foy. Importantly, the new era of professional women skateboarders provides room for new types of gods as I have already suggested. Indeed, Leticia Bufoni, Nora Vasconcellos, Lacey Baker and Lizzie Armanto have begun to forge an iconic status in skateboarding, while Jamie Reyes (Liao, 2018) and Elissa Steamer (The Berrics, 2018) appear to be having their legacies consolidated. However, the personalities I discuss are secondary to the ways in which they are imagined and positioned as icons, superhumans, sages, and gods. These discussions touch on philosophy, redemption, hate, and ritual. My contribution is not to provide concise biographies of the skateboarders I refer to—there are certainly vast resources where readers can piece them together in much more detail. Instead, I seek to highlight examples where these individuals are imagined in terms that allow us to observe the relationship religion has with skateboarding. Issues of spirituality and Christianity rub shoulders with criminality, celebrity, popular culture, and the profane secular world. Fundamentally, this is a treatment in myth and symbolism corresponding to how religion can be observed in skateboarding, and how it can generate powerful feelings amongst skateboarders.

The Prophet, Rodney Mullen

Born in Florida in 1966, Rodney Mullen has had an exceptional career in skateboarding. At the age of 14 he won the title of World Champion in freestyle skateboarding, defeating Steve Rocco. The deposed Rocco went on to become hugely influential in transformations of the skateboard industry beginning in the late 1980s. Mullen dominated freestyle competitions, developed a legion of skateboarding tricks that would become the staple of street skateboarding, co-founded the World-Industries, A-Team, Enjoi, and Almost skateboard companies, and developed new technologies for skateboard trucks and board pressings. He has achieved mainstream notoriety in his inclusion in the Tony Hawk skateboard video games from Activision, and collaborations with Vogue and Ted Talks.

While Tony Hawk has been the popular commercial face of skateboarding, Mullen has taken the uneasy role of the humble philosopher, channelling an emotive and cerebral advocacy for the importance of skateboarding. Mullen's autobiography (Mullen & Mortimer, 2004) describes the taut relationship he had with his father and an ongoing curiosity about religion and spirituality. The book provides, at times, a harrowing account of a tense family environment and the emotional and physical outlet that skateboarding provided. There are several allusions to religion throughout the text. Mullen states that 'from the start I was a skateboarding monk, relishing the solitude it afforded me' (2004, p. 35). At other points in the text he reflects on a shrine he made from artefacts sourced from a skate trip to California. He devotes four pages to reflecting on his spiritual wanderings, experimenting with Scientology, Buddhism, Hare Krishna, Mormonism, and the Church of Satan. Yet Mullen reconfirms his Christian faith, and it remains a subtle theme throughout the book.

Mullen's skateboarding and spiritual life speak of the same drive and ambition, a curiosity, often solitary, of self-discovery and empowerment. The fame and adulation that Mullen has received encompass an understanding of his talent, determination, and intellect. He represents an ethos of skateboarding that resonates as authentic. Mullen is creative, individual, and has prioritised his therapeutic need to skate throughout his life.

Aside from his own soul-searching, Mullen has left an indelible philosophical mark on skateboarding. This is at once palpable in his skateboarding, but also made explicit in his book and the numerous public talks and interviews he has provided. Mullen has repeatedly advocated for both the creativity and community that skateboarding provides. In one TED Talk he argues that the creativity of skateboarding is basically a challenge to the realms of possibility. What is done on a skateboard is primarily about imagination. When an unknown teenager from another part of the world learns an advanced trick that they have seen him do in a video, he declares they did not learn the trick from the video, they only learnt that it was possible (TEDx Talks, 2013).

Such talks are philosophical and inspirational, providing an expansive notion to what a skateboard can mean to an individual. It is as if Mullen is talking about faith and transcendence. In the writing of Bill Schaffer (2016) these ethics are explored in contrast to the philosophical writings of Spinoza and Deleuze. What is presented is a new form of philosophy termed 'Mullenology' which seeks to further develop critical understanding of Deleuze's notion of cantering. Schaffer also recognises that Mullen is engaged in presenting an ethics of skateboarding, exploring human potential in what the body can do, and the creativity afforded to a community that shares their progress in pursuit of further innovation (2016, p. 21).

A less philosophical account on the influence of Rodney Mullen is provided by Sean Wilsey in a searching autobiographical take on the importance of skateboarding. The author talks of his adolescence when he had a chance encounter with Mullen:

> We sat and talked for a while. He gave me some advice and I practiced while he watched. Then he signed a board that wasn't even his own pro-model. I left with the impression that he was a gentle and modest person. He'd've fit right into a monastery. (Wilsey, 2014, p. 107)

The author goes on to talk about a challenging inoperable injury to Mullen's leg. Faced with a crippling problem caused by a build-up of scar tissue, Mullen spent solitary evenings stretching his leg until he painfully tore apart the scar tissue and was able to skate again. Wilsey concludes: 'Rodney Mullen—self-torturing; flipping ballet moves alone in a gas station at midnight—is as close to an authentic holy man as an American can get' (2014, p. 108).

While Kotler's discussion of Danny Way likens him to a superman, Rodney Mullen is more commonly presented as an ascetic holy man or mystic. Physically talented, yet guided by an internal quest, a puzzle, that few can comprehend. In my conversations with skateboarders who have met Rodney, there are recurring motifs. He is frequently reported as being profoundly intellectual, soft-spoken, and somewhat incomprehensible in his brilliance. His legacy in skateboarding is remarkable, paving the way through his own disciplined study and innovation for a variety of tricks that now form a foundation of street skateboarding. Much has been written about the cultural values of skateboarding, and commonly the tropes of individualism and creativity are central (Wheaton, 2013; Wheaton & Beal, 2003). In Rodney Mullen we can fashion an idol that embodies these core values, an exemplar of creativity and individualism, but so too an entrepreneur, a millionaire, and also an outsider.

However, even with such a legacy Mullen can be a contested figure. Some might criticise his gentle manner, or regard his freestyle roots as an aberration of skateboarding. In one critique in *Wired* magazine, a former freestyle skateboarder takes issue with Mullen's unbridled optimism about skateboard culture. She argues that the meritocracy of skateboarding is patriarchal and exclusive (Sierra, 2015). It is these very themes which echo throughout this chapter, as many may note few women are celebrated as skateboarding icons. It is also this meritocracy that works as a cultural centrifuge, being to those with the appropriate cultural capital a force of powerful inclusion. So potent is this meritocracy that even skateboarders who have transgressed in appallingly violent, destructive, and irresponsible ways are often forgiven and even idolised for their contributions to skateboarding. It is only in recent years that voices within skateboard culture are critiquing veteran idols, and in some cases vilifying them and pressuring sponsors to part ways with seasoned professionals. These transformations are part of a broader cultural movement of social justice in which parity and redress are pursued by de-platforming individuals. One must ask if the end of this protectionism is another signal of skateboarding's progression or demise. Indeed, while it signals sensitivity and redress, it can also be destructive and exclusive. It reneges on the celebrated promise that skateboarding is for everyone, and offers no path to salvation.

The Prodigal Sons, Christian Hosoi and Jay Adams

Amongst all skateboarders, it is Christian Hosoi who has the most outlandish and evocative connection to both religion and idolatry. His 2012 autobiography, titled *Hosoi: My life as a Skateboarder Junkie Inmate Pastor*, is littered with the excesses of 1980s skateboard celebrity lifestyle, the godlike adulation Hosoi receives from fans, his prolonged and distressing fall from grace. This is all recast in triumph by Hosoi in his resurrection as a born-again Christian. Again, his life story can be seen to fit with Campbell's hero's journey, and echoes with evocative parallels to Christianity. His name, his signature trick, his gifted ability to soar into the heavens high above the ramp, and above all else his unshakeable faith in himself, all give Hosoi a veneer of majesty few others have. Hosoi's co-author pens the introduction to his autobiography labouring the religious mythologising of his subject by describing Hosoi's followers as 'worshipful' likening him to 'some sort of fast-rolling messiah' (Hosoi & Ahrens, 2012, p. 3).

A brief overview of Hosoi's well-known story sets the stage for our discussion. Born in 1967 to parents with mixed Japanese and Hawaiian ancestry, he is named Christian Rosha Hosoi (each of the names connecting to a religious tradition in Christianity, Judaism, and Buddhism). Hosoi enjoys an unconventional childhood growing up in Los Angeles and living for a brief time in Hawaii. His father Ivan, an artist, is influential, and clearly the first and most ardent of Hosoi's fans. Strikingly permissive, Ivan is described on numerous occasions rolling and smoking joints with his son. Hosoi's use of cannabis begins at the age of 10, and he first tries LSD at the age of 12. He quickly rises to be a skateboarding prodigy, thanks in part to his father's unwavering support. By the mid-1980s Hosoi is making and spending hundreds of thousands of dollars, living in a grand house, and bankrolling his friends. He has numerous sponsors and mingles with celebrities, hanging out in night clubs with the likes of Eddie Murphy, David Arquette, and Robert Rusler. Changes in skateboarding no longer favour the vert ramp style that Hosoi is famous for and the 1990s see him spiral into obscurity. He becomes addicted to crystal methamphetamine and eventually is arrested in January 2000 for smuggling US$60,000 (1.6lb) worth of the drug into Hawaii. He serves four years and whilst inside prison becomes a born-again Christian. On release he revives his skateboarding career, acquires new sponsors, and becomes involved in a Christian ministry in LA.

Sports Sociologist Becky Beal (2013) is one of the few academics to interrogate the interplay of religion, criminality, and celebrity in skateboarding. Discussing Hosoi's career, she reviews articles about Hosoi's celebrity in the 1980s, his fall from grace, and resurrection. Drawing from a 2006 documentary on Hosoi titled *Rising Son: The Legend of Skateboarder Christian Hosoi* (Montaño, 2006), she explores the theme of redemption. In analysing media sources Beal argues that while both Hosoi and his father are shown to be morally flawed, skateboarding, as both an industry and community, is represented as a source of redemption. Beal quotes Hosoi's wife who received an outpouring of support from the skateboarding community: 'I was just shocked, the (skateboard community) were there for Christian, they were there for me, whatever he needed, they gave it to him' (Beal, 2013, p. 103). Beal goes on to argue that there is a correspondence in Hosoi's redemption through skateboarding. He is embraced by a family that never deserted him, that pressed him to change his ways while immersed in drugs. The skateboard industry is presented in Beal's account as a patient forgiving entity, a force in itself. She rightly notes that this has a functional purpose—it reflects and consolidates principles at the heart of the skateboarding community. Skateboard companies supporting Hosoi can be understood as having a vested interest; while it helps him with renewed sponsorships, his social capital is enhanced, and the process communicates the solidarity of the skateboarding community. I understand this dynamic as part of the conservative politics of skateboarding, as protectionism that is manifest in a prefigurative politics (O'Connor, 2015). This is a politics that illuminates the core principles of skateboarding by enacting them. This is how skateboarders emphasise that their sport is not simply a sport; they demonstrate that it is also about helping kids in Afghanistan learn to skateboard, building local skateparks, supporting the local skateshop, celebrating iconic skateboarders. The message we see in Hosoi's redemption is that skateboarding protects and advocates for its own—that within skateboarding there is forgiveness, family, and support. This sense of community parallels that which religion has traditionally fostered, and that which it seeks to both develop and maintain in the twenty-first century. As Ostwalt (2012) argues, we are living in an era where religion becomes more secular, and, conversely, where secular life takes on religious features. The redemption of Hosoi in the skateboarding community underlines this dynamic. Ironically, Hosoi finds Jesus, but is saved by skateboarding.

The narrative provided in Hosoi's autobiography largely attributes his redemption to his celebrity and faith in Jesus Christ. While he celebrates the fact that the Red Hot Chilli Peppers performed with T-Shirts printed with 'Free Hosoi,' he stops short of attributing his successes to skateboarding alone. He states that 'skateboarding is awesome, but the best things in my life have nothing to do with it. It's all about my family and spreading the love and joy of my faith' (Hosoi & Ahrens, 2012, p. 271). Here Hosoi transgresses the skateboarder code. Skateboarding is almost dismissed out of hand and in its place family and religion take centre stage. Perhaps this is a savvy move, as the reinvented Hosoi seeks to make a name for himself beyond skateboarding in his role as a pastor in Huntington Beach. Regardless, he can count on the loyalty of skate-boarders who are reluctant to exile even the most transgressive of their community, as our next example demonstrates.

The 2001 release of the *Dogtown and Z Boys* documentary serves as a moment when the popular appeal of skateboarding came of age. The growth of the X Games, the rising commercial appeal of skateboarding and other lifestyle sports culminated in a documentary that served to cement the important legacy of a handful of skateboarders. The charis-matic and rebellious Jay Adams was already a legend within the world of skateboarding, and the documentary revised his iconic status.

Born in Venice Beach, Los Angeles, in 1961, Adams came to personify a rebellious and carefree style as the youngest member of the Zephyr skateboard team. In opposition to a number of skateboard teams, the Zephyr skaters eschewed a uniform and a repertoire of predictable orches-trated moves and pursued innovative stylised skateboarding. Jay Adams has come to be revered not simply because of his style and natural ability on the board, but also for his dismissal of the celebrity and wealth that skateboarding could provide. Following his death in 2014 at the age of 53, he received the Transworld Skateboarding Legend Award. In a short video documentary Tony Hawk explains that Jay Adams

[w]as really the epicenter of the attitude of skateboarding which is fuck everyone do it yourself. Do it cause it's fun. Try anything and don't care about the success or the consequences of it you know. And then I think that that still resonates and he really was the, you know, he was patient zero of all of that movement. (Transworld Skateboarding, 2015)

These sentiments were echoed in a simple editorial by *Transworld Skateboarding* magazine's editor Jamie Owens following the death of Adams. A full page depicts a recent photo of Adams skateboarding, crouched low to the ground, hands out, feeling the transition of the pool he skates. It is a picture evocative of his surfing style, and by selecting a contemporary picture, rather than one of the many from his youth, there is a nod to the lifelong commitment Adams had to skateboarding. The brief text of the editorial reads thus (Owens, 2014):

> *The reason why we're not a Little League sport.*
> *The reason why there's attitude.*
> *The reason why we hop fences.*
> *The reason why we're creative.*
> *The reason why there's aggression.*
> *The reason why style matters.*
> *The reason why we're reckless.*
> *The reason why we don't follow the rules.*
> *The reason why we say, "Fuck You."*
> *The reason why we skate the way we do.*
> *The reason why is Jay Adams.* (Owens, 2014)

In just 70 words, Owen distinguishes Adams as an antecedent in much that is considered essential and immutable in skateboarding culture. Adams had the phrase '100% skateboarder' tattooed on his back, and in many people's estimation this is an apt definition of the man and the attitude he embodied. Adams is praised for never selling out, and for shunning commercial opportunities to make considerable sums. Hosoi declares that as a result he earned something more valuable—'the undying respect of his friends, because most other people would have sung that jingle and taken the cash' (2012, p. 77). On skateboarding message boards there is a similar, almost unchallengeable reverence for Adams. Such admiration is particularly potent amongst middle-aged skateboarders, those who had been influenced by Adam's in their own youth. Often recycled in posts on online forums is the quote from Adams saying 'you didn't quit skateboarding because you got old. You got old because you quit skateboarding.' While many argue that he never actually said this, the pure prioritisation of skateboarding is often idealised, as too is Jay Adams.

What intrigues me about the example of Jay Adams is the willingness of the skateboard community to dismiss the abuses and misdemeanours of skateboarders because of their wider contributions to the culture.

Adams, although becoming a born-again Christian, struggled through his life with substance abuse, and was incarcerated for physical assault. Indeed, there are many professional skateboarders who have trodden a similar path, and many that continue to be lauded. Thus, Adams is an example here of a tarnished individual, supported and forgiven by a community to which he has been seen to contribute. Much from this example dovetails with points made by Beal (2013) in her discussion on the legacy of Christian Hosoi. While Hosoi has immersed himself in the ministry of Christ, Adams had a chequered and erratic religious rebirth. As Hosoi notes in his autobiography, Adams 'isn't always perfect in his walk, but when going strong, it's an amazing testimony to God's power' (2012, p. 289).

The most controversial of the numerous transgressions of Adams dates back to 1982. After attending a Suicidal Tendencies gig in Los Angeles, Adams and his friends stole a sandwich and hung out at a restaurant in Santa Monica Boulevard. Their rowdy behaviour resulted in them getting kicked out of the establishment. On the street Adams spotted a gay couple walking arm in arm and verbally abused them. One of the men shouted back, and Adams responded with his fists. Allegedly Adams fled after a few punches and kicks, while a crowd of others joined in and beat the men. One of the couple, Dan Bradbury, was killed in the attack. Adams was sentenced to felony assault and spent six months in prison.

The story as Adams tells it relinquishes him from the blame of murder, but many are sceptical about his testimony. What has grown to be more controversial is the inherent homophobia that is implicated in the event. Although Adams has claimed that the attack was not motivated by the couple's homosexuality, it appears that it was a convenient target for an already volatile and aggressive Adams. The way in which this story is handled and approached is intriguing in seeking to understand the cult of celebrity skateboarders, their position in the subculture, and their legacies.

Following the death of Jay Adams, there was little mention of the murder of Dan Bradbury. This point is explored in an article in which the incident is framed as a hate crime (Smith, 2014). The issue the article poses is that we should not lionise a skateboarder who was involved in the murder of a homosexual man. In a broader scope this is a significant point as skateboarding has been criticised for its hyper-masculinity and its homophobia. It has only been in the years following the death of Adams that the landscape has significantly changed with increasing numbers of women skateboarders turning professional, and Brian Anderson coming out as gay in 2016.

The responses I have from my ethnographic work with skateboarders indicate an intriguing tension in the way the legacy of Adams is understood. Matt, one of my respondents in his early thirties, declared that he understands that people adore Jay Adams, but only wishes that Adams had been asked about the 'deification' that surrounds him while he was alive. Recasting the popular Christian motif WWJD (what would Jesus do), Matt reflects on online forums where people pose the rhetorical question 'what would Jay do?'

> It's like almost cross-referencing what would Jesus do? I feel like Jay would be offended by that because he was religious and he was more into Jesus than skateboarding in my opinion, and he would probably say something like, I just skateboard, you know?

Many of my respondents felt that they did not idolise skateboarders, they appreciated them, their style, their moves. But they in no way confused the skateboarder to be more than their contribution to skateboarding. Jordan in his early forties explained that hero worship and lauding skateboarders was not important to him:

> I think I see their flaws, you know, especially Jay Adams or Christian Hosoi. And these are guys that are really good at this thing that they do, but they're also, sort of, horrible people in their ways, like in their relationships or they've made awfully bad decisions, too. So, yes, I try to just focus on the skills and not the person.

This was contrasted further by a woman skateboarder in her fifties, who compared skateboarders to other popular culture celebrities. She, herself homosexual, was able to balance the adoration awarded to Adams with both forgiveness and a measure for the contributions of Jay Adams:

Well okay, the first thing is none of us are perfect, some of us are less perfect than others, he possibly killed somebody or was involved in killing somebody and I think it was a homophobic scene ... but is it not the same in art and music? Do we not forgive Michael Jackson for whatever he may or may not have done because he was a genius? Do we not love the song by Rick James 'she's a very funky girl'? Rick James was known to beat his girlfriends, James Brown, same, wife beater. Now of course I would prefer to think that the artists I love led a good life like Prince, I love Prince, he led a good life. But they don't always do, and here's the thing, are we going to look away from great art according to the character of the person or do they leave behind their legacy which is, they put it all in their art. Or their skateboarding or their music and maybe it's a shame that they weren't able to be together in their private lives. But are we going to say what they brought to skateboarding art or music does not count because they were flawed people? I'm not a very religious person but who are we to judge? Jay Adams went to jail, he paid dearly for these stupid acts that he ... I'm not going to judge him, he paid but I wish that he didn't do what he did. But what he brought to skateboarding you can't look away from it, he changed it forever.

Thus, in Jay Adams we have an example of a flawed idol. His legacy is his contribution to skateboarding, and this is somewhat separated from his drug abuse, criminality, and violent past. The cult of celebrity aids us in understanding Adams, but so too does the subcultural conservatism of skateboarding. Here there is a boundary construction in which Adams is seen to be 'one of us,' and regardless of his transgressions, it is important to keep both the culture and the community loyal and connected. Considering Jay Adams as a god is therefore a flawed way to comprehend the dynamics. Referring to the argument of Ostwalt (2012), we may propose that appreciation of Adams relates more broadly to the myth and symbolism of skateboarding. He is seen to embody something essential of the values and politics of the culture. Part of this translates to what Ostwalt (2012, p. 211) has observed with regard to motorcycle culture and the mystique surrounding it in popular culture. It is a celebration of the anti-hero, the outlaw, and the maverick. Acknowledging Adams' contribution, his ethic, and his attitude is a powerful way to comprehend part of skateboard culture, part of the mythology and lore that contributes to how skateboarders conceive of themselves as a collective.

New Heroes

Professional skateboarder Paul Rodriguez stands out as an icon of twenty-first-century skateboarding. He received his eponymous name from his actor and comedian father and is of Mexican heritage. Rodriguez is the forerunner of a new generation of skateboarders that developed in the early 2000s. He is clean-cut, middle-class, multicultural, commercial, and athletic. Competitively, he has achieved broad success, winning four X Games gold medals, the Street League title three times, and also one Battle of the Berrics title. He is gifted on a skateboard, but is also level-headed, ambitious, and business-savvy. He was one of the first professional skateboarders to recruit a manager (former snowboarder Circe Wallace) and take on a commanding role in cultivating his skateboarding career. His legacy might best be measured in the way he has pioneered the legitimation of sponsorship from large sportswear companies. His relationship with Nike has been groundbreaking, as he was the first skateboarder to have a signature shoe with the company. In 2017 Rodriguez became one of only five athletes to have more than ten Nike signature shoe models released, placing him alongside Michael Jordan, LeBron James, Kobe Bryant, and Kevin Durant. More significantly he is the only non-basketball athlete to have ten Nike signature shoes, and an elite member of the 1% club of Nike-endorsed athletes to receive a signature shoe (Nike, 2017). Rodriguez is also interesting because he has managed to nurture a popular and commercially mainstream career whilst also continuing to be recognised as authentic and receiving broad subcultural support within the skateboarding community.

At a further tangent Rodriguez is relevant to our discussion because of his conspicuous Christianity. In the high-profile Street League and X Game competitions, he is often shown praying into his cap before he attempts tricks. In one interview he is asked if his action of praying into his cap is 'TV time,' a deliberate performance to showcase his sponsors as he moves his cap with their logo over his face and whispers a prayer. He responds that 'personally, I don't want to get too philosophical, but I believe in a higher power, so I say prayers. And so, for me, and by the way, I do this when I street skate as well. The more nervous I am, the more intense that gets. It's become an OCD.' He confesses he covers his face to not make it look too public and to try to have some personal time (The Nine Club, 2016). In another interview he speaks about a tattoo of Jesus that he has on his right forearm. He explains that he believes in Jesus and has the tattoo as a reminder of his good works (AlliSports, 2012). Rodriguez, like other American athletes, has invoked a muscular Christianity as part of his sporting identity. It is public and confessional but not burdened with moral overtones and evangelism. One could contrast American Football star Tim Tebow, who is notorious for his religiosity on the field (Feezell, 2013). Unlike Tebow, Rodriguez has largely been able to avoid controversy and criticism about his religious commitment.

Unlike the other icons we have explored in this chapter, Rodriguez represents skateboarding's new trajectory—polished, commercial, and athletic. It is void of the philosophical quest of Mullen, and untarnished by the indulgences and misdemeanours of Hosoi and Adams. Unlike these characters, Rodriguez has thoughtfully planned and managed his career. He represents less the subcultural anti-hero of skateboarding's punk and DIY origins and much more the cultivated skateboard athlete of the twenty-first century.

Gods as Folk Heroes

Imaging skateboarding as having a polytheistic cosmology or a pantheon of various personalities with differing skills and attributes is appealing. In part it provides a religious paradigm to contrast a legion of identities. However, I would argue that the creation of gods in skateboarding has less to do with the divinity of specific skateboarders, and more to do with the divinity of the skateboarding community. This is demonstrated by the fact that there is no ultimate skateboarding deity, all gods are acknowledged, and thus it is a community of gods that matter. We see this in a *Thrasher* (Callahan, 2013) feature on skate gods and in Tait Colberg's analogous comparison of skateboarders to artists, scientists, and musicians. It is the ensemble that truly matters, not the individual. Godmaking in skateboarding can be contrasted with Durkhiem's argument that religion is society worshipping itself. Indeed, the reverence awarded to skateboarders is simply a reverence for skateboarding itself. This is further demonstrated in the ways in which praise and respect are also cast upon home town heroes.

Within every city, or small town, there are a collection of skateboarders who are regarded as mythic characters. In my own childhood there was a local skateboarder called Jay (Jason) Bates. He lived in the nearby city, and skateboarders in our neighbouring town dreamed up imaginary scenarios in which he would be a triumphing hero. If a set of steps were too daunting for us to jump down, we would claim that Jay Bates could do it. If he were not tucked away in the rural English countryside of Mid-Devon, we imagined Jay would certainly be riding for Powell Peralta. To us, his skills and abilities were beyond our comprehension. Seeing him skate was like staring at the sun. In my interviews with skateboarders, young and old, this dynamic is replicated. Just about everyone mentions a local skateboarder that they hold, or have held, in high esteem. Professional skateboarders also tell these tales. Any number of guests on *The Nine Club*, or interviewed on the blog *The Chrome Ball Incident*, refer to friends they grew up with who they regard as 'the best.' In Gregory Snyder's (2017) book on professional skateboarding, his brother Aaron talks of a gifted friend who was influential in his skateboarding career, and one he regards as divinely talented and wise.

Veteran skateboarder and author David Thornton expands on the discussion of skateboarding's local heroes:

> These are the skaters that either never vied for glory at contests, or, for whatever reason, didn't get noticed on a national level. ... These skaters have been, on a smaller scale than the Zboys, glorified by stories told at skate spots over the years. These are the dudes that, despite the lack of fanfare, ripped as hard as the pros and inspired their local scenes through athleticism, creativity, and bravery. (Thornton, 2016, pp. 95–96)

He elaborates further on pools he has visited and ramps he has travelled to far and wide, each location replete with stories about the achievements of its locals dating back decades. Thornton argues that individuals are able to become legends through their subcultural 'contributions to local history' (2016, p. 96). This discussion is evocative of the notion of the Moroccan Marboutism described by Clifford Geertz (1968, pp. 48–49). A cult of saints is attached to renowned holy men and their tombs, attracting pilgrims drawn to these places, and the tales of the mystics attached to them. Such tombs are further related to fraternities, brotherhoods, and have a close connection to lineage. This, in part, mirrors the legitimacy of Hadiths, the saying of the prophet Muhammad in Islam, where authority is assumed in connection to those who were able to verify the given actions and sayings of the prophet. Similarly, in Thornton's description of local legends, there is often testimony that claims a local 'was the first to … '; the veracity of such tales is often bolstered by reference to others who bore witness to the infamous event. Thus, skateboarding, which has long been a mediated subculture, is still deeply influenced by an oral history that creates and maintains legends both locally and globally.

In an interesting twist, Thornton's notion of the local hero comes to rest with his own reflection on parenthood. He recognises the delicate negotiation that must take place in adulthood, transforming skateboarding from a necessary outlet of defiance, pushing the boundaries, to a discipline of confidence and respect. He sees his role as a father as dual: to campaign for a legitimate place for his son to skate, and also to impart the codes of street skating between the ambiguous lines of the law. He concludes that 'society makes gods of our sports stars and celebrities. It is our job as fathers to guide our children until they become old enough to realize that an appropriate role model was right beside them all along' (Thornton, 2016, p. 104).

Conclusion

I have argued throughout this chapter that the notion of skate gods is evident in the way skateboarders discuss and revere notable personalities. In observing various examples of this expression, we have foregrounded some ways in which religion and skateboarding intersect. My argument is that skate gods are not imagined to be real, but the sacred terms that are attached to specific individuals serve to symbolise their place in skateboard mythology. We observe Danny Way as a superman, Rodney Mullen as a holy man, and Christian Hosoi as the prodigal son. We also observe how skate gods have been a significant aspect in folklore, creating local meaning and forming part of an oral history of skateboarding shared within the community.

It is this final point, on the power of skateboarding as a community, that unites the various themes explored throughout the chapter. Whatever our initial impressions are of the phrase 'skate gods,' the people and the experiences that it tends to relate to resonate with the notion of communitas. Mullen is celebrated for his contribution, Hosoi and Adams forgiven, and it is a skate community that creates a local hero. Placing this discussion in the broader literature on skateboarding as a sport, religion, and popular culture will be fruitful. Just as mainstream sport personalities have been revered and made into secular gods, so too have professional skateboarders. It is thus important for the academic study of sport to take skateboarding more seriously as a cultural force with its own meanings that extend to both religion and ritual. As an example of the role of religion in popular culture, there is much here that connects to the arguments made by Conrad Ostwalt (2012), that as religion secularises, similarly secular activities begin to take on more religious features and elements. As a result, people derive not just meaning, but guidance and community from popular cultural commodities that in some form become sacralised.

References

@anthonypops. (2018, 5:06 am April 6, 2018). Frequent No Complyers Who Aren't Familiar W/Ray Barbee's Contributions to Skating Are Appropriating the Culture. *Twitter Post*. Retrieved from https://twitter.com/anthonypops/status/982001575018291201

AlliSports. (2012). Paul Rodriguez Tattoo Story—Allisports Under the Gun. *YouTube Video*. Retrieved from https://www.youtube.com/watch?v=YdwYZ4isYZA

Beal, B. (2013). The Ups and Downs of Skating Vertical: Christian Hosoi, Crystal Meth, and Christianity. In L. A. Wenner (Ed.), *Fallen Sports Heroes, Media, and Celebrity Culture* (pp. 92–106). New York: Peter Lang.

Callahan, J. (2013, March). Skate Gods. *Thrasher*, 32–33.

Campbell, J. (2004). *The Hero with a Thousand Face: Commemorative Edition* (3rd ed.). Princeton: Princeton University Press.

Colberg, T. (2012). *The Skateboarding Art*. Morrisville, NC: Lulu Press.

Eliade, M. (1959). *The Sacred and the Profane*. New York: Harcourt.

Feezell, R. (2013). Sport, Religious Belief, and Religious Diversity. *Journal of the Philosophy of Sport, 40*(1), 135–162. https://doi.org/10.1080/00948705.2013.785423

Geertz, C. (1968). *Islam Observed: Religious Development in Morocco and Indonesia*. Chicago: Chicago University Press.

Hosoi, C., & Ahrens, C. (2012). *Hosoi: My Life as a Skateboarder Junkie Inmate Pastor*. New York: Harper One.

Kotler, S. (2014). *The Rise of Superman: Decoding the Science of Ultimate Human Performance*. New York: New Harvest.

Kozlovic, A. K. (2002). Superman as Christ-Figure: The American Pop Culture Movie Messiah. *Journal of Religion & Film, 6*(1), 1–25. https://digitalcommons.unomaha.edu/cgi/viewcontent.cgi?article=1771&context=jrf

Liao, J. (2018). Catching Up with Jamie Reyes, the Forgotten East Coast Pioneer. *Online Magazine*. Retrieved from http://www.jenkemmag.com/home/2018/09/05/catching-jaime-reyes-forgotten-east-coast-pioneer/

Montaño, C. (Writer). (2006). Rising Son: The Legend of Skateboarder Christian Hosoi [Motion Picture]. In J. Freedman (Producer). QD3 Entertainment & Quiksilver.

Morrison, G. (2011). *Supergods: Our World in the Age of the Superhero*. London: Jonathan Cape.

Mullen, R., & Mortimer, S. (2004). *The Mutt: How to Skateboard and Not Kill Yourself*. New York: Reagan Books.

Nike. (2017, June 20). Paul Rodriguez Celebrates His 10th Nike Sb Signature Shoe. Retrieved from https://news.nike.com/news/nike-sb-paul-rodriguez-ten

O'Connor, P. (2015). Skateboard Philanthropy: Inclusion and Prefigurative Politics. In K. J. Lombard (Ed.), *Skateboarding: Subcultures, Sites and Shifts* (pp. 30–43). London: Routledge.

Ostwalt, C. (2012). *Secular Steeples: Popular Culture and the Religious Imagination* (2nd ed.). London: Bloomsbury.

Owens, J. (2014). First Words: The Reason Why. *Transworld Skateboarding, 32*, 1.

Schaffer, B. (2016). No One Standing above You: Rodney Mullen and the Ethics of Innovation. In K. J. Lombard (Ed.), *Skateboarding: Subcultures, Sites and Shifts* (pp. 17–29). London: Routledge.

Schweikher, E., & Diamond, P. (2007). *Cycling's Greatest Misadventures*. Solana Beach, CA: Casagrande Press.

Senrud, C. (2018). The Patron Saints of Skate. In I. Michna (Ed.), *Jenkem Vol. 2: More Skateboarding, Smut, Shenanigans* (pp. 214–219). Brooklyn, NY: Jenkem Magazine in association with WINS.

Sierra, K. (2015, February 23). Silicon Valley Could Learn a Lot Form Skater Culture. Just Not How to Be a Meritocracy. Retrieved from https://www.wired.com/2015/02/silicon-valley-thinks-can-learn-skater-culture-terrible-idea/

Slap Magazine. (2018). If Skateboarding Were a Religion. *Online Forum.* Retrieved from http://www.slapmagazine.com/index.php?topic=101943.0

Smith, J. (2014). Maybe We Shouldn't Be So Quick to Idolize a Gay-Bashing Skateboarder. Retrieved from https://www.vice.com/en_us/article/jmbbk3/maybe-we-shouldnt-be-so-sentimental-about-a-gay-bashing-skate-boarder-658

Snyder, G. (2017). *Skateboarding La: Inside Professional Street Skateboarding.* New York: New York University Press.

TEDx Talks. (2013, October 16). On Getting Up Again | Rodney Mullen | Tedxorangecoast. *YouTube Video.* Retrieved from https://www.youtube.com/watch?v=DBbmNAZWq-E

The Berrics. (2018). Baker Adds Elissa Steamer to the Team. Retrieved from http://theberrics.com/elissa-steamer-baker/

The Nine Club. (2016). Paul Rodriguez | *The Nine Club* with Chris Roberts—Episode 12. *YouTube Video.* Retrieved from https://youtu.be/xkmD86Ol44U

The Nine Club. (2018). Adidas "Das Days" Live | *The Nine Club* with Chris Roberts. *YouTube Video.* Retrieved from https://youtu.be/PKYTCl1OczE

Thornton, D. (2016). *Nobody: Essays from a Lifer Skater.* UK: Amazon.

Transworld Skateboarding. (2015, February 22, 2017). Tws Legend Award: Jay Adams—Transworld Skateboarding. *YouTube Video.* Retrieved from https://youtu.be/9WBWpknhjEc

Viceland. (2017). Skate Profile: Deathwish—Neen Williams *King of the Road/Web.* Retrieved from https://www.viceland.com/en_us/video/king-of-the-road-skater-profile-deathwish-neen-williams/592f3bb38f79e2df7ec1a4ce

Wheaton, B. (2013). *The Cultural Politics of Lifestyle Sports.* New York: Routledge.

Wheaton, B., & Beal, B. (2003). Keeping It Real': Subcultural Media and the Discourses of Authenticity in Alternative Sport. *International Review for the Sociology of Sport, 38*(2), 155–176.

Wilsey, S. (2014). *More Curious.* San Francisco: McSweeney's.

5

Iconography

My first decent skateboard was the Variflex 'Joker,' the board I learnt to
ollie on. I saw it in the window of my local bike shop with the outrageous
price tag of £50 (US$70). The graphic on the bottom of the board was a
human skull with a court jester's hat, framed by the outline of a playing
card. This corny graphic blew my 12-year-old brain. I returned almost
daily over the course of several weeks while I saved, begged, and borrowed
to supplement my slowly growing horde of cash. I was entranced by the
beauty of the board and excited by its menacing graphic. This board, like
countless others throughout the 1980s, played on a popular motif of
skulls and monsters. The artwork of Vernon Courtlandt Johnson (VCJ),
and his partnership with Powell Peralta skateboards, is often presented as
one of the best examples of this genre of board graphics. By the early
1990s the skateboard industry, and its visual culture, transformed with
Steve Rocco at the helm of World Industries. His companies released
boards with sophisticated graphics parodying both the skateboard industry and the ills of contemporary society. Skulls became passé, but satirical
religious imagery became a regular feature of board art and is so right up
to the present day. In Sean Cliver's book *Disposable: A History of Skateboard
Art*, these transformations are clear to see. Skateboard graphics appear to

© The Author(s) 2020
P. O'Connor, *Skateboarding and Religion*,
https://doi.org/10.1007/978-3-030-24857-4_5

be preoccupied with death, devils, skeletons, and religious iconography. It is easy to dismiss this association as trivial, inconsequential, and superficial, yet it is not.

Skateboard graphics are clear and distinct visual examples of religion in skateboard culture. This topic connects explicitly to the theme of observation. Corresponding with my polythetic notion of religion, and our present theme of observation, the artwork and iconography of skateboarding can be interpreted in a variety of ways. They relate to the family of ideas that includes symbolism, language, and can also be understood as artefacts. The issue of symbolism and iconography is relevant beyond the skateboard graphic. The cross insignia of independent trucks treads a line between Nazi insignia and Papal sacrality. The countless logos of skateboard companies, void of religious connections, end up invoking devotion and even worship. Many skateboarders have tattooed their bodies with the logos of the favourite skateboard brands mirroring Geertz's (1973, p. 90) claim that religion is a system of symbols that elicit 'long-lasting moods and motivations.' These examples highlight that skateboarding must be understood, at least in part, as a visual culture. But as we see in this chapter, the visual is also understood in an embodied and tactile schema. Taking seriously the prominence of art in skateboarding requires that I employ some of the techniques of art criticism. Embracing the principles of scholarly work on visual culture, that images must be understood not just in terms of their creators, but also their consumers, I discuss iconography, allegory, and symbolism in skateboard graphics (Gaiger, 2006; Morgan, 2005). Here I draw on the history, contexts, and artists of numerous works as well as incorporating the opinions of various collaborators in my ethnographic work. I argue that, if we are to understand skateboarding—its values, its meanings, its devotees—then we must turn to the art and iconography of skateboarding and explore what it seeks to communicate, and also how it is received. However, art might be too lofty a term to describe what skateboards are adorned with.

A body of work on religion and popular culture informs this discussion and details how the relevance of religion in the iconography of skateboard graphics and logos is one of the most important ways to frame and discuss the relevance of religion in skateboarding. The premise here is that we should begin by taking skateboard graphics at more than face value. For instance, my anecdote about the skull graphic shows an interest in grisly art and its association with death, danger, taboo, and the unknown. How might the skull be decoded by a teenage skateboarder? Does it connect with the subversive association of skateboarding as an alternative pastime and way of life? Is it evocative of the voluntary risk-taking, or edgework (Lyng, 2005), of skateboarding that courts danger for supposed freedom, empowerment, and control? Is the skull a message suggesting that skateboarding is a macho 'boys' activity (Yochim, 2010) and is coding a form of gendered boundary construction? Or do skulls simply look edgy and cool?

Skateboard graphics communicate both skateboard culture and a commentary on skateboarding's place in the broader visual coding of mass popular culture. The fact that skateboard art is made to be disposable is an important part of the nihilism of skateboard philosophy. Skateboarders young and old choose a board considering its shape, the company, the professional whose name is on it, and of course the graphic. They diligently and ritually set their boards up taking care over the placement of the grip tape. Yet once the board is ridden, it is inevitably going to become scratched, battered, worn, and eventually discarded. Skateboards, as all skateboard collectors will reluctantly admit, are made to be ridden. Skateboards, just like their human riders, are born to die. This is both a pragmatic reflection and an immediate and accessible metaphor for the art adorned on skateboards. The ephemeral quality of life does not detract from either its meaning or beauty. Thus, it may be more correct to refer to skateboard graphics not so much as art, which is to be preserved and admired, but rather as decorative design that is disposable and superficial.

Douglas E. Cowan writes extensively on the way religion is represented in horror movies (2008, 2012a). He suggests that part of what we must turn our attention to is the 'sociophobics,' or social construction of fear, that horror movies draw upon. Consistently, religion is part of this construction of fear; it represents at once something that is meant to be sacred and safe, and at the same time it is associated ritually and symbolically with death. Cowan argues that we must take the relevance of religion in film seriously because films are important cultural products of our era. Movies are mass-produced, involve considerable investment, and are painstakingly and minutely crafted in intricate considered detail (2008, p. 95). Terry Ray Clark argues that we should think carefully about why and how 'popular cultural practices and products, especially those considered as forms of entertainment, are laden with religious ideology' (2012a, p. 1). He encourages readers to reflect on the way popular culture interacts with both the sacred and profane. The message he clarifies is that the sacred and profane are empty conceptual categories that we impart with meaning. The sacred could be a crucifix for a Catholic, a cow for a Hindu, and a set of steps for a skateboarder. Conversely, it is not difficult to imagine that a crucifix, cow, or steps could be considered profane, mundane, and meaningless.

Skateboard art thus requires careful consideration. It is religious and the ways in which it is so are worthy of exploration. Some art clearly draws on sociophobics; this is the art of pentagrams, skulls, and devils. Perhaps the best example of this is the Natas Kaupas *Devil Board* for skateboard company 101, which we shall discuss in more detail later. Other representations of religion are subversive social commentary *Skate Switch for Jesus* or Jeff Grosso's *Crucifried* board for Anti Hero. A third category can be reserved for devotional boards, ones that include religious symbolism as part of the faith of the rider. Examples of devotional boards can be seen in Gabriel Rodriguez's *Jesus* board also for 101, and many of Jamie Thomas' boards for Zero that have crucifixes or other Christian imagery. These are the overt images of religion and there are many more examples of *diacritic* religious symbolism. This is a term I borrow from John Bowen (2012), who argues that a religious person may signal their ethnic group, piety, or political affiliation through body posture, choice of headwear, or type of prayer uttered. For example, the Jake Johnson's *Catharine* (from 2015) board from Mother (later Quasi) included reference to a biblical passage Romans 12:2 on the top of the board. It drew a connection to religion in a subtle way. In conversation with Johnson he revealed that this was in part a connection to the faith of his mother whose image is reproduced on the board. However, the passage speaks of individuality and resistance to conformity. Thus, a biblical passage is used not so much to invoke religion, but also to underline an ethic that may be considered relevant to the rider, the board company, or simply the act of skateboarding.

One thing is evident—Christianity and its associated sociophobics are dominant above all other religions in skateboard art. Following the argument of Ostwalt (2012) this is typical of a culture with its roots in the USA. The separation of Church and State in the USA has simply served to heighten the way in which Christianity is popularly communicated. Christianity has had to compete in the marketplace with all other cultural products. Simply put, its absence in government has ultimately led to its ubiquity in all forms of public life. Where the separation of Church and State has been less absolute in Europe, Heelas, Woodhead, Seal, Szerszynski, and Tusting (2005) argue, there has been a more noticeable decline in commitment to Christianity. However, a number of skateboard graphics over the last 30 years move beyond the Christian imagery that is often so dominant. Some examples relate to a whole host of Daoist, Rastafarian, and Hindu symbolism from Jef Hartsel's various board graphics to the esoteric extraterrestrial conspiracy artwork of Alien Workshop. Professional skateboarders often have a say in their graphics, and artists who work on skateboard designs are often skateboarders themselves. These are all reasons why the religious component of skateboard art should be scrutinised. Why are there so many religious skateboard graphics?

This link has been addressed in a 2003 *Transworld Skateboarding* editorial titled 'Cashing in on God.' The magazine lists various companies and professional skateboarders with notable religious graphics, questioning why there is a need for such representations. The critique is levelled at the way in which religion is used as a marketing gimmick, playing towards both the sacred and the profane. 'In the span of a year, Zero released peaceful, positive graphics of Jesus, the Virgin Mary, a Christian cross, and Bob Marley alongside images of Osama Bin Laden, skulls, blood, knives, demons, pentagrams, and the phrase "Zero or Die"' (Transworld Skateboarding, 2003). The editorial asks if religion is being used simply as 'fashion' and if young kids buying boards even care about religion. While providing various commentaries from skateboard artists, professional skateboarders, and even skateboard shop owners, the editorial assumes a critical position of the use of religious symbolism in skateboarding. This is remarkably similar to the distaste that football fans have voiced about the overt religious posturing of former NFL quarterback

Tim Tebow (Feezell, 2013). When one questions the place of religion in popular culture, one must consider what the objections are. They may ultimately seek to reinforce the divisions between the sacred and the profane, and reserve religion for some separate space. Fundamentally, such objections serve to dismiss the importance of religion at all levels of nearly all of human culture. Anthropology and psychology have shown religion to be a universal human concern albeit represented in distinctly different forms.

Skateboarding art shows us a religious sociophobic preoccupation that is still significant even if regarded as a marketing gimmick. In some ways the reliance on religious imagery, and particularly Christian symbols, serves as a form of 'Christotainment' (Steinberg & Joe, 2018). However, religious iconography in skateboarding is also social commentary, depicting a pope with devil horns, or a nun burned at the stake, skateboard graphics are often designed to provoke (Carayol, 2014). In using satire, skateboard graphics reinforce skateboarders as an alternative heterodox culture, interested not simply in rejecting convention, but more importantly in questioning the norms of society and striving to see the world differently. Clark argues that 'the purpose of satire is to provide an opportunity for an audience to begin thinking for itself, to think more critically about a topic than it has done so before' (2012b, p. 17). Such graphics provide us with further resources to understand the suspicion of religion in skateboarding.

Let us consider a 2010 Alien Workshop board by artist Mike Hill (see Fig. 5.1). The graphic is very simple, depicting a television set with two hands cupping it in praise and adoration. The text underneath reads 'exalt the new god.' The graphic was originally released as a T-shirt design by the company in 1995 and was subsequently resurrected as a board design (Carayol, 2014, p. 180). If we consider what a teenage child might think when purchasing a board or a T-shirt, we might be able to envision some of the impact of skateboard graphics in the intellectual, spiritual, and aesthetic repertoire of young people. Even if casually dismissed the board has a blunt message, *television is worshipped*, but in its satirical nature it is not judgemental. The graphic provides room for reflection on our notion of what god, and indeed the sacred, might be. But in a much subtler way the graphic informs skateboarders that their pastime is not simply a sport,

Fig. 5.1 *Exalt the New God*, Alien Workshop, Artist Mike Hill (from 2010)

but also critical social and self-reflection. If we apply comparative terms, can we readily imagine a football, cricket bat, or rugby shirt with a similar motif? This underlines the fact that skateboarding is so very difficult to contain and define.

In the following sections I will build on the points I have addressed thus far. Skateboard graphics are often religious, and this is not an issue to dismiss. Popular culture can be an important arena for religious exploration, and a space to deal with and encounter our sociophobics. I underline the fact that it is because these boards are ridden and destroyed they carry additional layers of importance. What does it mean to ride with a devil on your board, how does one feel about defacing a cross, the Virgin Mary, or a pentagram? At their very best, skateboard graphics can be both devotional and satirical, encouraging us to become uncomfortable, to challenge our beliefs, and to reconfigure them. In this way skateboard graphics are a synecdoche for skateboarding, an activity that demands alternative ways of viewing the world and of considering what is possible. In order to explore these ideas, I have selected four examples of board art to discuss in depth, each connecting with and explained through a different theme, sociophobics, satire, allegory, and devotion.

Natas Kaupas Devil Board

The 1991 Natas Devil Board is one of the most famous skateboard graphics of all time. The fact such notoriety is attached to a board with such deep religious symbolism serves to underline my point about the role of religion in skateboard graphics. The board, however, is not famous simply for its graphics alone, but also for the folklore that surrounds it and is attached to a group of skateboarding icons.

Firstly, the board designed by artist Marc McKee depicts a cross-legged Baphomet holding in his right hand a naked decapitated baby by its leg. In his left hand he levitates the baby's burning head. In the background six religious figures, seemingly priests and a naked woman, are depicted hanging from a wooden cross (Fig. 5.2). One of the figures is entirely naked, penis on display, and adorned only with a papal mitre which has 'Pope Hat' scrawled on it. Several naked torsos are falling through the background and skulls litter the land where a pentagram with the name 'Natas' is placed. A final touch is that the board graphic is printed upside down, this serves to invert the cross and make a nod to the reverse spelling of the rider's name. McKee claims that the art is heavily influenced by the cover art of the album *Reign in Blood* by the Metal band Slayer (The Nine Club, 2018). The artwork was intended to be a commentary on superstition, playing very much into the sociophobics argument of Cowan (2008). Shortly after Natas accepted the graphic he received a career-ending injury breaking his ankle. Carayol (2014) notes that the injury assures some that the board graphic is cursed despite the fact that Natas was not actually riding the board when he got injured.

Fig. 5.2 *Devil Board*, Natas: 101, Artist Mark McKee (from 1991)

Natas Kaupas is widely regarded as a skateboarding icon lauded for his innovative approach to street skateboarding, pioneering moves largely in isolation of other skateboarders, embracing alternative fashion and music, brokering industry deals at the age of 16, and the first skateboarder to launch a pro skateboard shoe. His magazine appearances and video parts in the late 1980s developed a large fan base. His Lithuanian name was, however, regarded with exotic curiosity, and superstition, by some. Many parents objected to skateboards with the name Natas on them as they believed the name was sinister, a backwards spelling of Satan (ON Video, 2003). His boards were banned for more than a decade by the Los Angeles Unified School District (Carayol, 2014, p. 162).

Marc McKee reports that originally he designed the board for professional skateboarder Jason Lee, a rider for Blind, one of the companies under Steve Rocco's World Industries umbrella. McKee thought that the devil graphic would appeal to Lee because he had requested a Bella Lugosi Dracula graphic but had been denied this by Rocco. McKee reports that Lee wanted something gothic, but probably not satanic. Blind team Manager Mark Gonzales, in jest, warned Lee not to take the graphic as it would beckon bad luck. Rocco then offered Lee $10,000 to accept the artwork as a graphic for his pro model skateboard, to which Lee originally agreed and then refused, returning the money to Rocco. In the end, Natas stepped in to take the graphic for his own board, claiming it as a joke because of the controversy surrounding his name.

The superstition that McKee sought to evoke in his artwork is indeed valid in how the board has been received, not just by Jason Lee, but by the skateboarding population. Professional skateboarder Chris Roberts, in conversation about the board with McKee, says 'it's a crazy graphic. My friend had one growing up and we didn't want to touch it' (The Nine Club, 2018). This commentary highlights the important issue that skateboard graphics exist on a board which is purchased with the chief aim of being ridden. One of my middle-aged male informants claimed that they liked the board, not just because of the graphic but also because of the shape. They also felt that riding on the devil was a statement, like 'dancing with the devil,' taunting those who dismiss and reject skateboarding as an aberrant and dangerous pastime. This introduces an important disruption to the division between the profane and the sacred. Skateboarders cherish their boards and yet they are transient objects used wholly in the profane world. Boards are playful, symbolic, yet functional. Another informant, a German woman in her early thirties, claimed that she would not ride the board as it is too masculine and that she would not want Satan 'under her feet.' A 22-year-old male skateboarder from the USA was enthusiastic about the board graphic and immediately identified the design as being McKee's. While he found the board humorous and advocated that such art serves an important subversive aspect in skateboarding, he confirmed that he would never ride such a board.

His choice not to ride the devil board rested on the fact that it was too controversial, and while he confessed that he is not religious, he does not want to 'stir the pot' and deliberately offend people. He also confirmed that he would never ride the board because of its shape and size. Of further interest is the fact that two of my informants read the image of the pope on a rope as a hanged Klu Klux Klan member. This in part may be a confused reference to a Jim Thiebaud board from Real, which depicts a hanging Klansman. Curiously the art for that board was composed by Natas Kaupas working alongside Kevin Ancell (Carayol, 2014, p. 146). So, it seems the Devil board is read in multiple ways by skateboarders, not simply as a piece of art, but also a tactile physical object that they would use, and as part of a world of interconnected skateboard graphics in dialogue with each other. They consider the board in terms of its symbolism, its controversy, its shape, and its size. The fact that the artwork is to be ridden extends the sociophobics of the art. Is it more daring to ride with the devil on your board? Additionally, skateboarders consider their boards like one might consider an item of clothing, as a statement about themselves which they identify with, and who they are. As a material object the board can also be understood as an artefact, something to be observed, held, and experienced.

A final point to make on the board is its connection to Steve Rocco's World Industries empire. Much has been written and discussed about the marketing savvy of Rocco who in many ways instigated a new level of interest in skateboard graphics. This unfolded in three main ways. Firstly, his board companies employed controversial graphics often spoofing existing copyrighted art and company logos. These graphics might be thought-provoking, but their main goal was to be cool enough for teenagers to buy them. Secondly, he inflated the demand for board art by releasing graphics every few months. Older established companies like Powell Peralta, Vision, and Santa Cruz would keep the same graphics for their professional riders for a year or more. Rocco's quick turnover of graphics was also compounded by the fact that his companies would invariably receive cease and desist requests from the copyright holders the art infringed upon. Lastly, the riders in Rocco's companies also eschewed the plastic rails previously used by vert riders to protect the underside of their boards and, as famously depicted in the video *Rubbish Heap*, began the practice of focusing boards. To focus a board is to deliberately snap it in two, making it unrideable. All of these practices contributed to an artistic environment in skateboarding where art was often provocative, ripped off, on rotation, and 'supposedly' disposable. It is within this context that the Natas devil graphic should also be read.

Crucifried 2017, Jeff Grosso, Anti Hero by Christian Cooper

Christian Cooper's artwork for the 2017 Jeff Grosso board *Crucifried* from the company Anti Hero reaches back towards the Baroque religious European art of the seventeenth to eighteenth century (Fig. 5.3). Cooper deliberately wanted to utilise this genre of art to draw on its norms of

Fig. 5.3 *Crucifried*, Jeff Grosso: Anti Hero, Artist Christian Cooper (from 2017)

religious iconography and allegory. He also wanted to push the limits of detail included in a skateboard graphic and react to the simple and often 'mundane' skateboard graphics that have increasingly become the norm. My commentary on this board is largely a dialogue with the artist himself, who generously provided elaboration on each of the details included on the board, and also with Jeff Grosso, who provided his own comments on the board and his thoughts on religion. Much of what I include here is paraphrased from Cooper's own words describing his art. He claims that 'the religious component was almost a test to see if anyone was paying attention,' but also reveals that Jeff Grosso initially requested to have board art in which he appeared crucified.

Before discussing the board in more depth it is important to highlight who Jeff Grosso is, and more precisely why a board depicting him as both a sinner and a martyr holds currency for skateboarders. Typically crucifixion scenes represent two notions: the passion of Christ's suffering and his ultimate resurrection. Both of these elements are evocative of Grosso's biography which includes lost years of alcohol and drug abuse, and a recent resurrection as an irreverent prophet for skateboarding's old guard. In my research with middle-aged skateboarders, Jeff Grosso's popular YouTube series for Vans, *Love Letters*, is a consistent theme. Three of my informants report owning or riding a Grosso board, and one cites Grosso's videos as a direct reason for why he started skateboarding again after a ten-year break. Grosso's popularity was discussed by 44-year-old Sarah, who also regularly watches his videos.

> There is that perception that he holds the soul, like the old-school soul of skateboarding. I think most people respond to a strong opinion. So, people like how he says it and means it and doesn't seem sad and lost you know, so that's compelling. I think that he's considered like a guard of a thing that is important. But at this moment a little bit eclipsed by the story of like competition money contest thing. … The stuff that Grosso is speaking to is the true line of skateboarding I think.

In line with the other icons of skateboarding that I explored in Chap. 2, Jeff Grosso is similarly an esteemed character in skateboarding and one who is valued because of his earnest adoration of skateboarding and his disdain for the pitfalls of the contemporary skateboard industry. Grosso discussed with me the context for the *Crucifried* board and referred to one of his previous board graphics from 1987 with Santa Cruz skateboards. He asked the company artist Jim Phillips to produce art depicting a battle between heaven and hell. This was a time in which Grosso was becoming deeply involved in drugs and there was speculation surrounding his ability to succeed as a professional skateboarder. 'It was like hey look this is what's going on with me guys.' Thirty years later, the *Crucifried* graphic does much the same thing. Following a drawn-out back injury Grosso had become 'strung out' on pain medication, was recovering from various surgeries, and was dealing with a painful divorce. Finally getting back on his board and overcoming these challenges, the idea for the artwork came through a discussion with a friend. It was initially going to be a sort of resurrection, to say Grosso is back. But it was Grosso who decided he should be crucified, providing a layered meaning not just of resurrection, but also of the willingness to perish for skateboarding and to stand up for what he believes in. Grosso elaborated on these issues at length, highlighting that while he believes in a Godlike power, the notion of organised religion is distasteful to him. Fundamentally he sees religion as a form of social control, manipulated by many to elevate and empower themselves at the judgement and expense of others. The board graphic was thus critical of religion, and also critical of the skateboard industry and how veteran skateboarders are selling out. He states:

> I want the new kid coming to skateboarding for the first time to have the exact same or at least a similar experience that I had. Because I felt ostracised and I felt alone and the other stuff that was available to me, organised sport, after school programmes, yada, yada, none of that fucking interested me. Skateboarding filled the void, you know, and became my best friend and it was my outlet. It was my way to get away from all of the bullshit at school and at home. And we need that, you know, kids need that. They need an alternative to the rest of the shit. I cannot understand why a bunch of fucking weirdos and misfits and freaks and geeks that came to skateboarding in the first place because they were all those things I just said, now have grown up and are going to sell skateboarding down the river and turn it into the exact same thing that we all hated.

Grosso's outspoken and opinionated videos have positioned him not only as a voice of old school authenticity, but also as a target for criticism and contempt. It is this dynamic that is represented in Christian Cooper's art. In my own imagining of the art, Grosso is a Jesus-like martyr, going against convention and those who have sought to commodify, profit from, and exploit what he might see as the pure faith of skateboarding. Think of Jesus casting out the moneylenders from the temple, standing up to the venality of the Pharisees. At the same time, I see the crucified Grosso as penance for the excesses of his younger life, and his passion or suffering of a world gone to ruin. In this second understanding I draw considerable interest in the elements of popular culture in Cooper's artwork. The Death Star hangs ominously in the sky as the burning International Space Station plummets to earth. Incorporated in these images are characters from the films *The Shining* and *Repo Man*, and the silver orb from the *Phantasm* film series.

Cooper's interest in presenting a religiously inspired graphic is remarkable for its connections to the arguments made by Cowan (2008, 2012a, 2012b) and (Cowan & Bromley, 2015) about the sociophobics of popular culture and their religious connections. Here, the artist has incorporated diacritic signals, many of which he acknowledges will be overlooked by people who enjoy the art and buy the board. For instance, at the foot of the crucified Grosso, four men are prostrated, as if they are performing the Islamic ritualised prayer of *Salah*. The rug on which they perform their prayer is adorned with the same pattern as the carpet from the Outlook Hotel, from Stanley Kubrick's *The Shining*. Cooper revealed to me that these elements were also connected to a link he had considered between grave desecration, relevant to the site of the Outlook Hotel in the film, and the opening up of Christ's tomb. The element of grave desecration is echoed in reference to the *Phantasm* films, where the bodies of the dead are exhumed and sent to an alien world to toil as slaves. Thus drawing on religious referents and Hollywood horror films, Cooper pushes existential questions about our place in the Universe.

Significantly, Cooper employs reference to religion beyond Christianity in this work. At the same time religious referents are enmeshed with pop culture and skate culture icons. Gandhi is depicted with a Ray 'Bones' Rodriguez, Powell Peralta deck on his lap. To the right of him there are poppies, which refer to Grosso's one time heroin addiction. Gandhi is said to represent both the idea of civil disobedience and the notion of religious pluralism that he promoted as the ideal for Indian independence. The artist claims that it is in part a commentary on how Hinduism is rarely an element of the dialogue in a post 9/11 world where the general feeling is one of religious warfare between Islam and the rest of the world. The fact that Gandhi holds what the artist and, he claims, many of his generation regard as 'the first truly high-impact graphic' is also a layered association between art, propaganda, and religion. This was the board that Grosso rode in his youth when he was a member of the Powell Peralta team. Indeed, the reproduction of this board and the original artwork from VCJ is an overt example of how skateboard art references and reveres previous board art. Similar to how academic work is built on a dialogue of the thinking and writing of previous scholars, skateboard graphics are designed and produced in a conversant manner, paying homage, respect, and acknowledgement to what came before. It connects with the family of ideas surrounding my schema of observation, drawing on myth, symbolism, and the way these elements sustain meaning.

Three further references to previous board art are included in the graphic. Firstly, a banner is displayed that reads 'God Hates Anti Hero'; Cooper explains that this is a reproduction of the 2014 board art for Anti Hero professional skateboarder Grant Taylor. This was a response to the Westboro Baptist Church demonstrators and their homophobic placards such as 'God Hates Fags.' He acknowledges that his artwork can be viewed as heretical and questions if indeed God does hate Anti Hero for releasing such a graphic. Secondly, Cooper extends this question by showing a pigeon perched on the crucifix with its droppings defacing the roman numerals representing 18. This requires elaboration for those unfamiliar with the skateboard company Anti Hero. The number 18 represents the nickname for the company taking the numerical alphabetical positions of both A and H. This is in itself a risqué nod to the far right's cult symbolism of Adolf Hitler and distinguishes the skateboard company as irreverent, nihilistic, and self-destructive. The pigeon itself represents the art of Todd Francis who has been a long-time collaborator with Anti Hero and has himself produced numerous controversial graphics. Pigeons are accordingly a common trope in Anti Hero boards. Cooper states that the pigeon droppings pose the question as to whether 'we are just shitting on ourselves by making the art we make.' Finally, to the left of the crucified Grosso is a ragdoll holding aloft a building block cube. This represents Grosso's very first pro board graphic from the company Schmitt Stix in 1986 originally designed by John Lucero. This is reportedly Grosso's favourite graphic of all time (Cliver, 2004, p. 159), but in this context it is surrounded by a fallen Disneyland sign and the Olympic rings. The placement of the graphic in this context is a reference both to the mutual distaste of both the artist and Grosso for the inclusion of skateboarding in the Olympics, and a slight to business practices where skateboard companies collaborate with Disney. The artist resists the notion that such practices are artistic collaborations and is critical of what might be considered a form of 'product placement' in skateboarding. Simply put, Disney's involvement in skateboarding is nothing but pecuniary, and while all skateboard graphics are in some way marketing devices, they have traditionally emerged from the subculture of skateboarding itself.

In general, there is a philosophical underpinning to many of the referents in the graphic. On the right side of the image there is an alien rolling his eyes in disgust, positioned next to the character Miller from the cult 1984 film *Repo Man* directed by Alex Cox. In the film Miller expresses some bizarre ideas about UFOs, time travel, and the synchronicity of the universe. At one point he also claims the iconic actor John Wayne was a homosexual, for which he is vehemently challenged. Cooper links the offence taken at the John Wayne comment as akin to blasphemy and notions, as highlighted previously, that the sacred and the profane are empty categories which we fill with our own collective social meanings. Both Cooper and Grosso have shared a fascination for extraterrestrials, and the placement of the alien being signals that such interests are religious in content seeking the ultimate answers to the cosmos. Indeed, visible on Grosso's left forearm is his Alien Workshop tattoo, a board company that he never rode for, yet was fascinated by their alien conspiracy themes. Miller's inclusion from *Repo Man* also dovetails with the connections made to the Westboro Baptist Church, and a bear-suited man and his sexual partner from the Shining. All of these elements connect to homophobia and the sordid hypocrisy of the Catholic church in condemning various sexual practices as aberrant while also harbouring paedophiles.

On the tail of the board, at the bottom of the graphic, there are two further religious connections. On the right-hand side there is a police mugshot of the punk icon Doc Colbin Dart, who was the lead singer in the band the Crucifucks in the late 1980s and early 1990s. Dart subsequently changed his name to 26 for spiritual reasons and claims that he is the messiah. He has, at times, been rabidly outspoken against the US government and lives a peculiar hermit-like existence caring for animals and shunning news on contemporary society. On the left there is a copy of *Time* magazine with the pope on the cover. This depicts a papal fascia from which the logo of the Independent Truck company is based. Jim Phillips was responsible for designing the logo for the fledgling truck company in 1979. He was originally inspired by the 'surfer's cross,' a practice by which surfers would signal their cultural belonging by wearing an adapted German Iron Cross. Connecting to the surfing legacy of skateboarding, Phillips incorporated the cross into his logo design. This was initially rejected as it looked too 'Nazi'; however, Phillips sought to verify the ancient origins of the symbol and found it used in the Pope's regalia, convincing colleagues that the logo was acceptable (Denike, 2004, pp. 22–25). In such an example Cooper provides an additional layer to an intricate dialectical relationship between skateboarding, religion, and popular culture. Again, Grosso's Independent Trucks insignia tattoo is also visible on his left wrist.

Cooper planned his art to give off an uneasy feeling, incorporating not just religious paraphernalia but also unnerving elements of popular culture, situated in a smouldering apocalyptic landscape. His process is also worthy of mention; working entirely digitally, Cooper's classical art training has had to be revised for work in the contemporary field. The *Crucifried* graphic is at once an artistic endeavour, a commentary on religion and popular culture, an Anti Hero product, and an ode to Grosso's skateboarding history. Beyond all this, the work is also about the friendship and shared passions of both Cooper and Grosso. It is both a cerebral and emotional work. Once again it is evocative of a challenge to a profane and sacred divide as Cooper's art includes an interplay of Grosso's biography, philosophy and religion, pop culture, and a critique of the skateboard industry. The real beauty of this achievement is that some will hang it on their wall, while others will ride it to destruction.

Grosso comments that the board has been a commercial success and has sold very well. At the same time, he reflects on the fact that the artwork is also provocative to his fellow veteran skateboarders and good friends, Christian Hosoi, Steve Caballero, and Lance Mountain, who are all devoted Christians. While he notes that some people will take offence at the graphic, his response is 'you know what? Fuck you. I have got to tolerate your bullshit too.'

Devotional Art

Finally, I turn to devout religious art. There are numerous examples of religious graphics from Christian skateboarders, and also companies such as Siren, Untitled, and Reliance. There are also many professional skateboarders who are publicly Christian who have not had explicitly religious graphics, such as Lance Mountain, Steve Caballero, and Ray Barbee.

Jamie Thomas is widely regarded as a skateboarding icon. He has a legacy connected to groundbreaking video parts, and companies. He has been a successful skateboard entrepreneur founding Zero skateboards, Fallen footwear, and Black Box distribution. Often regarded as an outsider, Thomas left his home in Alabama as a teenager and made his way to San Francisco in 1992. For months he lived out of his car and eventually found sponsors and built a career.

Born in 1974 and brought up in Alabama, Thomas confesses that religion was all around him as a youth. He lived in a conservative town and there was pressure and expectation for him to be religious. He was drawn to seeking out his own identity and drifted from the church and even rebelled against it in his teenage years (Haseltine, 2002, p. 36). At this time Thomas also got into trouble with the police through involvement in a racket of stealing car stereos (The Nine Club, 2017). It was not until Thomas was a successful professional skateboarder that he returned to Christianity. In 1999 the sudden death of fellow pro skateboarder Tim Brauch had a profound impact on Thomas. He claims that 'I wasn't looking for Jesus. I was fine with everything being about me. But yeah, I went to Tim Brauch's funeral and had a heavy realization that I was extremely selfish and I asked the Lord for forgiveness' (Thrasher Magazine, 2015).

Following his conversion Thomas decided to release a board graphic with a cross in 2000. He reported on several occasions that he was warned not to release a Christian graphic, that it would not sell, and that there would be a backlash. However, the board that has the passage John 3:16 reproduced in the background of the graphic, was one of Thomas' biggest sellers (Skateboarder, 2013). In an interview with *Thrasher* magazine he reports:

> When I first accepted the Lord, I felt like it was my responsibility to share my faith. I was also so hyped on the Lord that I felt it was what best represented me. I felt like everything else was cheap or blasphemous, but yeah I got a lot of heat because people said I was trying to cash in on God. Ironically, before I released the graphics everyone told me not to do it because they wouldn't sell and I felt so strongly about it that I did it anyways. When it comes to sharing your faith, you're going to get hate because spirituality is so personal. No one wants their spiritual space invaded. Over time, I realized that everything I did didn't have to advertise my faith or spirituality, so I started doing it more subtly. (Thrasher Magazine, 2015)

Following this public display of his faith Thomas found that he was regularly sought after for public speaking. There was no end of requests for him to do outreach work and share his story with youth congregations. He reports that while he initially felt obligated to do this work, he increasingly decided that his activities were an appropriate vehicle for his own ministry, which as he details earlier, have become increasingly discrete.

In contrast to the other boards discussed in this chapter, Thomas' *Cross* board requires very little elaboration. The message is clear: it is an item of faith and devotion. The choice of the Biblical passage is, however, worthy of note. John 3:16–3:18 reads as follows:

> For God so loved the world, that he gave his only Son, that whoever believes in him should not perish but have eternal life.
> For God did not send his Son into the world to condemn the world, but in order that the world might be saved through him.

Whoever believes in him is not condemned, but whoever does not believe is condemned already, because he has not believed in the name of the only Son of God.

—(John 3:16–18 ESV)

This is in itself a common passage repeated at Sunday service and Mass on a weekly basis. However, in the context of skateboarding it reads not only as an item of faith but also as an instruction and judgement. This is significant for the fact that skateboard culture is invested in testing boundaries, norms, and authority. It is indeed rare for such a high-profile skateboarder to have such an explicitly religious message, condemning those who do not believe. Much of skateboarding art is suggestive, and laced with ambiguity. Thomas' board does, however, conform to the risk-taking graphics of our other examples, pushing the envelope not in terms of symbolism and allegory, but in the earnest conviction to his new faith.

Responses to Thomas' board must therefore be read in the context not just of religious iconography, but also of implicit risk-taking. The online SLAP message board is a popular haunt of skateboard gossip and industry speculation. Occasional threads which provide an earnest discussion on religion are regularly shot down with irreverent banter. Examples of threads on the forum include 'Are religious pro's lame?,' 'Religious Skaters,' and 'Skating reveals my evidence of the one and only living God.' The author of the latter thread declares that,

[s]kating is a deep connection to the soul, and a way to achieve perfect bliss. Bliss like this is my evidence of having a God moment on earth, these moments are reminders that there is a God, and he designed things originally to be pleasurable, and in a state of natural high. It is a reminder that Jesus is alive and he is eternal, his love conquers all evil. (Taluk, 2018)

Responses to this post, almost without exception, deride it and make jest of the comment. One reply states that 'I bet Jesus would push mongo' (pushing with your front rather than rear foot which is widely regarded as uncouth and ineffectual), another suggests that the author might like to experiment with drugs, a further jests that the author is an evangelical skateboarder—'Oh shit waddup Hosoi'—while another asks 'Is god with me while I'm doin blow and banging strippers??? I'm genuinely curious' (Taluk, 2018, pp. replies #35, #33, #39, #34). Such responses show that while skateboarding can be regarded in various camps as a subculture, sport, lifestyle, and art form, it is not openly a place for religious expression. Thus, Thomas' board deals less with the broader sociophobics of US society (devils, pentagrams, skulls, aliens) and more with the particular sociophobics of skateboarding and its authenticity police. Arguably, the skateboard industry is phobic of religious devotion in its products. This is a theme also discussed by Jef Hartsel who claims that Steve Rocco would always be resistant to any Rastafarian board graphics that he proposed whilst he was a pro for World Industries (Swisher, 2017).

Similarly, Brian Sumner, a professional skateboarder with Birdhouse in the late 1990s, became a fervent born-again Christian after struggling with substance abuse. Birdhouse released several religiously inspired graphics for him. These included various depictions of Jesus, a cross, and Mother Mary. Jeremy Klein was art director for Birdhouse during the mid-2000s when Sumner was born again. He resented having to do religious graphics and commissioned his own pro model on Birdhouse, depicting an abusive Mother Mary choking a child, and surrounded by other bloodied and bruised children (Carayol, 2014, p. 161). Sumner, now sponsored by Christian skateboard company Reliance, continues to have devotional boards with recurring themes of a battle between Christ and the devil. Another subversive reaction to religious graphics is the model *Skate Switch for Jesus*, by Michael Sieben for Roger Skateboards. The graphic depicts a large cross inverted. The comedy of the board is that by riding switch (often resulting in the board's orientation being reversed), the graphic is transformed, and the cross is rectified to its devout and correct position. Again, Sieben's board highlights that skateboarding graphics are to be ridden and not simply gazed upon.

Some devotional boards have, however, become widely lauded and embraced in part because they are read as being authentic in terms of artistic and cultural contributions. One of the most famous boards comes again from artist Marc McKee and 101 Skateboards, this time for professional skateboarder Gabriel Rodriguez (Fig. 5.4). The inspiration for the

Fig. 5.4 Jesus, Gabriel Rodriguez: 101 by Marc McKee (from 1991)

board comes from Rodriguez's own home where his mother had a collection of Catholic imagery on display. Natas picked out one of the images of Jesus and told Rodriguez that it would be the graphic for his pro model board. In this sense, the circumstances surrounding the graphic are not so much religious as cultural, speaking of the Rodriguez home and their Catholic heritage. The graphic itself is reproduced in a style which appears neither sycophantic nor satirical. One of my respondents Joe, in his mid-forties, was quite critical of devotional religious graphics. He called for a 'separation between church and skate' and disliked both the Jamie Thomas board and the Jeff Grosso boards. He suggested that the Rodriguez board is much loved because it is subtle and you can take it primarily as a piece of art.

I think it goes back to the iconography though. If you see Jamie Thomas' board and you see Gabriel Rodriguez board, you're more drawn to Gabriel's board because of the whole, the art and the person at the end, Jesus. There's just so much going on in that board that you're drawn to. The artwork is spectacular. Even if you're not a religious person, you're appreciating that board for what it is. It's a beautiful piece of artwork. That's what really drew me to that one. I remember when that board came out, I was like wow that's really rad.

The Rodriguez Jesus board is of further significance with regard to the fact that it, along with the Devil board, was the first skateboard whose graphics explicitly engaged with religious iconography. Emphasising the legacy of the Devil and Jesus images, both of these religious themed boards from McKee originally released in 1991 were again re-released by Dwindle as part of their heritage series in 2016. The repertoire of taste developed and expressed by skateboarders appears to demand that religious graphics do more than simply confess devotion, that they must have some artistic value, or be part of a larger social observation and commentary. One could argue therefore that the suspicion or critique of religious expression in skateboarding is not about cashing in, or expressing devotion, but more chiefly about being consistent and authentic to the values and mores of skateboard culture.

Conclusion

This chapter broaches a topic that could itself be of book length. There are hundreds of explicit religious graphics on skateboards over the last 40 years. There are scores more with tacit, subtle, nuanced religious connections. I thankfully resisted the desire to catalogue them all. What I have sought to do instead is to provide a deeper exploration of some of the dynamics that we see in religious skateboard graphics: sociophobics, satire, allegory, and devotion. I have strived throughout to place these works of art in context, to include the voices of the artists involved, and to also include comments from my respondents, skateboarders who are likely to buy and ride such boards.

In conclusion I attempt to push these themes forward and make some analytical and critical statements. Firstly, I wish to argue that the skateboard graphic and its canvas, the skateboard, introduce an important differential in our understandings of art. As I have mentioned, the skate-board is intended to be ridden, the graphic is ultimately disposable. Of course, a robust market in skateboard collecting has arisen to challenge this notion. But I insist that first and foremost the skateboard graphic is, as Sean Cliver's (2004) book emphasises, disposable. Jeff Grosso also makes this point:

> Like what's cool about skateboard art, especially now, is it's temporary. You make these really fucking grand and outlandish statements and it will be gone in a minute. So you're really not offending anyone because it's just a fucking skateboard. Get over yourself.

This presupposes an intriguing relationship that skateboarders have with their boards and these graphics. They choose boards invariably because they like the shape, the company, the rider, and the graphic. Riding (read as defacing) the board is in its own way a form of devotion, or almsgiving. Indeed, professional skateboarders earn money through board sales. So, in the world of skateboarding there is a pride that skate-boarders have ridden collectable boards, rather than storing them for financial investment. Boards are meant to be ridden.

This inverts notions of sacrilegious behaviour inherent in the deface-ment of artefacts and images of the divine. Let us consider the Japanese practice of Fumi-e (踏み絵), or 'stepping on pictures' that was used in the seventeenth-century persecution of Nagasaki Christians during an era when their religion was outlawed. Typically these were stone tablets with images of Christ or the Virgin Mary. It was understood that Christians would refuse to disrespect the images and thus not tread on them. The boundaries of religious offence are rife with ambiguity. Is it a sign of devotion to get a tattoo of the Buddha? Are prayer mats sold in Mecca sacred or commercial exploitation?

Saudi graphic designer and artist Yusef Alahmad produced a series of skateboards with Arabic calligraphy. These sophisticated designs with clean and clear graphics test the boundaries between art and decorative design, the sacred and the profane. Originally producing them as artistic pieces, Alahmad received interest from people who wanted to purchase the boards. Some of his Instagram followers were keen to point out that

Fig. 5.5 Blue Board Ysuef Alahmad reproducing Ayat 23:29

a board that reproduced an ayat from the Qur'an (Fig. 5.5) should not be stood on or defaced. The ayat alluded to skateboarding praising god for a safe and fortuitous disembarking. However, the response from many Muslims was clear—the sacred text should be revered and skateboarding would not dishonour it. This example relates to the notion of Fumi-e and highlights how the ritual orthopraxy of Islam and the sacrality of the Qur'an for Muslims problematise devotional skateboard graphics for Muslim skateboarders. Indeed, because of the tension between idolatry and respect in Islam the medium of skateboard graphics represents a potential challenge. One way this has been navigated is by engaging with political issues that connect to a religious identity. For example, the G-Hard skateshop in Kuala Lumpur produced a political graphic for the boards they sold at their store in which a Palestinian child is depicted throwing a stone at an Israeli tank, the child's skateboard tucked under his foot in defiance.

To skateboarders the feel of their board is a pleasure. It might ultimately be destroyed and discarded, but there is a register of affect in riding a skateboard. Borden has noted that some skateboarders consider their boards as a fifth limb, an extension of their body. To others they are artefacts imbued with magical powers, what Ostwalt (2012, p. 209) refers to as 'spiritual talisman' in reference to the motorcycle, replete with supernatural powers that transform the rider. Thus, skateboard art connects to an embodied schema, a way of being in the world. When skateboards display religious iconography this embodied relationship must also be considered. Jamie Thomas, Gabriel Rodriguez, and Brian Sumner see no affront to riding a skateboard with Christ's image. This is seen as an act of devotion. Similarly when non-religious skateboarders choose graphics that are devotional, that parody or critique religion, they are also expressing a religious sensibility.

The fact that a skateboard is a canvas for art, symbolism, and social commentary conveys much to indicate that skateboarding cannot easily be defined, or perhaps confined, as a sport. It would be unthinkable to have a discussion about religious iconography and tennis racket design, rugby balls, or golf clubs. Even within lifestyle sports skateboarding is remarkable in the vibrancy of its visual culture. The prominence of popular culture symbolism in board art is undeniable. Distinct in the visual culture of skateboarding is the fact that skateboards are lifestyle paraphernalia communicating aesthetics, and orientations of style and identity. Boards represent all these factors and are also items of consumption, ultimately to be physically ridden and eventually destroyed. Board iconography is a vibrant topic in which religion can be observed in skateboard culture. I argue further that the relevance of religious motifs on boards can also be extended far beyond our trope of observation, highlighting that skateboarding itself is potent in its ability to challenge and disturb the dualism surrounding the sacred and the profane. The topics explored throughout this chapter further contribute to a rendering of lifestyle religion, emphasising the individuality, choice, and consumption involved in such new religious expressions.

References

Bowen, J. (2012). *A New Anthropology of Islam*. Cambridge: Cambridge University Press.

Carayol, S. (2014). *Agents Provocateurs: 100 Subversive Skateboard Graphics*. Gingko Press.

Clark, T. R. (2012a). Introduction: What Is Religion? What Is Popular Culture? How Are They Related? In T. R. Clark & D. W. Clanton Jr. (Eds.), *Understanding Religion and Popular Culture: Theories, Themes, Products and Practices* (pp. 1–12). London: Routledge.

Clark, T. R. (2012b). Saved by Satire? Learning to Value Popular Culture's Critique of Sacred Traditions. In T. R. Clark & D. W. Clanton Jr. (Eds.), *Understanding Religion and Popular Culture: Theories, Themes, Products and Practices* (pp. 13–27). London: Routledge.

Cliver, S. (2004). *Disposable: A History of Skateboard Art*. Berkeley, CA: Gingko Press.

Cowan, D. E. (2008). *Sacred Terror: Religion and Horror on the Silver Screen*. Waco, TX: Baylor University Press.

Cowan, D. E. (2012a). Religion in Cinema Horror. In T. R. Clark & D. W. Clanton Jr. (Eds.), *Understanding Religion and Popular Culture: Theories, Themes, Products and Practices* (pp. 56–71). London: Routledge.

Cowan, D. E. (2012b). Religion in Science Fiction Film and Television. In T. R. Clark & D. W. Clanton Jr. (Eds.), *Understanding Religion and Popular Culture: Theories, Themes, Products and Practices* (pp. 41–55). London: Routledge.

Cowan, D. E., & Bromley, D. G. (2015). *Cults and New Religions: A Brief History*. Chichester: Wiley-Blackwell.

Denike, B. (2004). *Built to Grind: 25 Year of Hardcore Skateboarding*. San Francisco: High Speed Publications.

Feezell, R. (2013). Sport, Religious Belief, and Religious Diversity. *Journal of the Philosophy of Sport, 40*(1), 135–162. https://doi.org/10.1080/00948705 .2013.785423

Gaiger, J. (2006). Dealing with the Visual: Art History, Aesthetics and Visual Culture. *The British Journal of Aesthetics, 46*(1), 102–104. https://doi. org/10.1093/aesthj/ayj010

Geertz, C. (1973). *The Interpretation of Cultures: Selected Essays*. New York: Basic Books.

Haseltine, D. (2002). *I.Am.Relevant: A Generation Impacting Their World with Faith*. Lake Mary, FL: Relevant Books.

Heelas, P., Woodhead, L., Seal, B., Szerszynski, B., & Tusting, K. (2005). *The Spiritual Revolution: Why Religion Is Giving Way to Spirituality*. Oxford: Blackwell.

Lyng, S. (2005). *Edgework: The Sociology of Risk-Taking*. New York: Routledge.

Morgan, D. (2005). *The Sacred Gaze: Religious Visual Culture in Theory and Practice*. Berkeley, CA: University of California Press.

ON Video (Writer). (2003). Winter 2003 [DVD]. In 411 Productions (Producer). *ON Video*.

Ostwalt, C. (2012). *Secular Steeples: Popular Culture and the Religious Imagination* (2nd ed.). London: Bloomsbury.

Skateboarder. (2013). Skateboarder Magazine—Jamie Thomas: Memory Screened—February/March 2012 Issue. *Adventure Sports Network*. Retrieved from https://www.adventuresportsnetwork.com/sport/skateboarding/jamie-thomas-memory-screened/

Steinberg, S. R., & Joe, L. (2018). *Christotainment: Selling Jesus through Popular Culture*. Routledge.

Swisher, E. (2017). Chrome Ball Interview #107: Jef Hartsel. Retrieved from http://chromeballincident.blogspot.com/2017/10/chrome-ball-interview-107-jef-hartsel.html

Taluk. (2018). Skating Reveals My Evidence of the One and Only Living God. *Online Forum*. Retrieved from http://www.slapmagazine.com/index.php?topic=98325.0

The Nine Club (Producer). (2017, October 16). Jamie Thomas | *The Nine Club* with Chris Roberts—Episode 68. *YouTube Video*. Retrieved from https://www.youtube.com/watch?v=hc5AlRTTNx0

The Nine Club. (2018). Marc Mckee | *The Nine Club* with Chris Roberts—Episode 79. *YouTube Video*. Retrieved from https://youtu.be/nwuEkSnl2VY

Thrasher Magazine. (2015, September 30). 20 Years of Jamie Thomas.

Transworld Skateboarding. (2003). Cashing in on God. *Transworld Skateboarding*. Retrieved from http://skateboarding.transworld.net/news/cashing-in-on-god/#kCwZHzRt0IU4k9wa.97

Yochim, E. C. (2010). *Skate Life: Re-imagining White Masculinity*. San Francisco: University of Michigan Press.

Part II

Performance

6

Video Journeys

A fundamental recognition of skateboarding involves acknowledging the process of motion. Simply rolling on the board is the traversing of space. Tricks are all kinetic, involving propelling, rotation, and explosive releases of energy. Academic work on skateboarding acknowledges the importance of moving through space, and thus travelling. It often entails a local journey that skateboarders embark on as they visit their nearby spots. Skateboarders in Northern England have been shown to construct nightly nomadic practices where they gather with friends and travel to and through key spots in their evening skate (Jenson, Swords, & Jeffries, 2012). Sometimes these journeys are broader in scope. Much of the reportage on skateboarding in magazines speaks of the road trip in which skateboard teams embark on 'life in the van.' This journeying has been made the subject of an annual 'King of the Road' (KOTR) competition in *Thrasher* magazine and now syndicated as a reality television show on the Viceland network. In KOTR, three teams of skateboarders visit various cities across the USA and attempt to complete challenges or tricks at specific locations. Many of these challenges include homage to professional skateboarders, their tricks, and importantly their spots (Viceland, 2017). Similarly, skateboard videos play on the importance of place and

© The Author(s) 2020
P. O'Connor, *Skateboarding and Religion*,
https://doi.org/10.1007/978-3-030-24857-4_6

the notion of travelling pilgrims. This chapter is concerned with both journeying and the media which capture and communicate this.

The iconic 1987 skateboard video by Powell Peralta *The Search for Animal Chin* (Peralta, 1987) involves a group of skateboarders searching for the mythic Animal Chin who they believe to be a wise skateboarding sage. By the end of the film Chin is revealed to be the embodiment of joy and adventure in skateboarding, not a person or place. In the 2015 video *We Are Blood* (Evans, 2015), a group of professional skateboarders take a road trip across the USA, and then tour Brazil, Barcelona, and Dubai. While the film is a polished piece of commercial skateboarding, in part funded by Mountain Dew, its theme is the solidarity and connection that skateboarders share across the world and that the skateboard is itself a passport to skateboarding communities at home and abroad. This was emphasised by one of my informants in Hong Kong. At 24 years of age he claimed that his skateboard meant that he could go to any city in the world and find skateboarders and a community to help and support him. Returning to Yochim's (2010) argument about the corresponding tie between skateboard media and skateboard culture, we can understand that the journey is important in skateboard videos because it is important in skateboard culture and vice versa. In this chapter we also take a symbolic journey into the canon of skateboard videos.

This is the first chapter to explore our polythetic notion of religion through performance. Here we are interested in a family of ideas that connect to factual motivations, *mysterium tremendum*, ritual, pilgrimage, and communitas. Performance is addressed by looking at the contribution of skateboard videos to presenting skateboarding as a mystical journey, a sojourn of self-discovery and communitas, connecting with others and building community. This is not a simple observation of religious components; in fact, the religious connection in the videos that I discuss is not overt or readily apparent. Some might argue that these videos, and skateboard videos more generally, are not religious at all. Even the video offerings from some Christian skateboard companies like Untitled skateboards simply focus on skateboarding. Thus, this chapter is not about observation like the former chapters; it is not concerned with how religion is visible. Rather this chapter is about how religion is performed in terms of practice, meaning, and motivation.

Building a Community Through Video

Skateboard videos are a prominent part of skateboard culture. They have, at least since the mid-1980s, worked as an early form of social media where skateboarders could keep up to date with new developments, and also contribute to the culture by making their own short films. Now, nearly every teenage skateboarder keeps up to date with their favourite professionals and their own friends via Instagram clips and YouTube videos that are regularly posted online. However, a skateboard video is also a term commonly associated with the filmed projects of various skateboard companies, be they board brands, shoe companies, or other various teams. Skateboard videos tend to have a discernible formula—a team is the focus, but the video typically unfolds with a series of individual parts, documenting the skills, style, and attitude of one skateboarder at a time. It is generally understood that the final part of a skateboard video is regarded as the 'best' part or performance, with the opening slot being reserved for the second best. A variety of scholarship has addressed skateboard videos. Yochim (2010), for instance, analyses *Dogtown and Z-Boys*, an award-winning documentary on skateboarding's origins, and *Hallowed Ground* from the Hurley clothing company. Much of the extant sport research on skateboard videos is uneven, giving particular attention to the documentaries of Perlata and also reading the media through the guise of masculinity and race (Kusz, 2007, 2018; Willing, Green, & Pavlidis, 2019; Yochim, 2010). More broadly, skateboard videos have been understood not only as a marketing tool for companies, but also as a means to communicate authenticity about skateboard culture, its values, and norms (Atencio, Beal, & Wilson, 2009, p. 7; Borden, 2019, p. 117; Wheaton & Beal, 2003). As a result, skateboarders often pay considerable attention to the content and production of these videos; they critique the music, trick selection, editing, and locations included in these films. I make scant mention of the importance of music in this chapter, but skateboard videos draw heavily on the emotional vitality engendered by the music that accompanies the images. This is significant because, as Edith Turner (2012, p. 43) identifies, 'music is a fail-safe bearer of communitas' conveying emotion and being ephemeral. Beyond the music the importance of location can also not be understated. Snyder (2017) highlights that skateboard filmers or videographers must have a remarkable memory for who performed which trick in which video as duplicating footage is often seen to reflect poorly on both the company and the skateboarder depicted. As such great importance is placed on skateboard videos, this chapter explores how media productions communicate both spiritual and religious themes.

Within the field of religion and popular culture there is a variety of scholarship that employs content and media analysis to deconstruct the way religion is portrayed in cinema. For example, in *Sacred Terror*, Douglas E. Cowan (2008) addresses the use of religious symbolism in the horror genre. He identifies a series of intriguing motifs such as the prominence of churches as places of shelter in films, and also the dominance of the occult. Cowan argues that these elements correspond with our latent fears about religion, death, and the unknown. This is more broadly described as sociophobics, or the social construction of fear (Cowan, 2012a). In various other works, religion is explored through the science fiction genre (Cowan, 2012b; McDowell, 2012; McKee, 2007) with particular attention paid to both the Star Wars and Star Trek franchises. In her exploration of invented religions Carole Cusack (2010) notes how *Jediism* and *Matrixism* have emerged from Hollywood science fiction films. Conrad Ostwalt (2012) also explores the impact of the *Matrix* trilogy and the Christ-like saviour Neo. While recognising the popularity of religious analysis of modern film, Ostwalt also highlights that these critiques are often focal on similar themes, be that a messiah, redemption, penance, or transcendence. In contrast, he explores secular apocalyptic disaster movies, and draws our attention to how these portray modern risk and the evils of secular life (Ostwalt, 2012, pp. 176–177). This analysis complements the sociophobics of Cowan, highlighting that the narrative of film can provide both caution and instruction with regard to religion and spirituality.

A vast array of work on religion and film has been instructive in writing this chapter (Blizek, 2009; Lyden, 2003; Lyden & Mazur, 2015). Following the schema provided by Okuyama (2015) I complement my sociological analysis by employing a semiotic reading of the two main videos I address in this chapter. Her work draws from Levi-Strauss (1995) and Barthes (1972, 1973), two scholars who have contributed to a semiotic analysis of myth. The functional approach of Levi-Strauss highlights that myths can be reduced to component parts representing oppositions such as good and evil. These he describes as mythemes, essential building blocks in myths. In agreement, Barthes highlights that modern trends replicate mythological archetypes—heroes, villains, beauty, justice, all come to be significant in our modern media (Okuyama, 2015, p. 26). Influenced by these insights I explore symbolism in skateboard videos that depict a cultural worldview.

Rather than speedily explore the vast number of videos available on skateboarding I have chosen to analyse two titles in depth. These videos are distinct in that the notion of communitas forms part of their concept and narrative. They are arguably exaggerations of the skateboard video format and while they break with a number of conventions, they are both critically acclaimed, groundbreaking, and wholly understood as authentic products. These two videos, *The Search for Animal Chin* (Peralta, 1987) and *We Are Blood* (Evans, 2015), are filmed 30 years apart and demonstrate a profound advancement in the professionalisation, sportification, and globalisation of the skateboard industry. Despite the time differential, both films promote skateboarding as a fun communal activity that is both exploratory and deeply rewarding. Both films are listed in the Internet Movie Database (IMDB) and at the time of writing have respective ratings of 8.0 and 7.7. I proceed to introduce each film, provide a brief synopsis, and then present an exegesis of their religious themes grouped around the ideas of communitas, transcendence, and ritual quest. At various points I refer to other skateboard videos to extend my discussion. I conclude that for skateboarders, videos operate as both a point of communion and also as an extension of text. Thus, skateboarders watch and discuss videos as a way of maintaining community, but many also find meaning and solace in the close detail that they pay to these films. These videos provide lessons about life as a skateboarder understands it, and also reflections of their values, ethics, struggles, and joys.

The Search for Animal Chin

Released in 1987 *The Search for Animal Chin* is a road trip skateboard video that features the Powell Peralta team. The film is notable in that, while being the third Bones Brigade video, it was the first to provide a narrative structure and have skateboarders perform basic (this might be too generous) acting in scenes. The Bones Brigade is made up of the skateboarders Steve Caballero, Tommy Guerrero, Tony Hawk, Mike McGill, and Lance Mountain. These young men spend the video skateboarding together rather than having their own separate video parts. The premise of the video is that a legendary skater known as Won Ton Animal Chin has gone missing and the Bones Brigade tour across the USA trying to find him. As the film unfolds we learn that the mystical Chin is really a metaphor for the joy of skateboarding. The finale of the film focuses on the discovery of an enormous vert ramp in the desert. The film has achieved iconic status in skateboarding, with people popularly alluding to its tag line 'have you seen him?' Part of the attraction to *Animal Chin* is the fact that it is undeniably cheesy, camp, and corny. This was true of the film on its first release and continues to be the case 30 years later. The film does not take itself too seriously and as a result prefigures the message that it holds: *skateboarding should be fun*.

The video begins like the first Bones Brigade video, with Stacy Peralta watching a spoof television show talking about skateboarding. One of the men on the screen provides a cynical take on skateboarding, declaring that skateboard graphics with 'death, gore, dismemberment' are key to winning the youth demographic and that 'after all, that is what skateboarding is all about.' An annoyed Peralta hurls the television out of the window and then opens a fortune cookie. The camera focuses on the note inside which reads 'have you seen him?' Text then scrolls up the screen introducing Animal Chin as the first person to bolt skates onto a piece of wood and construct a skateboard. At once we are introduced to the mythologising of skateboarding's origins. A spoof news report declares the fictitious 62-year-old Chin as missing and that the skateboard world is mourning his absence. Text appears on screen that explains that true believers in Chin are committed to the quest of searching him out and the Bones Brigade are among these 'true seekers.' The video then opens to the first scene of skateboarding action as the Bones Brigade visit the famous Hawaiian skate spot known as the Wallows.

This opening montage provides a few cues to the broader sentiment of the film. It addresses the commercialisation of skateboarding and the concern that the true meaning of skateboarding is something both purer and simpler. In the fictitious Chin, who becomes a very evident MacGuffin (a device used to move the plot along), we have an attempt to mythologise skateboarding. As the prototypical skateboarder, Chin is portrayed as the most authentic skateboarder. These themes are all given a mystical veneer through East Asian aesthetics. Chin appears to be an elderly Chinese sage with a long beard, pictured donning a bamboo hat. The music in the introduction, and during transitions, is similarly an ode to Westernised oriental riffs. Thus, in establishing some form of skateboard mythology, *Animal Chin* employs Orientalism to construct it, deliberately sidestepping the more familiar Californian origins of skateboarding.

As the movie proceeds, the Bones Brigade travel to San Francisco and skate the streets, searching Chinatown for Chin. They visit a suburban backyard ramp, and then hit the road heading to the famous Pink Motel. After skating the pool at the motel, they sleep and are haunted by dreams of falling off their skateboards. Here we are provided with another mainstay of all skateboarding videos—a 'slam section.' Sometimes occupying a discrete segment, in other cases interspersed throughout videos, these are a collection of short scenes in which skateboarders fall whilst attempting to perform tricks. These scenes emphasise the authenticity of skateboarding, that it is tough and dangerous, and that everyone fails. These often spectacular tumbles, or slams, also serve to highlight that there is no fourth wall in skateboard videos. Viewers know that the process is filmed, and they experience the filming sometimes seeing the filmer and other crew in video scenes. *Animal Chin* breaks with this convention a little by sustaining a fictive narrative interspersed with the filming. As the story proceeds the Bones Brigade wake the next morning and pick up a junked 1959 Cadillac. They refit it to accommodate their skateboards, then head to Las Vegas to Johnny Rad's party at the Blue Tile Lounge. Here they are given their most promising clue from Johnny Rad—news of an enormous ramp that has appeared in the desert. He describes it as follows:

> There is something you've got to know. If you look too hard for Chin you are never going to find him. You got to relax and enjoy your skating. Isn't that how it all started out? … I heard about this ramp. It is in this field between two junk yards just south of a town called Guadeloupe. … I don't even think it is man-made. I am talking skate Martians or something came

down and made this thing. … I think that is where Animal Chin is hanging out.

As thanks they give Johnny Rad the keys to their Cadillac and head back on the road, this time solely with their skateboards. Next, we see the Bones Brigade skateboarding along a desert road pushing on the final leg of their quest. A voice-over from Johnny Rad explains that he went searching for Animal Chin once, 'not the man, but what he stands for.' He emphasises the message of 'fun' and declares that this is an art that must be developed. The skateboarders spot a giant stone carving of a skateboard and rush to investigate it. Tony Hawk declares 'it is like a skate god must have skated on this thing.' The carving has ancient Chinese pictographs on it and at the foot of the monument is a carving in English with the name Guadeloupe. They scan the horizon and spot the promised giant skate ramp. A climatic ramp scene follows which showcases the skills of the Bones Brigade and includes some spectacular synchronised manoeuvres including a shot where all four of the Bones Brigade perform an invert (handplant) on the spine of the ramp at the same time. The closing scene sees the skateboarders sitting round a camp-fire at night and making a promise to continue searching for Chin. A final voice-over announces that 'as long as skaters keep searching for Chin, they've already found him.'

Animal Chin is a video that must first be placed in the context of its time. During the mid-1980s, skateboarding was in the midst of a renewed wave of popularity. Michael J. Fox brought a whole new generation to skateboarding in his depiction of teen skateboarder Marty McFly in *Back to the Future* (1985). Hollywood also experimented with their own skate-board themed films: *Thrashin* (1986), and then *Gleaming the Cube* (1989), and scenes in *Police Academy 4: Citizens on Patrol* (1987). Members of the Bones Brigade had cameos in nearly all of these films which further highlights the popularity of skateboarding in the mid-1980s. Powell Peralta was the leading board company at this time and the celebrity status of skateboarding appears to be part of what *Animal Chin* is reacting to. Furthermore, *Animal Chin* influenced the way in which skateboard videos were made. Narrative structures and skits became more common following its release. In 1989, Santa Cruz skateboards produced *Streets on Fire*, which has a loose narrative in which skateboarder Jason Jessee is in prison. At the end of the film Jessee is sent to the electric chair, a punitive measure for the crime of skateboarding. In Blind's *Video Days* (Jonze, 1991) a car forms part of the narrative structure in which the skateboarders journey and ultimately die as the final scenes show it shooting off a cliff. The Birdhouse video *The End* (Mosberg, 1998) developed a short narrative around each of the skateboarders' video sections. In *The End* we see Andrew Reynolds getting drunk with an orangutan, Steve Berra, being hunted down by an evil invisible force, and Rick McCrank replying to a job advertisement as narrative elements mixed in with their skateboarding. Themes of mortality recur during *The End*—in Heath Kirchart and Jeremy Klein's section they drive a van around in a destructive rampage smashing into hedges, signposts, gates, and trees. Eventually their van crashes and explodes and we see them in pseudo-heaven as millionaires pampered with candy, video games, and buxom French maids. The Shorty's video *Guilty* (Henkels, 2001) includes the team dressed as convicts and brought before a judge. As skateboard videos have become more sophisticated in their filming and production, a variety of special effects have been employed often in the form of short narrative skits. The Girl/Chocolate videos *Yeah Right* (Evans & Jonze, 2003) and *Pretty Sweet* (Evans & Jonze, 2012) are classic examples of this, both of which include cameos from celebrities such as Owen Wilson and Jack Black. The *Spirit Quest* video also includes some highly original filming techniques and special effects that merge the movement of skateboarders with various animals (Read, 2016). Most recently the film *Jobs? Never!!!* (Greco, 2018) includes a narrative element through some of Los Angeles' urban decay. These films all provide a journey, a new exploration of skateboarding and its possibilities.

It is also important to identify that Stacy Peralta, the director of *Animal Chin*, has long been interested in constructing a skateboard mythology throughout his moviemaking career. He reached his zenith with *Dogtown and Z-Boys* (2001), producing a documentary that essentially identified a group of men as the forefathers of skateboarding's rebellious mystique. In further documentaries, both in the *Bones Brigade: An Autobiography* (Peralta, 2012) and *The L.A. Boys* (Kennedy, 2016), Peralta positions himself right at the centre of modern skateboarding folklore.

This is significant not simply as an egotistical act—Peralta really was in the midst of some very formative moments in skateboarding—but because it highlights that film is a powerful way in which the origins and icons of skateboarding have been reified.

The legacy of *Animal Chin* is indisputable and in many ways the video has served as prescient. In 2016, the *Animal Chin* skate ramp was reconstructed at Woodward West skate camp, 30 years after its initial construction. The original Bones Brigade members, then in their late forties and early fifties, reunited to skate the ramp again. Remarkably they were able to perform many of the same tricks that appeared in the 1987 video, and were able to replicate the synchronised four-person invert that included Steve Caballero, Tony Hawk, Mike McGill, and Lance Mountain (see also O'Connor, 2017, pp. 1–2). Speaking in 2016, Tony Hawk states that the story was 'obviously based on the search for fun,' and Steve Caballero confesses that 'Chin is just like a mythical person to represent fun. It's been thirty years and we are still searching for him every day' (Ride Channel, 2017). Thus, the arguably superficial notion promoted in *The Search for Animal Chin*, about a lifelong search for fun, is triumphantly enacted in the demonstration of these middle-aged men still searching for Chin. When the *Animal Chin* ramp was originally constructed in 1986, it was ahead of its time, incorporating design elements such as a vertical spine, channels, and extensions on a large scale. The ramp was only constructed for the video and after three days of filming it was destroyed. Tony Hawk describes how this added to the enigma of the film:

> I understood the sense of exclusivity for the video, it would seem right that it would be this crazy thing that we all got to skate and then no-one else would get to try it. There was this mythological element to it. There has been for thirty years. No one has rebuilt that ramp which is shocking to me. (Ride Channel, 2017)

The resurrection of the *Animal Chin* ramp extends the mythology of the original video. While the message of the video was about preserving the essence of skateboarding, the return to the ramp and the video by the original Bones Brigade members some three decades later shows that skateboarding is something liberating and meaningful to adults approaching their senior years. The YouTube videos that depict the 2016 return to the *Animal Chin* ramp are touching, and somewhat inspirational. We witness five middle-aged men recapturing their youth and sharing a passion that has guided them through their lives.

We Are Blood

In a variety of ways, *We Are Blood* is an exceptional film that strives to push the boundaries of skateboard videos in a new direction. Much like *Animal Chin*, this video takes the form of a road trip narrative, but its scope is global, crossing five continents and including a legion of both professional and non-professional skateboarders. *We Are Blood* is a timely reflection of where skateboarding now is—globalised, multicultural, and inclusive. The video employs a documentary format led by the narrative of professional skateboarder Paul Rodriguez, who has an impressive resume of both commercial and competitive success in the industry. We also hear the narrative in Portuguese from Brazilian skateboarder Tiago Lemos, from Brandon White, a deaf skateboarder who tags along for the road trip, and on two occasions from women skateboarders. The message presented by *We Are Blood* is explicit—skateboarders share a global fraternity; they are not simply practitioners of a sport, they are connected in their passion, drive, and commitment to skateboarding. This is expressed as both a brotherhood and as something ineffable, innate, and organic. Directed by Ty Evans, a videographer recognised for his technical innovation in video technology, the film is crisply produced and rendered in high definition with tracking shots and drone footage of the highest calibre. The video is also remarkable for its duration; at 90 minutes it is far longer than most skateboard videos and takes a meandering path from North America to Brazil, China, and then to a spectacular finale in the futuristic cityscape of Dubai. Much like *Animal Chin*, the video supplants the traditional finale of 'the best' skateboarding, for an extravagant location.

The video begins with a car driving through downtown Los Angeles. We see the towering skyscrapers and then the street life of the homeless and marginal denizens of the city. Abruptly, the speeding car hits a skateboarder who momentarily rides into the street. The camera zooms in on the fallen skateboarder as time slows on a drop of blood falling from his wounded arm. We take a molecular journey into the drop of blood down to the level of DNA. We then follow a group of skateboarders in a slow-motion montage as they apply DIY techniques to transform a disused warehouse into a skate spot. They emerge on the roof of the building and hold their boards aloft to the sky as the video title is displayed in shiny silver bold block lettering. As the camera returns to the street scene we learn that the injured skateboarder is Paul Rodriguez, who provides a voice-over to scenes of his recovery. He states that it is crazy what skateboarders put themselves through, and then clarifies that 'we have to, it's in our blood, it's in our DNA. Skateboarding is what drives us. It keeps us moving forward. It's our passion, our family, our life. It's the common bond that every skateboarder shares.' Rodriguez goes on to explain that while skateboarding is now a global phenomenon, it all began in Los Angeles, at which point the first montage of skateboarding begins with scenes across the city set to the high-energy Metallica song Battery. Various professionals are depicted, Omar Salazar skates a ditch at a frantic speed. We see him at the end of the run visibly elated and reporting to the camera 'that is exactly why skateboarding is the best.' The next scene shows a group of skateboarders purchasing a large recreational vehicle (RV) off an elderly lady. They convert the inside of the vehicle, paint it, and cover it with skateboard stickers. Rodriguez's voice-over informs the viewer that skateboarding is about moving, the 'freedom of the road'; it is the 'journey not the destination.' The skateboarders inside the RV travel to Las Vegas and then San Francisco, and we see beautifully filmed vivid scenes of skateboarding at each spot. At 16 minutes into the film we hear Tiago Lemos as he celebrates the gift of skateboarding providing him with the opportunity to see so much of the world. He casts his eye across the desert apparently taking in the wonder of nature and the surrounding mountains. The next voice-over tells us that skateboarders see the world differently, that they care about the design of cities in a way that others do not. We then travel to Barcelona, which is described as a 'Mecca for skateboarding' and that people travel to from all over the world to skate the ledges at Museu d'Art Contemporani de Barcelona (MACBA). Next, we travel to the hills of Barcelona as an excavator digs up a skatepark that has been buried for 30 years, before the camera speeds away to New York. In Manhattan we briefly follow Anthony Pappalardo, a former professional skateboarder, as he seeks out novel places to skate. He confesses that skateboarding is 'my sacred thing' and that regardless of his status in life, he will always skate.

At this juncture in the film we have travelled far and the peripatetic nature of the production is firmly established. What follows over the next hour is a series of several aphorisms delivered by Rodriguez. We learn that skateboarding in China involves many challenges, such as several encounters with security guards and police. We hear that there is 'always someone trying to stop us.' Next, we encounter more adversity for skateboarders as a brutal high-definition slam section plays out. The nomadic skateboarders visit the Skatopia commune, Brazil, and then, back in the USA, veteran pro Jamie Thomas joins the road trip in the RV. Thomas reflects on turning 40, and we learn that skateboarding is a symbol of 'hope,' 'inclusion,' and 'family.' For the finale of the video the skateboarders are transported to Dubai, where they are provided with access to some of the most engaging architecture, taking in office plazas and futuristic skyscrapers. This part of the video is also an advertisement for the Dubai tourist industry. Part of the funding for *We Are Blood* was provided by XDubai, a lifestyle sports company promoting various sports events and the city itself. We witness beautiful panoramic shots of Dubai and see our touring skaters skydiving and driving dune buggies in the desert. The concluding scene in Dubai depicts the skaters performing tricks on a bench positioned on the helipad of the iconic Burj Al Arab hotel. As the film draws to a close we are back in Los Angeles as hundreds of skateboarders take to the streets and the bonds shared between all skateboarders are confirmed once more.

We Are Blood is by all accounts an epic skateboard video that is distinctly ambitious. It employs state-of-the-art technical production and innovative filming, it is global in its focus, and it also strives to communicate a message about skateboarding, its culture, and above all else its community. Ty Evans describes the film as a production about travelling the world, 'showing the brotherhood,' and 'sharing this love for skating' (Eisenhour, 2015, p. 109). For Paul Rodriguez the meaning of the film is arguably even deeper; he states that

> [i]t's addressing what it is that unites us. It's hard to even put into words, but what is it that keeps us coming back for more? Why did I start doing this when I was 12 and now, here I am at 30 still just as in love with it? What is it that makes me able to go to Brazil and meet a kid from a favela who loves it just as much? You don't even have to speak the same language, and it may be someone that without skateboarding you would probably never even be meeting each other but through this common bond you end up clicking with that person, all because of skateboarding. (Eisenhour, 2015, p. 114)

There is much in this quote that is open to critique. Certainly, the notions of multicultural exchange and mobility overlook the profound power differential between Rodriguez, a Nike-endorsed professional, and a street kid in Rio. However, it is precisely this buoyant optimism and the pure joy of skateboarding that skate videos seek to capture. Just as *Animal Chin* before it, *We Are Blood* is a reflection of the current state of skateboarding, its personalities, styles, values, and the media technology deployed to harness and document its culture. Both videos can be seen as synecdoche for the broader world of skateboarding, demonstrating innovation and a restless desire for progress and exploration. I believe both videos toy with spiritual and religious components and inform us how skateboarding can be understood as a spiritual practice and also a nascent twenty–first-century lifestyle religion. The most distinct examples of this conform to communitas, transcendence, and the spiritual quest.

Communitas

Communitas is a Latin word that describes an unstructured community, or, in the purest sense, the ideal egalitarian mode of community. The concept of communitas has been developed in academic work on the ritual process by Victor Turner (1977). He has argued that rituals include a liminal moment in which a feeling of community arises, not out of ordered structure, but out of a transient feeling that elides social position and amplifies a shared commonality. This is as relevant in the rites of passage performed by a pre-industrial tribal community as in the charismatic praise observed in a church congregation or mass prayers performed by pilgrims on hajj in Mecca. Ostwalt departs from Turner's narrow formulation of the concept and provides an exploration of the value of communitas in secular culture. He understands communitas as intense feelings of communal solidarity, purpose, and equality. Significantly he identifies that there is a more general malaise in modern North American society that believes authentic community to be disappearing, or even absent. Lifestyles that provide access to communitas are thus increasingly appealing as they promise inclusion, equity, and validation (Ostwalt, 2012, p. 206). Edith Turner (2012, p. 2) argues that 'communitas is a group's pleasure in sharing common experiences with one's fellows' and that this 'may come into existence anywhere.' Accordingly, it is communitas that provides part of the attraction to lifestyle religion. Shared social context creates a forum for people to relate in expressive and sincere ways to each other, while not necessarily demanding their adherence to a set of rules and commitments that may be seen as restrictive, compromising their freedom, individuality, and ethics.

My first level of analysis argues that both of these videos provide a powerful sense of communitas. It is observed on screen in the authentic joys, triumphs, and failures of the depicted skateboarders. In *Animal Chin* we are voyeurs as the Bones Brigade travel in search of Chin, but we partake in their fun. Throughout the video we see the team riding together, sharing jokes, and celebrating their triumphs with one another. Along their journey they encounter friends who provide them with motivation and help as they continue on their quest. The final ramp sequence provides a celebration of their journey and even the novice comes to understand that these individuals are not athletes in the traditional sense of the word—they are simply immersed in playful exploration. Thus, community is on display and equality is tacit but self-evident. Each of the Bones Brigade has a different personality, yet they are not competing with other skateboarders, they are in unison. We are thus pulled into their world and partake in these experiences. Much is scripted, but the skateboarding, even when planned, is spontaneous and connects the viewer with something larger than what they see, the feeling of skate-boarding. In *We Are Blood* none of these themes is subtle; the voice-over from Paul Rodriguez instructs us on the fraternity of skateboarding. In describing the bond as innate, within our blood and DNA, communitas becomes unquestionable. In exploring how non-skateboarders would respond to *We Are Blood*, I showed the video to a mixed group of liberal arts undergraduates in my *Value of Sports* class at Lingnan University. I asked 22 students to write down some of the themes and symbolism that they observed as significant in the video. I performed a content analysis of the responses which indicated that they understood the most salient themes communicated as 'skateboarding as life,' 'skateboarding as global,' and 'skateboarding as community.' By promoting the kinship of skate-boarding as a global condition *We Are Blood* provides a powerful expression of communitas in skateboarding. While many elements of the video detailed some arcane skateboarding practices, all of my students identified the message of the film as an expression of the powerful and visceral identity of skateboarders tied to a community of global reach. This in turns leads us to question, as Rodriguez does earlier, how this feeling could derive from something so basic. How are these feelings conjured simply through the practice of skateboarding? We are left recognising the communitas and also experiencing something of the ineffable, what Turner would recognise as a liminal state.

For Victor Turner (1977, p. 112) communitas is a quality observed in alternative lifestyles such as the beat generation and the hippies. These lifestyles demonstrate their own community and importantly occupy a liminal positioning, even a 'lowly' status in society. In part, by rejecting social status, shunning fashion, and enduring hardships, Turner argues that we are transported to an in-between state that provides the necessary disjuncture for communitas. The skateboard videos I address, and universally all others, focus on liminal states and provide countless demonstrations of 'lowly' moments as skateboarders endure pain, falling, cutting, grazing themselves, bleeding, and even breaking bones. The ritual humiliation of the slam section provides a lesson. It at once informs us of the hardiness of the skateboarders, their ability to endure pain, and their commitment to their craft. It also demonstrates that this humiliation is temporary, something that can be endured and even relished because it is not permanent. This is emphasised in the editing of skateboard videos where numerous slams of a skateboarder attempting a trick are often shown before the final landing is revealed. Inevitably the pain has been forgotten and the skateboarder is shown vindicated, elated, and celebrating with friends. This connects to Turner's discussion of communitas during the Hindu festival of Holi (1977, pp. 185–188). At this time, social order becomes suspended and lowly caste members debase those of higher castes in jovial festivity. In both humiliation and pain, Turner identifies that individuals can at once be elevated into a disembodied community and in the process experience forms of ecstasy. Thus, through communitas a door to transcendence is opened.

Edith Turner (2012, p. 15) pursues these ideas further and broaches the issue of inauthentic communitas. Here, attempts to create communitas are flawed when they become structured, intentional efforts to create a feeling rather than expressive moments of affective sharing. While the videos are planned and organised in often meticulous detail, they are still able to conjure feelings of communitas. How? Firstly, both of the videos, and I might argue more broadly the canon of skateboard media, capture the spontaneity of skateboarding. Even when a particular manoeuvre is planned in advance, its performance is always in some way richly communicative of the risk involved, and the style and personality of the skateboarder. At a deeper level the physical expression relates to the shared knowledge and recognition of the social symbol of the body, a materiality that we all embody and share. To many skateboarders, competitions, particularly the high-skilled and high-stakes SLS tour, are unable to elicit such excitement and communitas, being deliberately structured and premised on points and an ultimate winner. Such hierarchy actively works against communitas, which is about equality and connection and is similarly almost entirely absent from the message and tone of the two videos discussed earlier. Secondly, communitas works because these videos are shared with friends, they are often watched together, and certainly form the context of much discussion. They become part of the corresponding culture of skateboarding, a currency by which skateboarders communicate and share experiences with one another. Videos provide a journey for skateboarders, connecting them with community, culture, and heritage. This is a point that I return to in the next chapter, and which echoes throughout this section of the book on performance.

Transcendence

The notion of transcendence relates to other-worldly or physical states. It is associated with spirituality, religious experience, enlightenment, near-death experiences, recreational drug use, physical pleasure, and the natural highs of physical play and endurance. In religious studies the notion of transcendence is often associated with Rudolph Otto who speaks of the experience of the numinous or holy as producing profound effects on individuals, as transcendental, frightening, and expansive. We may similarly consider that the medium of film is an exercise in transcendence. Great care and expense go into crafting an experience for moviegoers that may allow them to abscond from their everyday lives and experience and immerse themselves in wonder, fear, bewilderment, and awe in a cascade of audiovisual narrative. In much the same way the skateboard videos I address present stories of wonder while detailing impressive and groundbreaking feats of physical innovation. Borden notes that great investment went into the production of *Animal Chin* that included mobile cameras and aerial photography from helicopters. This, he argues, along with the formidable ramp that was built for the video, was part of the spectacularisation of skateboarding that the film cautions about (Borden, 2019, p. 132). Indeed, Borden is correct, while the message is the simple fun of skateboarding, it is demonstrated in a formidable and expensive way. However, skateboard videographers have a challenging task; what they seek to capture is exhilarating and dangerous, and their audience are practitioners. Thus, their films must communicate not simply the community and the manoeuvres, but also some of the excitement, elation, and risk involved. Skateboarding videos are therefore exercises not only in cultural authenticity but also in transcendence.

One way to frame this is through the sociology of voluntary risk-taking, a concept termed edgework by Stephen Lyng (1990, 2005). Edgework, like communitas, is about another liminal space that is encountered between control and chaos. Typically, edgeworkers perform risky activities, but demonstrate considerable skill and understanding about both their abilities and the tools at their disposal. Part of the attraction is that it provides an escape. The negotiation of danger can become an empowering experience as individuals gain some control over both the alienation of everyday banality and the ubiquitous nature of contemporary risks (Miller, 2005, p. 154). Ostwalt (2012, p. 223) states that 'it should be no surprise that faith communities center on high-risk activities and the attendant feeling of transcendence that survival of such activities bring[s].' While edgework holds great potential for community building, it has also been framed as part of the conceptual apparatus of neoliberal self-sufficient meritocracy. Most importantly, edgework can also be understood as a path to self-discovery. In asking what the value of dangerous sport is, Russell (2005) distinguishes self-affirmation as key and notes that dangerous sports provide 'ways of transcending the boundaries imposed on us by ordinary life' (Russell, 2005, p. 14). This is further explored in Thorpe's (2011) analysis of snowboarding and bodily affect. Some snowboarding practices are shown to conform to the maxims of edgework, courting chaos and death as practitioners negotiate big mountainboarding and backcountry routes. But entwined with these pursuits are the exhilarating sensations of being present in the moment and intensely focused. The importance of embodied knowledge and focus connects edgework to Csikszentmihalyi's (1975) concept of flow where temporal states are disrupted and sensations are heightened. Such sensations are sometimes described in spiritual terms. Self-styled *Indie Spiritualist* Chris Grosso (2014, pp. 9–10) describes a moment of transcendence as a spectator at a Van Halen concert. Immersed in a concentrated state during a 15-minute guitar solo, Grosso describes the experience of Samadhi, a Sanskrit term for a state of meditative concentration akin to the notion of flow.

I argue that these skateboard videos, and countless others, in their efforts to provide an authentic representation of skateboard culture, have a transcendental effect on some of their viewers. While I believe the fusion of exhilarating skateboarding, music, and the engaging filming is transformative in itself, the fact that this is coupled with layers of communitas makes it all the more significant and transcendental. Thus, in my interviews with middle-aged skateboarders I was reminded time and time again of the importance of particular skateboard videos, be they Blind's *Video Days* or Alien Workshop's *Photosynthesis*. These videos clearly conveyed emotional significance to my participants. The significance of these videos also proceeds in another direction, that of personal biography, or more appropriately the quest, or journey of life.

Ritual Quest

Aptly, the conclusion to this chapter returns to the performance of the journey. This is an important frame by which we can understand skateboarding, both in its micro practice of rolling and the macro global movement of skateboarders seeking out new terrain in cities throughout the world. The topics of this chapter, *Animal Chin* and *We Are Blood*, are both stories about journeys, but they are also expressive in being tales about the quest of life, learning about ourselves, our drives, and our joys. They speak of community and transcendence and show that the performance of skateboarding can be part of a larger journey in life. In a semiotic analysis, the signs and symbols of these skateboard videos represent in a microcosm a series of elements that reflect some of the core values of skateboarders. The importance of place, of community, and perseverance in the face of adversity are all strikingly evident.

Indeed, all of skateboarding is a journey, even if this is to the corner store at the end of your road. A popular trope in skateboard videos are the happenchance encounters with people who occupy the same space as skateboarders. Often this will include some marginal characters, homeless people, drug addicts, or revellers returning home after a night on the town. This sentiment is evident in *Animal Chin* as a host of unusual (but scripted) characters are encountered. Journeying in skateboarding provides a means of social encounter at a tangent from more quotidian urban exchanges. The skateboard frequently acts as a third person in encounters, a means for discussion and communication, an ice-breaking device like no other.

In terms of religious journeying, skateboarding has provided access to cultures and communities for legions of elite and mobile skateboarders across the world. This is beautifully depicted in the globe-trotting encounters of Patrik Wallner, who has travelled extensively on skateboard trips across Europe and Asia for more than a decade. Wallner has documented professional skateboarders in North Korea, Bhutan, and Yemen. His book *Visualtraveling* is compiled from journeys to 101 nations and includes some remarkable images of faith and religious festivals. One of Wallner's trips to India in 2013 coincided with the Maha Kumbha Mela festival, which occurs once every 144 years and is an augmented version of the already enormous Kumbha Mela pilgrimage held every 12 years (Wallner, 2018, p. 107). A short documentary of the event combines evocative footage of skateboarding throughout India juxtaposed with scenes from the festival. Professional skateboarders Sean Malto, Sebo Walker, Mark Suicu, and Nestor Judkins are shown navigating their culture shock in India while also drawing crowds through their spectacular skateboarding. Their skateboards appear to be as essential to their journey as their passports—these simple tools provide them with access to people and places and are able to transcend the boundaries of language and cultural difference. The journeying skateboarder in such accounts is close to the globe-trotting snowboarder (Thorpe, 2014) and the North American surfer (Laderman, 2014). Yet I argue that skateboarders in their journeys both global and local are humbled by the fact that their destinations are typically the streets where everyday folk meander and toil. I read the symbolism of the skateboard journey in religious terms to be cosmopolitan, ecumenical, and multifaith. These accounts may be suggesting that the skateboard is at times a vehicle to learn about others and in the process oneself.

A key focus of this discussion has been the importance of media in capturing and communicating these elements of skateboard culture. Skateboard videos more generally are cherished because they are seen to represent the authenticity of the culture, providing a reflection of the practices and challenges that colour the lives of skateboarders. These video journeys then become text for skateboarders, something to share with others, and in the process build and extend their community. The importance of media for lifestyle religion is distinct. This relates to the arguments of both Thorpe (2014) and Taylor (2007), who recognise new and increasing spiritual practices in lifestyle sports as connected to media.

The argument here, that media is central in the way in which skateboarders perform religion, is further developed in the following chapter exploring pilgrimage.

References

Atencio, M., Beal, B., & Wilson, C. (2009). The Distinction of Risk: Urban Skateboarding, Street Habitus and the Construction of Hierarchical Gender Relations. *Qualitative Research in Sport and Exercise, 1*(1), 3–20. https://doi.org/10.1080/19398440802567907

Barthes, R. (1972). *Mythologies* (A. Lavers, Trans.). New York: Hill & Wang.

Barthes, R. (1973). *Elements of Semiology* (A. Lavers & C. Smith, Trans.). New York: Hill & Wang.

Blizek, W. L. (2009). *The Continuum Companion to Religion and Film*. London: Continuum.

Borden, I. (2019). *Skateboarding and the City: A Complete History*. London: Bloomsbury Visual Arts.

Cowan, D. E. (2008). *Sacred Terror: Religion and Horror on the Silver Screen*. Waco, TX: Baylor University Press.

Cowan, D. E. (2012a). Religion in Cinema Horror. In T. R. Clark & D. W. Clanton Jr. (Eds.), *Understanding Religion and Popular Culture: Theories, Themes, Products and Practices* (pp. 56–71). London: Routledge.

Cowan, D. E. (2012b). Religion in Science Fiction Film and Television. In T. R. Clark & D. W. Clanton Jr. (Eds.), *Understanding Religion and Popular Culture: Theories, Themes, Products and Practices* (pp. 41–55). London: Routledge.

Csikszentmihalyi, M. (1975). *Beyond Boredom and Anxiety*. San Francisco: Jossey-Bass Publishers.

Cusack, C. M. (2010). *Invented Religions: Imagination, Fiction and Faith*. Farnham, UK: Ashgate.

Eisenhour, M. (2015). We Are Blood. *Transworld Skateboarding, 33*, 104–117.

Evans, T. (Writer). (2015). We Are Blood [DVD].

Evans, T., & Jonze, S. (Writers). (2003). Yeah Right! [DVD]: Girl Skateboards.

Evans, T., & Jonze, S. (Writers). (2012). Pretty Sweet [DVD]: Girl Skateboards.

Greco, J. (Writer). (2018). Jobs? Never!! [Video]. In Hammers USA (Producer): Supra

Grosso, C. (2014). *The Indie Spiritualist*. New York: Atria Paperback.

Henkels, R. (Writer). (2001). Guilty: Shorty's.

Jenson, A., Swords, J., & Jeffries, M. (2012). The Accidental Youth Club: Skateboarding in Newcastle-Gateshead. *Journal of Urban Design, 17*(3), 371–388. https://doi.org/10.1080/13574809.2012.683400

Jonze, S. (Writer). (1991). Video Days [VHS Video]: Blind Skateboards.

Kennedy, C. (Writer). (2016). The L.A. Boys. The Berrics.

Kusz, K. (2007). *Revolt of the White Athlete: Race, Media and the Emergence of Extreme Athletes in America.* New York: Peter Lang.

Kusz, K. (2018). The Next Progression: Centering Race and Ethnicity in Skateboarding Studies. In K. Butz & C. Peters (Eds.), *Skateboard Studies* (pp. 66–85). London: Koenig Books.

Laderman, S. (2014). *Empire in Waves: A Political History of Surfing.* Los Angeles: University of California Press.

Levi-Strauss, C. (1995). *Myth and Meaning: Cracking the Code of Culture.* New York: Schocken Books.

Lyden, J. C. (2003). *Film as Religion.* New York: New York University Press.

Lyden, J. C., & Mazur, E. M. (2015). *The Routledge Companion to Religion and Popular Culture.* New York: Routledge.

Lyng, S. (1990). Edgework: A Social Psychological Analysis of Voluntary Risk Taking. *American Journal of Sociology, 95*(4), 851–886.

Lyng, S. (2005). *Edgework: The Sociology of Risk-Taking.* New York: Routledge.

McDowell, J. C. (2012). "Unlearn What You Have Learned" (Yoda): The Critical Study of the Myth of Star Wars. In T. R. Clark & D. W. Clanton Jr. (Eds.), *Understanding Religion and Popular Culture: Theories, Themes, Products and Practices* (pp. 104–117). London: Routledge.

McKee, G. (2007). *The Gospel According to Science Fiction: From Twilight Zone to the Final Frontier.* London: Westminster John Knox Press.

Miller, W. J. (2005). Adolescents on the Edge: The Sensual Side of Delinquency. In S. Lyng (Ed.), *Edgework: The Sociology of Risk-Taking* (pp. 153–171). New York: Routledge.

Mosberg, J. (Writer). (1998). The End: Birdhouse Skateboards.

O'Connor, P. (2017). Beyond the Youth Culture: Understanding Middle-Aged Skateboarders through Temporal Capital. *International Review for the Sociology of Sport, 53*(8), 924–943. https://doi.org/10.1177/101269021 7691780

Okuyama, Y. (2015). *Japanese Mythology in Film: A Semiotic Approach to Reading Japanese Film and Anime.* New York: Lexington Books.

Ostwalt, C. (2012). *Secular Steeples: Popular Culture and the Religious Imagination* (2nd ed.). London: Bloomsbury.

Peralta, S. (Writer). (1987). *The Search for Animal Chin* [VHS].

Peralta, S. (Writer). (2001). *Dogtown and Z-Boys* [DVD].

Peralta, S. (Writer). (2012). *Bones Brigade: An Autobiography* [Video].

Read, C. (Writer). (2016). *Spirit Quest* [Video]: Mandible Claw.

Ride Channel. (2017). Animal Chin 30 Years—Tony Hawk, Steve Caballero, Mike Mcgill & Lance Mountain 2/4. *YouTube Video*. Retrieved from https://youtu.be/k51n4hhmu6w

Russell, J. S. (2005). The Value of Dangerous Sport. *Journal of the Philosophy of Sport, 32*(1), 1–19. https://doi.org/10.1080/00948705.2005.9714667

Snyder, G. (2017). *Skateboarding La: Inside Professional Street Skateboarding*. New York: New York University Press.

Taylor, B. (2007). Surfing into Spirituality and a New, Aquatic Nature Religion. *Journal of the American Academy of Religion, 75*(4), 923–951. https://doi.org/10.1093/jaarel/lfm067

Thorpe, H. (2011). *Snowboarding Bodies in Theory and Practice*. New York: Palgrave Macmillan.

Thorpe, H. (2014). *Transnational Mobilities in Action Sport Cultures*. New York: Palgrave Macmillan.

Turner, E. (2012). *Communitas: The Anthropology of Collective Joy*. New York: Palgrave Macmillan.

Turner, V. (1977). *The Ritual Process: Structure and Anti-Structure*. Ithaca, NY: Cornell University Press.

Viceland. (2017). King of the Road. Retrieved from https://www.viceland.com/en_us/show/king-of-the-road

Wallner, P. (2018). *Visualtraveling: The Eurasia Project*. Hong Kong: Patrik Wallner.

Wheaton, B., & Beal, B. (2003). 'Keeping It Real': Subcultural Media and the Discourses of Authenticity in Alternative Sport. *International Review for the Sociology of Sport, 38*(2), 155–176.

Willing, I., Green, B., & Pavlidis, A. (2019). The 'Boy Scouts' and 'Bad Boys' of Skateboarding: A Thematic Analysis of the Bones Brigade. *Sport in Society*, 1–19. https://doi.org/10.1080/17430437.2019.1580265

Yochim, E. C. (2010). *Skate Life: Re-imagining White Masculinity*. San Francisco: University of Michigan Press.

7

Pilgrimage Spots

In 2017, Bayer the German multinational pharmaceutical company launched a marketing campaign in Los Angeles focused on leaps of innovation. At the Bayer event guests mingled around a specially designed and constructed set of steps and drank cocktails. These steps led to nowhere, a functional piece of architecture removed, it would seem, from its context and erected to be part of a promotional gaze. The steps were designed by Nina Freedman of Dreamland Creative Projects architecture and design labs. The novel design included a hollowed-out underside built into the steps. This became a room with relaxed lighting and cushions where guests could mingle and lounge. In the evening, a light screen built into the steps projected the promotional video, transforming the set of steps into a giant video screen (see Fig. 7.1). The website for the Bayer Leaps project also includes inspirational text and crypto-religious quotes (Bayer, 2017).

The instillation was a reproduction of a set of 25 steps, the exact size and dimensions of those at the Cité des Congrès in the French city of Lyon. These steps are a famous location in skateboarding known as the 'Lyon 25' that graced the cover of the May 2016 issue of *Thrasher* magazine depicting Aaron 'Jaws' Homoki as he became the first skate-

© The Author(s) 2020
P. O'Connor, *Skateboarding and Religion*,
https://doi.org/10.1007/978-3-030-24857-4_7

BAYER LEAPS STAIR NIGHT VIEW WITH LEAPS STORY MOVIE ON STAIR

Fig. 7.1 Bayer Leaps stairs photo Nina Freedman

boarder to ollie down the steps and ride away. Using the motif of a leap of faith Bayer centred its marketing campaign on the visually dramatic leap made by Jaws. In truth, Jaws was performing a pilgrimage of sorts in attempting this trick, making both a journey to a notorious spot and offering homage to an older skateboarder. The origins of the Bayer campaign can be traced to feats of the talented Swedish skater Ali Boulala. His attempts to jump down the steps were famously captured in the Flip video *Sorry* released in 2002. The fact that Boulala was never entirely successful is made all the more tragic by events that followed. In 2007, Boulala was involved in a motorcycle accident that killed his friend and fellow professional skateboarder Shane Cross. He spent four months in a coma and then four years in prison for being the inebriated culpable driver of the motorcycle. The legacy of Boulala is also captured and acknowledged by Bayer in their promotional video in which both skateboarders are interviewed (Leaps by Bayer, 2017). Ironically, in the months before Bayer began their promotional campaign the steps at Lyon had become skateproofed with the introduction of defensive architecture to obstruct skateboard wheels (@aaronjawshomoki, 2017).

I use the Lyon 25 as an introduction to the theme of pilgrimage spots because it captures and compounds a variety of key issues. Mundane urban sites across the globe have become sacred to skateboarders. The notoriety of these sites is fuelled by media reproduction. The meaning derived from the media is often rich and associated with the biographies of skateboarders and also the history of the sites or 'spots' depicted. The popularity of skateboarding at the end of the second decade of the twenty-first century has resulted in the recognition and re-articulation of some of these sacred urban spots beyond the world of skateboarding. Yet, despite this notoriety, many meaningful locations are off limits to skateboarders, locations where their visits may be obstructed by deliberately hostile architectural features, security guards, laws, and fines.

The foundation for this discussion is the importance of space, which has been a central motif in much of the existing research on skateboarding. These works have tended to focus on how architecture is appropriated, reimagined, and even constructed for the purpose of skateboarding (Beal, 2013a; Blayney, 2014; Borden, 2001, 2019; Howell, 2005). Gregory Snyder explores the roots of urban sociology and considers how skateboarders are preforming urban theatre. He argues that, largely through subcultural media, skateboarders have a 'quasi spiritual' relationship with mundane urban space and that they experience a 'strong emotional attachment' to places which they may never visit (2017, p. 197). Sean Wilsey (2014, p. 113) similarly articulates that skateboarders have an urban spiritual purpose providing love to unloved places, 'emotion to emotionless terrain.' I want to contribute to this discussion by exploring the idea of urban space as not just playful, but emotional, and in some cases even spiritual. I argue that skateboard spots can also be understood as pilgrimage spots—locations in which meaning is invested and communitas is achieved. Sets of steps in a San Francisco office plaza, brick banks under the Brooklyn Bridge, and a handrail at a Hollywood school can be sacred to skateboarders in a similar way that 'Old Trafford' can be sacred to football fans. These places become meaningful through the actions of individuals and the media in which they are reproduced. Importantly, many of these sites are found spaces, but that does not mean that constructed space is not also important. *Thrasher*'s book on *Epic Spots* (Burnett, Phelps, Henry, & Creagan, 2008) includes numerous skateparks, sites constructed specifically for skateboarding. The book also documents the importance of DIY spots, places skateboarders have located, designed, and constructed themselves, almost always without permission. I argue towards the end of this chapter that skateparks are devotional monuments to urban space. Skateparks are thus hybrid entities that lovingly replicate swimming pools, steps, and handrails for ludic worship. However, I begin by situating skateboard spots in a discussion of sacred space and pilgrimage. I then proceed to unpack examples that demonstrate how sites in California, and then beyond, have become pilgrimage spots for skateboarders. While the focus here is on place, I underline throughout that it is performance that makes all of these locations meaningful.

Sacred Spots

The performance of pilgrimage must be framed through our polythetic understanding of religion. It relates to Geertz's qualification that religion includes factual motivation that conjures strong feelings in individuals, communities, and thus cultures. Place can be understood as fact, a material location that can be visited, and thus a physical entrepôt to the divine. Sites which are considered important are imbued with both feelings and thus motivation. I connect Pilgrimage to a family of ideas about the power of religious feeling, what Otto (1959) would refer to as *mysterium tremendum*, and in turn the manifestation of the sacred, which Eliade (1963) describes as *hierophany*. Both Jaws and Boulala enacted feats that dramatised the values of skateboarding and Bayer recognised the universal quality of these actions in terms of a spiritual performance of human potential and creativity. Places are thought to be important because they are where intense, holy, and sacred things occurred. For Mircea Eliade the symbolic value of place acts as an anchor between the sacred and the profane. His idea of the *Axis Mundi* suggests that a sacred place symbolises a central pillar in which the 'homogeneity of space' is disturbed (Eliade, 1959, p. 37). He elaborates that such important sites can be understood as an orientation, a point to which attention is turned and focused. Holy sites are seen to be locations that represent creation, and in returning to these sites in the rhythmic ritual of pilgrimage we are recon-necting the past and the present and instigating creation anew. While Eliade's ideas have been criticised, especially in the contradiction that holy sites are at once multiple and also essentialised as the centre of cre-ation, his sensitivity to the importance of place is influential.

Throughout this chapter I discuss pilgrimage but collapse the distinc-tion between secular and religious understandings of the act. Paraphrasing Geertz (1973, p. 90), my argument is that for some skateboarders places that we might recognise as banal functional urban terrain is deeply mean-ingful and sacred. Some enact pilgrimages to these sites 'clothing' their conceptions of the 'moods and motivations' they derive from skateboard-ing in an 'aura of factuality.' That is to say, these places are 'really' real to these individuals, representing deeply held truths and a locus in which they have been enacted. This engagement in sacred spots is at its essence a field of communication and communitas and builds on our discussion of video journeys in the previous chapter. Indeed, the motivations for many skateboard pilgrimages come from an engagement with skateboard media. However, the significance of sites of pilgrimage extends deep into human history and our initial ties to place. Lewis Mumford (1961) sug-gests that the very first cities were actually cities of the dead. These were ceremonial places where loved ones were given a permanent resting place which, in turn, became sites of significance motivating ritualised journeys of return and eventually human settlement in the vicinity of these monu-ments to the dead. Mecca has become synonymous with sites of pilgrim-age; the history of the city of Mecca provides an insight into a location where pilgrimage was entwined with trade and sustenance from the Zamzam well, even in the pre-Islamic phase (Crone, 1987). Thus, human activity precludes the development of many everyday sites into sacred places. The European pilgrimages of the thirteenth century and the 'Grand Tour' in the seventeenth century are presented by Urry (2001) as examples of noble and enriching pursuits that over the centuries departed from religious pilgrimage and became tourism. Indeed, in modern times the line between pilgrimage and tourism is increasingly blurred (Margry, 2008).

This is a dynamic which mirrors the way churches have become tourist attractions (e.g. the Sistine Chapel) and the development of 'Dark

Tourism,' where morbid sites such as the Auschwitz concentration camp or the 'Killing Fields' of Cambodia further complicate our understanding of both pilgrimage and sacred places. Similarly, Gammon (2004, p. 34) suggests that pilgrimage exists on a hypothetical continuum where piety is at one pole and the secular tourist is at the other. He highlights that even for pilgrims who journey for expressly religious purposes, travel may include other priorities. This can be demonstrated in various ways: Mitchell (2016), for example, discusses gay sex tourism, pilgrimage, and racial nostalgia in Brazil. Here, alike some examples of skateboarding, pilgrimage is part of a repertoire of pleasure, consumption, commercialisation, and tourism. In a further connection to Mitchell, it may also be errant to think of skateboard pilgrimages as devoid of sexual adventure in unfamiliar places, and homosocial desire. *Jenkem* Magazine has joked that the entire skateboard industry is built on 'guys having crushes on guys' (@ jenkemmag, 2017). The documentary on Skatopia provides insight to the sexual adventures of Brewce Martin where the Mecca of Skatopia draws in skateboarders, musicians, and strippers alike (House & Powers, 2010). Countless articles in *Thrasher* magazine detail tours to important locations juxtaposed with pictures of attractive nubile local women, be this in Cuba, Japan, or London. Even at a competition in Oceanside California the writer confesses 'I'm in it for the boobs' (Peterson, 2001, p. 78). Essentialising activities as sacred or profane is perhaps an unhelpful starting point. In Palmer and Siegler's (2017) anthropology of Daoist pilgrims in China the authenticity of spirituality is constantly tested by languid monks hamstrung by bureaucracy, many with a penchant for either power or sex, and wealthy American visitors consuming expensive tours and secluding themselves in mountain caves fasting and drinking their own urine. Thus, the notion of pilgrimage may be deeply entangled and muddied with profane activities and is ambiguous at best.

Secular pilgrimage is, however, a term that is often associated with sporting activities and their fans. An example can be found in Cusack and Digance's (2009) exploration of the annual Melbourne Cup horserace. They make a distinction regarding the social transformations which have seen commercial events 'sacralised' and religious places 'secularised' as little more than tourist attractions. Cusack and Digance tie their analysis to spiritual transformations and a contemporary departure from forms of organised religion. This extends to a body of work on the sociology of religion which observes a greater emphasis on identity construction and individuality, a theme that becomes our focus in the closing chapter of this book. Secular pilgrimages emerge as a way to share a communal experience of place made meaningful through historic expression. Cusack and Digance, like Mitchell, and Palmer and Siegler earlier, argue that contemporary pilgrimages connect to consumerist rituals and identity construction.

Here, there is arguably much material that can relate to lifestyle sports where the importance of mobility (Laderman, 2014; Thorpe, 2014) has been discussed at length. Place is sometimes secondary to the nomadic lifestyle of exploration and endless journeying for the perfect spot. Thorpe (2014, p. 136), for example, highlights how each lifestyle sport has a list of destinations made iconic through media coverage and personal stories. Place is important to the surfer, snowboarder, and skateboarder but in very different ways. Natural settings dominate the two former activities, while constructed and found space is important to the latter. Similarly, snowboarding and surfing can be regarded as middle-class pursuits in contrast to skateboarding, which although often imagined as a white and middle-class activity, is in no way essentialised by these dynamics (Thorpe, 2014; Wheaton, 2013). All of these activities are connected by the lack of importance they have with regard to stadiums and sports grounds which have tended to dominate discussions of sports pilgrimage (Gaffney & Bale, 2004; Gammon, 2004).

Academic work on skateboarding has identified the importance of place in skateboarding (Borden, 2001; Woolley, Hazelwood, & Simkins, 2011; Yochim, 2010) yet has stopped short of making a distinct connection to its emotional importance and the notion of pilgrimage. However, Beal (2013b) provides an astute explanation of both the importance of place and a list of iconic spots in skateboard culture. She highlights that skateboarders are invested in finding fresh places and creatively adapting sites for new uses. Yet this search also generates a wealth of significant places that stand out, that are revisited, and memorialised. Through acts of skateboarding, spots gain notoriety locally, and through media coverage and association with personalities they gain international recognition and subcultural meaning. Beal states that 'their iconic status is more about what the spot symbolizes than whether it is well designed. The sites need to embody the ideals of skateboarding: creativity, freedom, and do-it-yourself (DIY) ethos' (Beal, 2013a). While Beal does not frame these spots as pertaining to pilgrimage, she identifies them as being iconic precisely because they communicate important ideals and values about skateboarding.

An Enhanced Experience of Space

Evident in the subcultural media of skateboarding, and in various academic works, is the disposition that skateboarders are privy to some essential esoteric knowledge. This reveals itself in various ways, an aloof almost aristocratic attitude, an artistic and style-conscious modus operandi. In one skateboarding blog the writer refers to non-skateboarders as muggles (Neverwas, 2018). This term for non-magic folk from the Harry Potter series of J. K. Rowling highlights that skateboarders consider themselves as having an 'enhanced experience' of reality (Borden, 2019, p. 211), qualitatively different from other people. This in part may be due to the way skateboarders see ludic possibilities everywhere. Commenting on an art exhibition, Newman (2015, p. 129) notes that the skateboard artist 'shows us that the bleak rationalism of the urban environment can be resisted, its cultural signifiers reclaimed to create a more fulfilling set of daily encounters.' The notion that skateboarding is a tool in creating a more fulfilling life is significant here. It underlines how place becomes meaningful and even sacred.

We can confidently assert that skateboarders experience space differently from other athletes. Borden's (2001) groundbreaking analysis of skateboarding applies the spatial theory of Henri Lefebvre and shows that skateboarders create places of meaning that they derive from functional street architecture. One distinct example is the handrail that is designed for support and safety as one traverses down steps; for the skateboarder it is transformed into an item of dangerous spectacle to be slid and grinded upon with acute balance and timing. Not all skateboarding occurs in the street; stadiums and skateparks are increasingly prominent (Lombard, 2010; Thorpe & Wheaton, 2017), some even achieving heritage status

intimacy fostered with skateboarding spots and how the meanings these places have can be layered with biographical, spiritual, and even commercial significance.

In conversation with one skateboarder who has visited California and many famous skateboard spots, I learned of the difficulty of gaining access to some of these locations. For example, he described Wallenberg as a dangerous place to skate because the local skateboarders do not like tourists. He claimed that, if you go there you must be able to stand your ground and prove through competent skateboarding that you are worthy of visiting the spot. He mentioned that the best way to visit was to go with a local. He also noted that it was common to encounter professional skateboarders at these sites; some would even sell their equipment to skaters passing through (O'Connor, 2017). This same scenario is observed in an episode of Rick McCrank's *Post Radical* television show. Sitting at Wallenberg, McCrank and Frank Gerwer encounter a skate pilgrim who has travelled to the steps simply to take in the ambience. McCrank asks the pilgrim if he considers Wallenberg a sacred place, to which the pilgrim replies 'Yes. In its own weird way' (Craig, 2018; O'Connor, 2018b).

Wallenberg can be challenging to access, with skateboarders having to wait until the caretaker leaves for the day. The difficulty of gaining access to spots like Wallenberg connects to Preston's (1992) typology that pilgrimage sites are often remote and hard to reach. This makes such trips more complex; they may not be expensive to visit, unlike stadiums and big sporting mega-events, but they may similarly be difficult to gain access to. The need to work with local rules, the benefit of having a guide, the need to perform rites at a specific time, and the commercial opportunism encountered, all connect this account of Wallenberg to other pilgrimage stories. During the Muslim pilgrimage to Mecca, or Hajj, Saudi rules must be keenly observed: only Muslims can enter the holy city, pilgrims are required to have a Hajj guide, rites must be performed on the appropriate days, and the city is full of paraphernalia to purchase and take home (Bianchi, 2004). Just as a prayer mat purchased from Mecca might be valued for its connection to place (despite being made in China) one could argue that a set of wheels purchased from a professional at Wallenberg could be a meaningful artefact to a visiting skateboarder

(O'Connor, 2017). Similarly, both examples of pilgrimage contain a cachet of risk or danger. Hajj is fraught with risk; even within recent years, disease, dehydration, fire, and even stampedes have been serious threats to pilgrims. Accompanying these problems are social concerns, bureaucratic, residential, travel, but also robbery and fraud. As such pilgrims must only leave for Hajj after putting all domestic affairs in order, to also prepare for the morbid possibility that they may not return. Skateboarders encounter different risks, the most potent of all being injury, but perhaps also fines and detainment by security guards and police. After having made a long journey to a famous location, the last thing a skate pilgrim wants to do is break a bone miles from home and perhaps in a different country. This is not to make a false comparison between Wallenberg and Mecca, but to highlight that both forms of pilgrimage include a range of sacred and secular practices not focal on the place itself.

A further instance of the challenge of skateboard pilgrimages is the sense of reality when confronted with the imperfections of an iconic spot. Various people have mentioned to me that seeing famous locations in person only gives them deeper respect for the professionals who have skated there. Visiting an iconic spot can underline one's own limits and mere mortality. One of my informants described visiting Hollywood High as daunting, not simply because of its legacy, but also because of its size and difficulty to skate. This was also emphasised by Matt who spoke of the notorious San Francisco spot, the Hubba Hideout.

> It's just cool to see the place in which those tricks occurred, or how big some of those things were. So, you see like a big set of steps like Hubba, then you know how difficult that stuff really is. (O'Connor, 2017)

The Hubba Hideout set of steps acquired its moniker from the street slang for crack cocaine (Salo, 2011). The secluded design of the steps meant that it was a popular place for illicit transactions. It was here that people would score a 'hubba,' or small hit of crack, and often smoke 'hiding out' in relative privacy. However, it is the architectural features of the steps with sloped concrete ledges on either side that attract skateboarders and on which they grind and slide. The influence of the spot is vast. In skateboard vernacular, analogous sloped ledges have all come to be called hubbas. Skatespots and skateparks around the world with concrete, metal, or wooden sloped ledges are all called 'hubbas.' Indeed, international competitions similarly use this appropriated street slang to describe these now intentionally designed and constructed features. With the growth in mainstream appeal of skateboarding the Hubba Hideout has even been referenced in the *New York Times* in association with professional skateboarder Brian Anderson (Dougherty, 2016). Anderson's performance of a 'frontside blunt slide' on the hubba is reproduced in the 1996 skateboard video 'Welcome to Hell' and is sometimes described as the trick that secured him sponsorship. The notoriety of the place has been further heightened by the fact that Anderson has subsequently become a cultural icon beyond skateboarding, being the first professional skateboarder to come out as gay. Alike the Lyon 25, the Hubba Hideout has made its way into popular culture and is linked not just to skateboarding, but to the biographies of those who made the spot famous (O'Connor, 2017).

As important as place may well be, not all skateboarders have reverence for iconic locations. Sarah, a 44-year-old Californian pool skater, confessed that she did not feel a particular need to visit any iconic spot. She stated that 'there is no place that has been *that* built up in my mind or my consciousness that I, like, need to go there.' More important to her was the journey, the process of travelling to spots with her friends, rather than the fame of one location over another. She attributed this in part to her somewhat blasé familiarity with California. As a woman skater she had come to see that much of the skateboard culture in the area was far from sacred and was in fact too male-centred and sexist. For Sarah the cultural magnetism of skate culture in California was not potent and she confessed to feeling a little excluded from the scene in comparison to other places (O'Connor, 2017).

Emphasising the importance of video in skateboard placemaking and building on the discussion in the previous chapter, the documentary 'The L.A. Boys' (Kennedy, 2016) provides some powerful insights. This video tells the story of four skateboarders who grew up in Los Angeles and were featured in the 1989 skateboard video 'Ban This' (Peralta, 1989). The skateboarders—Guy Mariano, Rudy Johnson, Gabriel Rodriguez, and Paulo Diaz—all grew up skateboarding together, and back in 1989 Stacy

Peralta wanted to capture this fraternity in 'Ban This.' This was a savvy move on Peralta's part as skateboarding in the late 1980s had started to shift, becoming far more focused on street skills and the innovation of young pioneers. All four skateboarders went on to have careers as professional skateboarders and the documentary provides an emotional account of the friends reuniting 25 years later at the locations at which they skated in 'Ban This.' Now, as grown men we watch them recreate tricks they performed as teenagers and in one incident they find a dent they made on a metal grate that was captured in the filming of 'Ban This' a quarter of a century earlier. In truth, the documentary appears to be rather bland; it is simply a group of four revisiting some banal urban locations in Los Angeles. But the magic that is conveyed relates to the emotional investment in these spaces, the ways in which they were made meaningful and continue to be so (O'Connor, 2017). The documentary also highlights that skateboarding's history is not like that of other sports. It is not a history of pitches, stadiums, and courts. The pilgrimage spots of skateboarders are hidden in plain sight, inscribed with scratches, dents, and wax. These pilgrimage spots are found and socially constructed, remade through human creativity and innovation, and this is in part why they come to be emotionally and spiritually potent.

As I have already argued, California is for many a skateboarding holy land, tied to place, media, and people. For some it provides sites of pilgrimage but also an ethic and an ideal. The importance of media, particularly video, cannot be understated in the process of making spots iconic to skateboarders. Skateboard videos, and increasingly documentaries like 'The L.A. Boys' and 'Dogtown and Z Boys,' reinscribe the importance of place by paying homage to locations and their histories (O'Connor, 2017). But we must be sensitive to the fact that this is not specific to California, and that it is a process taking place the world over.

Morrison Hill: Hong Kong

The previous examples have explored the prominence of California, and also a European site. However, the global popularity of skateboarding has seen a number of East Asian locations rise to prominence over the last 20 years. As a result, skateboarders have to associate an array of global cities around the world with specific skateboarding spots. Again, these have been made famous through magazines, videos, and most recently in social media. China has attracted a slew of skateboard pilgrims seeking an endless array of marble ledges that cities like Shenzehn, Guangzhou, and Shanghai offer (O'Connor, 2017). As Tim Sedo (2010, p. 276) reports, one skateshop in Shanghai produced a T-shirt with the slogan 'Hey America, come skate Shanghai ... everyone is doing it!' sarcastically mocking the large numbers of skateboarding tourists passing through. I have encountered dozens of skateboarders stopping in Hong Kong while on their way to China. Many of these are solitary travellers, living a frugal existence propelled by a desire to skate some of the skateboard utopia they have seen reproduced in skateboard media. These skateboard pilgrims are a peculiar by-product of China's meteoric rise and rapid urbanisation. Skateboarders are drawn to these new monumental spaces, many of which are not policed by security guards, and some are even ghost cities, urban shells with few residents constructed for some future anticipated commerce. One skateboarder who had accompanied numerous professionals on skateboard trips to cities in China described these locations as culturally barren. He argued that China has the spots but none of the feeling. Veteran skateboard videographer Anthony Claravall replicated these comments seeing China as a skateboarding boot camp, a place simply to get video clips and photos, not really a place to enjoy yourself.

Hong Kong, as a Special Administrative Region of China since 1997, has a different history than other Chinese cities, and a different importance in terms of travel. Hong Kong is often a gateway to China, a key transportation hub, and a convenient place to get visas to travel into China. Many tourists and skateboarders alike stop off in Hong Kong as they travel through East Asia (O'Connor, 2018a, 2018b). Hong Kong also has a core skateboarding scene that reaches back to the early 1990s with longstanding connections to players in the skateboard industry based in California.

In Hong Kong one small bicycle track in Morrison Hill Road has long been used by skateboarders and has been awarded skatepark status by the Leisure and Cultural Services Department (LCSD). It has received international recognition because of its unusual architecture that includes humps and winding paths through plush vegetation (O'Connor, 2017). The path has a steep curved 'snake run' and is made all the more curious and attractive to skateboarders by the addition of cylindrical metal barriers throughout. Morrison Hill embodies the ideals that Becky Beal (2013a, p. 43) identifies in iconic skatespots. Its architecture is unusual and corresponds with the freedom and individuality that skateboarders tend to value. Similarly, as a found spot appropriated for skateboarding, it corresponds with the DIY ethos and creativity found within the culture. As a frequent visitor to this site since 2001, I have met numerous visiting professional skateboarders including X-Games champion Eric Koston and Zoo York rider Zered Bassett (who appears on the cover of this book). Morrison Hill has thus become a site for skateboard pilgrims and with each notable visit the spot becomes more widely known (O'Connor, 2017).

One evocative example of the way in which Morrison Hill is regarded by skateboarders can be provided through a recounting of events from October 2014. During this time Street League champion and owner of April Skateboarders Shane O'Neill visited Hong Kong and posted a picture of Morrison Hill on his Instagram feed for his more than 1.2 million followers (@shanejoneill, 2014). The post featured a shot of the skatepark with O'Neill's board in the background, and the text 'HONG KONG.' The message I read in this was simple, that to skateboarders across the world, Morrison Hill signifies Hong Kong. The dazzling skyscrapers and the busy harbour that adorn so many postcards of the territory are not chiefly important to skateboarders when they imagine Hong Kong. It can be argued that when they think of a city, or a country, they think of the architecture that they are familiar with, and the spots that have been made important to them through skateboard media. It was also significant that O'Neill, one of the world's most famous skateboarders, turned up to Morrison Hill without pomp or preparation and simply began skateboarding with the locals who occupy the park day in and day out. While many of these skateboarders were excited to skateboard with a visiting professional, O'Neill was arguably performing a type of ritualistic deference to the locals, that is, showing them and their spot respect by engaging with them. A further example of the importance of the location is provided by professional skateboarder Torey Pudwill. He visited Hong Kong specifically to film a line (a continuous run of tricks) in Morrison Hill skatepark that featured in a video he released funded by his sponsors (Red Bull, 2017). In short, Morrison Hill was the reason Pudwill visited Hong Kong.

In conversation with visiting professional skateboarder Jake Johnson at Morrison Hill in October 2015, I learned the spot was well known to professional skateboarders in the USA and it was a key location on any visit to Hong Kong. Johnson was enthusiastic about finally getting a chance to skate at what he regarded was an iconic spot. The fact that both Converse shoes in 2015 and New Balance Numeric shoes in 2017 chose to do skateboarding events at Morrison Hill underlines the importance of this place and how it is remade and reaffirmed by the skateboarders who visit (O'Connor, 2017). This association is further highlighted by video footage of skateboarders at Morrison Hill available on YouTube. One montage includes more than eight well-known professional skateboarders including Chris Cole, Stefan Janoswki, and Jamie Thomas (Rodgers, 2009). Again, beyond the world of skateboarding these names may carry little relevance, but as both the Bayer Leaps example and the *New York Times* report on Brian Anderson highlight, mainstream knowledge of skateboard spots is on the rise.

So can Morrison Hill be regarded as a pilgrimage spot in skateboarding? Returning to the literature on pilgrimage, it can be understood as having a form of spiritual magnetism and a type of 'sacred geography,' a place not made for skateboarders but embraced and admired by them (O'Connor, 2017). Significant placemaking has also occurred through association with various personalities, who while not supernatural are recognised for their skill (Preston, 1992). The popularity of this spot with both locals and professionals characterises Morrison Hill as a mandatory place for visiting skateboarders. The obligation to visit, as Preston has argued, is equally an important part of pilgrimage and a notable part of sacralised modern tourism (1992, p. 56). These accounts highlight that place in skateboarding is key, but differentiated from place in other sports since many of skateboarding's most important spots are not legitimate sporting facilities. In fact, they are prosaic, unremarkable urban locations that have become so much more.

A final note on Hong Kong is that too often iconic places are considered only in terms of their relevance to the core skateboard industry in California. There is similarly a great deal of regional importance attributed to skateboarding spaces. Dr Sander Hölsgens (2018) writes beautifully on the specificities of place for Korean skateboarders, especially as an extension of home. In a research trip to Hong Kong, Hölsgens encountered Korean skateboarders who saw a cultural value in documenting their travels to regional skateboard spots on their social media feeds. This underlines that it is not professional skateboarders alone, or at all, that make spaces significant and meaningful to skateboarders.

Skateparks: Found and Built

The versatility of the skateboard has meant that it is a tool of urban freedom. There is no need for a specific court or playing field to skateboard. One simply has to walk out of the door in order to find somewhere to skate. However, the desire to construct tailor-made places for skateboarding emerged as a prominent commercial activity in the 1970s. In this final part of the chapter I suggest that skateparks can also be meaningful sites of pilgrimage. But my main claim here is that skatepark construction, both officially approved projects and opportunistic DIY skatespots, are ultimately sites of urban devotion to the majesty of urban architecture. Skateparks are hybrid environments, taking cues from swimming pools, office plazas, handrails, and even parking lots. To exploit a religious vernacular here, skateparks are monumental forms of idolatry. They are temples to the urban environment, honouring concrete, steel, and wood in the playful ways they can be combined. Skateparks provide places for skateboarders, but as my discussion highlights, these places are very much in dialogue with the sacred notion of cities at large and exist in honour of them. Our Neolithic ancestors fashioned their surroundings to mimic the phallus and the vulva, to consecrate not just loved ones, but to also honour the stars, the seasons, and the tress. Simon Schama (1995) writes at length about our intimate relationship with the landscape and how it is revealed in our art and architecture. Skateparks can be seen as an expression of love for a more contemporary landscape, that of the city. Richard

Sennett (2002, pp. 18–22) speaks of the desensitised citizen in the modern city, sleepwalking through malls and passive in their automobiles, disconnected from the world they have created. The skatepark flips this scenario and provides a recreated site of reverence for all of the disregarded beauty of the city, not in its pomp and opulent architecture, but in its ludic potential. Skateparks are voluptuous sculptures of urban eros.

Iain Borden (2001) describes how skateparks emerged not simply as a commercial vehicle, but also as a combination of three other desires. Firstly, the associated danger of skateboarding meant that many felt it necessitated containment to be safely practised. This motivation was bolstered by a second, the increase of legitimate spaces due to the criminalisation of skateboarding on streets. Thirdly, the boom in skatepark construction in the 1970s was built off the introduction of urethane wheels and the desire to test these new products in the best possible environments. The lessons of poor park design in the 1960s contributed to a new awareness of what parks could be if designed correctly.

The very first skateparks that were built in the USA aimed to mimic the environments that skateboarders had come to use, often found spaces, drainage banks, hills, and empty swimming pools. The example of the skatepark bowl, which is basically a Californian-style backyard pool designed simply for skateboarding, is an excellent primary example of the hybridity of skateparks. One of the first bowls designed and built was at the Pipeline skatepark in California. It opened in 1977 and was celebrated as a terrain relevant to skateboarders. It also received criticism for not being similar enough to a swimming pool. Skateboarders noted the absence of pool tiles and coping blocks standard in backyard pools (Borden, 2001, p. 62). Rather than these features replicating the appearance of the pool, skateboarders desired these elements because of the ways in which their skateboards could be used with them. Coping blocks provided a surface to be grinded by the trucks, and the tiles provided an audible reverberation as wheels travel across them signalling that the skateboarder has risen to the steepest part of the bowl. These design elements of the backyard pool are valued features that resonate with an embodied experience of riding the pools, an experience that was similarly desired in skatepark bowls. In the British context, skateparks, like the Rom park in Essex, transplanted the typical Californian backyard pool from American skateparks. This fusion continues to be replicated across the world to this day. Bowls mimicking the classic Californian backyard pool are to be found across the globe in territories as diverse as Bali and Tehran.

The rise in popularity of new skateparks at the turn of the century also signals a further evolution of skateboarding. New parks, whilst still frequently housing bowls, also accommodate new skateboarding practices in replicating features of the city that skateboarders have often appropriated. Skateparks now commonly possess the features of stairs, handrails, concrete ledges, pole jams, manual pads, along with flat banks and transitions of varying angles, and gaps which manifest as void space between obstacles that skateboarders try to jump between.

By the year 2000 skateboarding had once again become consolidated as a popular, if not central, sporting pastime in North America and throughout the world. In an excellent analysis of the renewed popularity of skateparks Ocean Howell highlights that the number of skateboarders between 1995 and 2005 rose from 4.5 million to 20 million in the USA (2008, p. 476). The fluctuating number of skateparks in the USA details these changes. In 1982, there were 190 skateparks in operation throughout the country; ten years later this had fallen to just 120, only to rise again to 165 by 1997 (Borden, 2001, pp. 68–84). Howell notes that between 1997 and 2008 the number of skateparks had once again ballooned from 165 to 2100 (Howell, 2008, p. 475). As of 2014, estimates suggest that there are approximately 3500 skateparks in the USA (Transworld Skateboarding, 2014) and over 9630 skateparks globally (Concrete Disciples, 2017). A news release from *Transworld Skateboarding* magazine website (2014) reports that the Centre for Disease Control suggests the USA requires an additional 9000 skateparks to meet the needs of the current active skateboarding population and provide resources to encourage an active and healthy generation of young people.

The new era of skatepark construction has produced many superb parks which attract their own groups of new pilgrims. Jordan, an IT worker in his mid-forties, spoke about the annual skatepark trips he made with friends:

I also do a yearly trip to Colorado. Somehow Colorado has become a Mecca for skateboarding, because they have so many parks all within 20 to 30 minutes of each other, and flights in the off season for Denver are really cheap from Chicago. It is $180 for a round trip flight, and then we just rent an Airbnb. I think eight of us are going this year. Last year and the year before, I think it was only four people… and then maybe six people the year before that. … I do a lot of shutterbug, a lot of videos and photographs out there, just because we're skating these amazing parks, and we never know which is going to be the last trip.

These trips took on emotional significance for Jordan. These were times to be with his friends, to enjoy skating new terrain, and to document a pastime that he feels may be slipping away from him. As his concerns about ageing raise doubts about his future trips, his photography provides a means to capture the meaning and experience that he holds dear. His testimony utilises a specific type of language, referring to Colorado as a site of pilgrimage, a Mecca. He goes on to discuss how beautiful these new parks are and how pleasurable it is to skate them.

The renaissance of skatepark development is also matched by the recognition of skateparks as part of urban historical heritage. This was demonstrated in September 2014 when the Rom Skatepark in Essex England was listed as a heritage site (Brown, 2014). The history of skateboarding that is documented and reproduced in skateboard media brings with it a motivation to preserve these important locations.

In recent years there has been a considerable rise in this type of activism by skateboarders seeking to protect such iconic locations in skateboard culture (Blayney, 2014; Howell, 2005; Németh, 2006; Trotter, 2013). The campaign to save the Southbank Undercroft in London was a success that consolidated a cultural and commercial acknowledgement of the role of skateboarders in the civic life of the city (Borden, 2015). One of the evocative successes of the Long Live South Bank campaign was to capitalise on the communitas and grass-roots nature of placemaking (Ruiz, Snelson, Madgin, & Webb, 2019). The 'Bro Bowl' built in Florida in 1979 was the first skatepark in the USA to be listed on the National Register of Historic Places in 2013 (Skateboarding Heritage

Foundation, 2016). It has subsequently been demolished in a redevelopment of the surrounding area. The bowl was laser-scanned and reconstructed in an effort to preserve the site and its legacy (Pratt, 2015).

Beyond the skateparks that have been planned and funded by businesses and local government is a whole host of skatespots and skateparks that have been self-made. The DIY ethic in skateboarding is a prominent credo that at one pole links to the entrepreneurialism of millionaire skateboarders and at the other connects to penniless teenagers pulling together scraps of wood to make a ramp or slidebar. This element of skateboarding is replicated in stories of first skateboards, of milk crates being cut up, and roller skates being sawn into two and nailed onto two by four planks. The key example of this is the Burnside skateboard project in Portland, Oregon, where skateboarders in the early 1990s decided to build their own skatepark in a vacant area underneath a bridge in the peripheries of the city. The project was ultimately celebrated by the local authorities as it had a gentrifying effect on the local community, influencing a drop in crime and the clearing out of homeless people from the same area (Borden, 2001, p. 485; Howell, 2008). Burnside has become another iconic site of pilgrimage, a constructed site, and a concrete palimpsest to skateboarding. The Skatopia skatepark and commune in Ohio is perhaps one of the most infamous skate pilgrim locations. A *Rolling Stone* article describes the 88 acre skatepark as an attempt at skateboard utopia where there are none of the rules that have come to dominate skateparks across the world. The founder Brewce Martin imagines himself as a cult leader, drawing comparisons to Stephen Hawking, Socrates, and Robert Mugabe (Binelli, 2008). Skateboarders across the world make their way to Skatopia where they are free to skate and live as long as they contribute an hour of work each day. The skatepark was founded in 1995 and holds an annual skateboarding event called the 'Bowl Bash.' Skatopia provides further parallels to the scholarship on pilgrimage. Martin has constructed a liminal space, free from rules, that is open to all manner of marginal wandering skateboarders.

The love of urban space is beautifully demonstrated in Richard Gilligan's (2014) book on DIY skateparks. The coffee table book is essentially a collection of photos Gilligan has taken across the world at various small- and large-scale DIY projects. Originally extending from a photography project he did at Burnside, his collection of DIY skatespots is underscored by the very ephemeral reality of these spots, none of them appearing to be built to last indefinitely. Unlike the grandeur of a skyscraper, potent yet naive of its finite existence, the DIY skatepark is not built to look good, but purely to be enjoyed. Yet in Gilligan's book very few of the photographs include skateboarders, or any people at all. One plate details a location in Derry Ireland where 80% of the picture is green, a field strewn with trash. A small concrete driveway comes to an abrupt end with a short banked concrete transition. A thing of beauty? The vistas are laid bare for the reader to indulge not in the spectacle of skateboarding, but in its sumptuous terrain.

Conclusion

The fact that Bayer pharmaceuticals, a company unrelated to skateboarding, chose to celebrate the Lyon 25 and that the *New York Times* reported on the legacy of the Hubba Hideout suggests that the hidden places of skateboarding are slowly becoming better recognised and understood. I believe that increased emotional investment in and spiritual identification with iconic spots is also tied to the growing mainstream popularity and sportification of skateboarding. By this I mean that some skateboarders are seeking to demonstrate and consolidate parts of their culture which are being altered beyond their control. The emotional content of a life of skateboarding makes an impact and our exploration of pilgrimage spots touches on this. These places are sites of communitas. They are sites of cultural heritage both tangible and intangible (Ruiz et al., 2019). They also foreground a possibility that skateboarders might pursue cultural rights, perhaps ones that extend beyond specific places and pertain to self-expression and even ritual process.

These varied accounts of important places in skateboard culture connect to existing discussions of both space (Cresswell, 2004) and sport (Bale, 2003; Gaffney & Bale, 2004; Henning, 1997; Vertinsky & Bale, 2004; Wenner & Billings, 2017). They highlight that skateboarding is not unlike other sports in the sense of history surrounding placemaking.

Yet, skateboarding is differentiated in the types of spaces that become significant. Many of skateboarding's iconic places are overlooked urban spots. This means that they are anonymous to the average person, unlike the ways stadiums are distinct even to those disinterested or unaware of sports. Skateboarding's important locations may be denied to skateboarders; they may have to trespass, risk fines, or wait till late at night to visit them. Yet, they are also democratic; not everyone can score a goal in Wembley stadium, but any skateboarder can visit Wallenberg, or the Lyon 25 (O'Connor, 2017).

What is most significant in this discussion is that place in skateboarding is intimately tied to history; places become vessels of the past and are connected to photographs and videos. The importance of skateboard videos in placemaking is distinct, and is shown to be self-aware and self-referential. Skateboarders remember 'who did what and where' (O'Connor, 2017). This holds significance for professional skateboarders also, as it is they and their filmers and photographers who have to be mindful of the past and understand what is homage to previous performance, and what is disrespect. The discussion on the Lyon 25 underlines how tentative the line between the two may be.

By way of conclusion I return to the Lyon 25 and cite an enthusiastic and emotive account of Boulala's attempt to jump the steps. It provides pause in showing that triumph is not an integral part of the glory of skateboarding, that the ritual humiliation of failure is part of the communitas that makes the activity and its places both real and relevant:

Ali Boulala's Sorry part, literally ends with his destruction and failure. Now, a 25 stair ollie is a very tall order, but how amazing and refreshing is it to see a man not succeed as a way to close out his career's greatest achievement? You see, that's a skate video I can relate to. It doesn't make his part any worse, it makes it real. Us commoners don't normally get our big trick, most of us don't even try. … Ali Boulala's Sorry part is the realest account of skateboarding ever produced by a professional skateboarder. He gets drunk, he pukes, his dog humps his leg, he throws meat at a window, he does absolutely absurd things on a skateboard, and best of all? He bails. He gets hurt. He gets really hurt. And he doesn't win … he's just like us. He is our champion. (Ridge, 2015)

References

@aaronjawshomoki. (2017). The Lyon 25 Now Has Skate Stoppers in Front of It. *Instagram Post*. Retrieved from https://www.instagram.com/p/ BQwQrm9gXeA/

@brian_panebianco. (2017, June 2). Amazing… Retrieved from https://www. instagram.com/p/BUz8Lobg04-/?taken-by=brian_panebianco

@jenkemmag. (2017). Skateboarding: A Whole Industry Based on Guys Having Crushes on Guys. *Tweet*. Retrieved from https://twitter.com/jenkemmag/sta tus/942492879783477248?lang=en

@shanejoneill. (2014, October 23). Hong Kong. *Instagram Post*. Retrieved from https://www.instagram.com/p/uedrZEOF2A/

Bale, J. (2003). *Sports Geography* (2nd ed.). London: Routledge.

Bayer. (2017). Leaps by Bayer. Retrieved from https://leaps.bayer.com/

Beal, B. (2013a). *Skateboarding: The Ultimate Guide*. Santa Barbara, CA: Greenwood.

Beal, B. (2013b). The Ups and Downs of Skating Vertical: Christian Hosoi, Crystal Meth, and Christianity. In W. L. Benoit (Ed.), *Fallen Sports Heroes, Media, and Celebrity Culture* (pp. 92–106). New York: Peter Lang.

Berrics, T. (2017). Tiago Lemos Switch Backside Tailslide. *The Berrics*. Retrieved from http://theberrics.com/tiago-lemos-switch-backside-tailslide/

Bianchi, R. (2004). *Guests of God: Pilgrimage and Politics in the Islamic World*. New York: Oxford University Press.

Binelli, M. (2008). Welcome to Skatopia. *Rolling Stone*, pp. 43–51.

Blayney, S. (2014). *Long Live South Bank*. London: Long Live Southbank.

Boil the Ocean. (2017). Could Tiago Lemos' Incredible Switch Backside Tailslide Also Reflect Ledge Skating's Shrinking Middle Class? Retrieved from https://boiltheocean.wordpress.com/2017/06/04/could-tiago-lemos- incredible-switch-backside-tailslide-also-reflect-ledge-skatings-shrinking- middle-class/

Borden, I. (2001). *Skateboarding, Space and the City*. Oxford: Berg.

Borden, I. (2015). Southbank Skateboarding, London and Urban Culture: The Undercroft, Hungerford Bridge and House of Vans. In K. J. Lombard (Ed.), *Skateboarding: Subculture, Sites and Shifts* (pp. 91–107). London: Routledge.

Borden, I. (2019). *Skateboarding and the City: A Complete History*. London: Bloomsbury Visual Arts.

Brown, M. (2014, October 29). The Rom, Hornchurch, Becomes First Skatepark in Europe to Get Listed Status. *The Guardian*. Retrieved from https://www.

theguardian.com/culture/2014/oct/29/the-rom-hornchurch-first-skatepark-europe-listed-status

Burnett, M., Phelps, J., Henry, R., & Creagan, A. (2008). *Epic Spots: The Places You Must Skate Before You Die*. New York: Universe Publishing.

Concrete Disciples. (2017). Total Skatepark Info on Concrete Disciples. Retrieved from https://www.concretedisciples.com/skatepark-directory/all-countries

Craig, A. (Writer). (2018). Episode 6: A Rolling Obsession [Cable Television Show]. *Post Radical*.

Cresswell, T. (2004). *Place: A Short Introduction*. Oxford: Blackwell.

Crone, P. (1987). *Meccan Trade and the Rise of Islam*. Princeton, NJ: Princeton University Press.

Cusack, C. M., & Digance, J. (2009). The Melbourne Cup: Australian Identity and Secular Pilgrimage. *Sport in Society, 12*(7), 876–889. https://doi.org/10.1080/17430430903053109

Dougherty, C. (2016, September 28). Brian Anderson, Skateboarding Star, Comes Out as Gay. *The New York Times*. Retrieved from https://www.nytimes.com/2016/10/02/fashion/brian-anderson-skateboarding-gay-coming-out-vice-sports.html

Eliade, M. (1959). *The Sacred and the Profane*. New York: Harcourt.

Eliade, M. (1963). *Myth and Reality*. New York: Harper & Row.

FingerSkateSelective. (2009). Tech Deck Carlsbad Gap!!!!!!!!!!!!!!!!!!!!!!!!!! Retrieved from https://www.youtube.com/watch?v=qiVU0RaxyCw

Gaffney, C., & Bale, J. (2004). Sensing the Stadium. In P. Vertinsky & J. Bale (Eds.), *Sites of Sport: Space, Place Experience* (pp. 25–38). London: Routledge.

Gammon, S. (2004). Secular Pilgrimage and Sport Tourism. In B. Richie & D. Adair (Eds.), *Sport Tourism: Interrelationships, Impacts and Issues* (pp. 30–45). Clevedon: Channel View Publications.

Geertz, C. (1973). *The Interpretation of Cultures: Selected Essays*. New York: Basic Books.

Gilligan, R. (2014). *DIY/Underground Skateparks*. Munich: Prestel Verlag.

Glenney, B., & O'Connor, P. (2019). Skateparks as Hybrid Elements of the City. *Journal of Urban Design*, 1–16. https://doi.org/10.1080/13574809.2019.1568189

Haseltine, D. (2002). *I.Am.Relevant: A Generation Impacting Their World with Faith*. Lake Mary, FL: Relevant Books.

Henning, E. (1997). *Body Cultures: Essays on Sport, Space and Identity*. London: Routledge.

Hölsgens, S. (2018). *A Phenomenology of Skateboarding in Seoul, South Korea: Experiential and Filmic Observations.* UCL (University College London).

House, L., & Powers, C. (Writers). (2010). Skatopia: 88 Acres of Anarchy: Garden Thieves Pictures.

Howell, O. (2005). The "Creative Class" and the Gentrifying City. *Journal of Architectural Education, 59*(2), 32–42. https://doi.org/10.1111/j.1531-314X.2005.00014.x

Howell, O. (2008). Skatepark as Neoliberal Playground: Urban Governance, Recreation Space, and the Cultivation of Personal Responsibility. *Space and Culture, 11*(4), 475–496. https://doi.org/10.1177/1206331208320488

IGN. (2012). Tony Hawk's Pro Skater HD: School II. Retrieved from http://www.ign.com/wikis/tony-hawks-pro-skater-hd/School_II

Just Skate. (2015). Carlsbad Gap on Video Skateboarding #Short Documentary. Retrieved from https://www.youtube.com/watch?v=MAOKbRGrJhQ

Kennedy, C. (Writer). (2016). The L.A. Boys. The Berrics.

Laderman, S. (2014). *Empire in Waves: A Political History of Surfing.* Los Angeles: University of California Press.

Leaps by Bayer. (2017). Bayer | Leaps | Interview Aaron Homoki and Ali Boulala. *YouTube.* Retrieved from https://youtu.be/w7oUsm_fiA0

Lombard, K.-J. (2010). Skate and Create/Skate and Destroy: The Commercial and Governmental Incorporation of Skateboarding. *Continuum, 24*(4), 475–488. https://doi.org/10.1080/10304310903294713

Margry, P. J. (2008). *Shrines and Pilgrimage in the Modern World: New Itineraries into the Sacred* (P. J. Margry, Ed.). Amsterdam: Amsterdam University Press.

Mitchell, G. (2016). *Tourist Attractions: Performing Race and Masculinity in Brazil's Sexual Economy.* Chicago: University of Chicago Press.

Mumford, L. (1961). *The City in History.* New York: Harcourt.

Németh, J. (2006). Conflict, Exclusion, Relocation: Skateboarding and Public Space. *Journal of Urban Design, 11*(3), 297–318. https://doi.org/10.1080/13574800600888343

Neverwas, B. (2018). Stupidfest 2018—The Whole Story Part 5: Day Two Part One. *Blog Entry.* Retrieved from https://neverwasskateboarding.com/stupidfest-2018-the-whole-story-part-5-day-two-part-one/

Newman, D. (2015). New Mobile Methods: The Skateboarder as Contemporary Flâneur. *5*(1), 127. https://doi.org/10.3167/trans.2015.050112.

O'Connor, P. (2017). Handrails, Steps and Curbs: Sacred Places and Secular Pilgrimage in Skateboarding. *Sport in Society, 21*(11), 1651–1668. https://doi.org/10.1080/17430437.2017.1390567

O'Connor, P. (2018a). Hong Kong Skateboarding and Network Capital. *Journal of Sport and Social Issues*. https://doi.org/10.1177/0193723518797040

O'Connor, P. (2018b). Skateboarding and the Fetish of Sacred Places—Post Radical Episode 6. *Tumblr Blog*. Retrieved from http://everydayhybridity.tumblr.com/post/177079118127/skateboarding-and-the-fetish-of-sacred-places

Otto, R. (1959). *The Idea of the Holy* (J. W. Harvey, Trans.). Harmondsworth: Penguin.

Palmer, D. A., & Siegler, E. T. (2017). *Dream Trippers: Global Daoism and the Predicament of Modern Spirituality*. Chicago: University of Chicago Press.

Peralta, S. (Writer). (1989). Ban This [VHS].

Peterson, S. (2001, February). Drive by Suicide. *Thrasher*.

Pratt, D. (2015, June 16). Demolition of Historic Bro Bowl Skateboard Park Begins. *Tampa Bay Times*. Retrieved from http://www.tbo.com/news/politics/demolition-of-historic-bro-bowl-begins-in-downtown-tampa-20150616/

Preston, J. J. (1992). Spiritual Magnetism: An Organizing Principle for the Study of Pilgrimage. In *The Ritual Process: Structure and Anti-structure* (pp. 31–46). Ithaca, NY: Cornell University Press.

Red Bull. (2017, March 1). Torey Pudwill's Flatbar Frenzy. *YouTube Video*. Retrieved from https://www.youtube.com/watch?v=mZd6NsTDSsY

Ridge, R. (2015). The People's Champion. Retrieved from http://www.jenkemmag.com/home/2015/01/14/the-peoples-champion/

Rodgers, O. (2009). Pro Skaters at Morrison Hill. Retrieved from https://www.youtube.com/watch?v=k3hSt5WHBpQ

Ruiz, P., Snelson, T., Madgin, R., & Webb, D. (2019). 'Look at What We Made': Communicating Subcultural Value on London's Southbank. *Cultural Studies*, 1–26. https://doi.org/10.1080/09502386.2019.1621916

Salo, A. (2011). R.I.P. Hubba Hideout. Retrieved from http://espn.go.com/action/skateboarding/news/story?id=6054554

Schama, S. (1995). *Landscape and Memory*. London: Fontana Press.

Sedo, T. (2010). Dead-Stock Boards, Blown-out Spots, and the Olympic Games: Global Twists and Local Turns in the Formation of China's Skateboarding Community. In P. Rethmann, I. Szeman, & W. D. Coleman (Eds.), *Cultural Autonomy: Frictions and Connections* (pp. 257–282). Toronto: UBC Press.

Sennett, R. (2002). *Flesh and Stone: The Body and the City in Western Civilization*. London: Penguin Books.

Skateboarding Heritage Foundation. (2016, March). Save the Bro Bowl. *Skateboarding Heritage Foundation.* Retrieved from http://www.skateboardingheritage.org/programsmenu/brobowl/

Snyder, G. (2017). *Skateboarding La: Inside Professional Street Skateboarding.* New York: New York University Press.

The Nine Club (Producer). (2017, October 16). Jamie Thomas | *The Nine Club* with Chris Roberts—Episode 68. *YouTube Video.* Retrieved from https://www.youtube.com/watch?v=hc5AlRTTNx0

Thorpe, H. (2014). *Transnational Mobilities in Action Sport Cultures.* New York: Palgrave Macmillan.

Thorpe, H., & Wheaton, B. (2017). The X Games: Re-Imagining Youth and Sport. In L. A. Wenner & A. C. Billings (Eds.), *Sport, Media and Mega-Events* (pp. 247–261). Taylor & Francis.

Thrasher. (2015a). Bust or Bail 2: Clipper Pre-Game Interviews. Retrieved from https://www.youtube.com/watch?v=f38OMEYrfnk

Thrasher. (2015b). Bust or Bail 2: The Ripper at Clipper. Retrieved from https://www.youtube.com/watch?v=rHoGc3lrLU0

Thrasher Magazine. (2015, September 30). 20 Years of Jamie Thomas.

Thrasher Magazine. (2017). Skateline—Tiago Lemos, Miles Silvas, Guy Mariano, Alex Midler, Antonio Durao & More. Retrieved from https://youtu.be/Q-Zhy94WwLg?t=2m43s

Tonyhawkgames. (2016). Carlsbad-Gap-View.Jpg. Retrieved from http://tonyhawkgames.wikia.com/wiki/File:Carlsbad-gap-view.jpg

Transworld Skateboarding. (2014). CDC Report Supports More Skateparks. Retrieved from http://skateboarding.transworld.net/news/cdc-report-supports-skateparks/#JpL330GRxlXLaVP6.97

Trotter, L. (2013). *Walking with Skateboarders: The Southbank Struggle for Egalitarianism, Working Class-Ness and Capitalist Critique.* Retrieved from https://www.academia.edu/12748160/Walking_with_skateboarders_the_Southbank_struggle_short_version_for_LSE_Argonaut_magazine_

Urry, J. (2001). *The Tourist Gaze* (2nd ed.). London: Sage.

Vertinsky, P., & Bale, J. (2004). *Sites of Sport: Space, Place, Experience.* London: Routledge.

Wenner, L. A., & Billings, A. C. (2017). *Sport, Media and Mega-Events.* London: Routledge.

Wheaton, B. (2013). *The Cultural Politics of Lifestyle Sports.* New York: Routledge.

Wikipedia. (2017). Point Loma High School. Retrieved from https://en.wikipe-dia.org/wiki/Point_Loma_High_School#Leap_of_Faith

Wilsey, S. (2014). *More Curious*. San Francisco: McSweeney's.

Woolley, H., Hazelwood, T., & Simkins, I. (2011). Don't Skate Here: Exclusion of Skateboarders from Urban Civic Spaces in Three Northern Cities in England. *Journal of Urban Design, 16*(4), 471–487. https://doi.org/10.1080/13574809.2011.585867

Yochim, E. C. (2010). *Skate Life: Re-imagining White Masculinity*. San Francisco: University of Michigan Press.

8

Ritualised Play

Three taps, three times. This is part of professional skateboarder Andrew Reynolds' ritual when trying to offset his anxiety before he performs a trick. He refers to this as 'the madness.' It manifests in a variety of ways, perhaps riding his skateboard up to an obstacle repetitively, tapping his board on the ground in anticipation, or kicking a nearby wall. In one video we see him attempting a backside flip down the Wallenberg Gap and indulging in the madness as he prepares (Vice, 2012). Reynolds describes how the madness is even part of his obsession with the practice of setting up a new board, sometimes organising his wheels into patterns of three (The Nine Club, 2017a). This is a personalised ritual, and it is one that Reynolds recognises as part of his obsessive and compulsive personality. It appears to be anything but religious. The madness might be best understood as a superstition, a tactic of edgework to assert some control over the chaos of attempting to jump a four-foot-high and 16-foot-wide set of stairs on a precariously wheeled wooden board. But in some ways rituals are superstitions, they must be performed at certain times and follow specific procedures in order for them to be valid. Rites are performed to allay our anxieties about specific life events both big and small. They can be communal, providing the opportunity

© The Author(s) 2020
P. O'Connor, *Skateboarding and Religion*,
https://doi.org/10.1007/978-3-030-24857-4_8

to signify the importance of a particular moment, perhaps the shift from one phase in life to another. Similarly, all rituals contain the capacity for personalisation as Catherine Bell (2009, pp. 221–222) argues. It is precisely the capacity for ritual to be effective in forming and sustaining groupings while also being open to appropriation that makes it so powerful. Skateboarding is awash with ritual, ranging from the most arcane and personalised practices, like the madness of Andrew Reynolds, to the institutionalised global celebrations of the annual Go Skateboarding Day.

Ritual relates to repetition, communication, knowledge, and the body. In religion, ritual is physical worship, seen to signify moments of departure from everyday life and immersion in the holy or numinous. Ritual is thus associated with a different realm of reality, of play, performance, and efficacy. For Bobby Alexander (1997, p. 139) a simple definition of ritual identifies it as 'performance, planned or improvised that effects a transition from everyday life to an alternative context within which the everyday is transformed.' The notion of performance is our overarching motif in this second part of the book. It resonates with the way Geertz has explored religion as a cultural phenomenon, and, importantly, the emphasis he puts on ritual being an activity, a performed action, rather than a belief. Indeed, when Geertz (1973, p. 90) speaks of religion as 'clothing' 'conceptions' of an 'order of existence' with 'factuality' that make 'motivations' 'realistic,' he is addressing ritual as a means to make belief and worldview apparent. Thus, in enacting ritual people are involved in committing not just to a worldview, but in making that worldview part of their lived and experiential reality. Importantly, Geertz gave ritual considerable attention and developed the notion of thick description in his account of the Balinese cockfight (1973, p. 412). In his own words, to religious people rituals are 'not only models of what they believe, but also models *for* the believing of it' (1973, p. 114). Key in Alexander's definition is the fact that ritual transforms daily life. This echoes Durkhiem's understanding in which religious life is signified by a move from the profane to the sacred realm. The notion of transformation is paralleled in Borden's (2019, p. 285) work on skateboarding. He sees that the skateboard provides a means to transform the 'everyday' and, quoting Lefebvre, points to the possibility of a 'magnificent life.' The signal of a political and transcendent ritual quality to skateboarding is readily apparent in Borden's work (2001, 2019). This suggests that ritual could be an apposite answer to the ever-elusive quest of defining skateboarding itself.

These conceptions are exciting for us because they resonate with the way in which skateboarding is fundamentally a performance. Indeed, the problem that I broach in this chapter is not how to identify the relevance of ritual in skateboarding—it is self-evident and manifold. Rather the challenge is to order and interpret the prominence of ritual in skateboarding. In the following pages I provide a standard unpacking of the features of ritual and highlight how skateboarding conforms to these tropes. I point to both macro and micro rituals, the former being those that can be simply traced onto standard life events and existing religious architecture (birth, death, festivals) and the latter being idiosyncratic to skateboarding. Micro rituals are similar to what anthropologist John Bowen (2012, p. 54) describes as diacritic actions, particular performances used to communicate with, and understood by, only a select group. For Bowen these actions and motifs are like indexes by which others can infer a wealth of codified information. We learn through this chapter that skateboarders have a ritual life that is layered with such symbolic meaning. In analysis this renders the cultural world of skateboarding in a unique way, underscoring it as both philosophical and political. This chapter shows that, to many, skateboarding is a religion and that it is primarily a religion of ritual. The first half of this chapter provides evidence to underscore this argument. What is absent in the recognition of the ritualised patterns of skateboarding is what the overarching meaning of skateboarding might be. I argue that many popular accounts of ritual overlook the importance of play and thus I explore this component to argue that skateboarding can be understood as an emergent lifestyle religion of ritualised play.

Classifying Ritual

There is a vast body of work on ritual and numerous taxonomies regarding different forms of ritual expression. Ronald Grimes (1985) distinguishes 16 different categories of ritual, including practices of purification, magic, and pilgrimage. A more conservative schema is provided by

Catherine Bell in what she refers to as a 'pragmatic compromise between completeness and simplicity' (1997, p. 94). She provides six categories in which distinct ritual practices can be distinguished. Firstly, she identifies rites of passage that signal the transformation of one life stage to another. These include birth rituals, coming of age rites, and funerary practices. Secondly, calendrical rites that pertain to temporal repetition: an annual festival such as Easter for Christians, or Holi for Hindus. These need not be annual events. For example, the five pillars of Islam include rites that must be performed daily (prayer), monthly (almsgiving), annually (fasting), and once in a lifetime (pilgrimage). Of further significance, the Islamic calendar, like the Chinese ritual calendar, is based on the moon, and thus rituals need not occur in the same months or seasons year to year. The third category includes rites of exchange and communion. Symbolic offerings, sacrifices, and devotionals are some examples of such rituals. Rites of affliction become Bell's fourth category and represent acts to mitigate bad omens or spirits. Her fifth category of ritual is reserved for feasting, fasting, and festivals. While it is true that these acts might conform to calendrical rites, they can also be performed outside of such cyclical repetition. The emphases in these acts are to demonstrate the strength of the ritual community and to express commitment to it. Her final ritual category is that of political rites, which are used to make power visible, and in some cases to create and critique hierarchy. Inherent in any culture is some form of structure which communicates values and social order. Rituals of display, parade, and various honorific gestures all seek to codify this. In all six categories ritual can be understood as a cultural process, not exclusively limited to religion, deities, and transcendence.

John Lyden (2003, pp. 80–102) attempts to map his argument regarding 'film as religion' onto Bell's six criteria of ritual. He recognises that some fit more neatly than others, for instance, he suggests that calendrical rites are not particularly significant to filmgoers, especially when linking specific films and particular times of the year. He does, however, acknowledge that certain genres of film become more significant when traced on top of existing annual festivities. Think, for example, of when individuals tend to watch Christmas movies and also the prominence of horror films released, broadcast, and now streamed during Halloween. Lyden also argues that Bell's third, fourth, and fifth categories are less distinct and have, at times, some overlapping characteristics. Indeed, rites of exchange may be performed during festivals which in turn may signify a rite of affliction. These overlapping qualities are undeniably evident in all explorations of ritual. My argument about the communitas derived from skateboarding video journeys and the subsequent pilgrimages to sacred urban spaces touch upon many of these ritual processes. Bell's categories are helpful as a means to order our discussion of ritual; however, ritual in practice is far from tidy and distinct. Ritual is in part so meaningful because it can be layered with devotion, penance, sacrifice, pilgrimage, and feast.

The relevance of ritual is similarly potent within the sociology of sport. Carole Cusack (2010) lists the various ways in which sport and religion are contrasted and positions ritual as a dominant motif. She unpacks the ancient Pan-Hellenic games from which we derive the modern Olympics. It is clear that the historic games were sacred events in which elaborate ritual patterns were observed. Modern sports have replicated some of these rituals and introduced new ones. Cusack's exploration of sport and religion highlights that at the heart of religion there is an importance not of a deity, but of commitment to something. As a result, the pursuit of sport as an occupation need not be dismissed as a pointless indulgence, or a base activity of volatile competition. Indeed, Cusack (2019, p. 921) notes that in ancient Greece sport was a valid profession for an aristocrat, particularly because participation was in itself seen to be a noble pursuit. This aristocratic quality is similarly identified by Morissette (2014, p. 391) as a feature of lifestyle sports practitioners who appear aloof from winning, not hot-headed competitors but cool and immersed in the theatrics of performance. My emphasis in this chapter is not on skateboarding competitions, which in sum do not represent the most common experiences of the sport, but rather both the commitment to skateboarding as a meaningful pastime and the significance of its performance.

In order to make instances of skateboarding ritual distinct, I follow Bell's sixfold schema. Many of the examples and anecdotes explored here show that skateboarding is distinctly ritualised. In various accounts, skateboarding has been introduced to, and traced upon, existing rituals, remaking them meaningful to a niche community, and to individuals themselves. In other cases, skateboarders have developed their own distinct rituals that strengthen community, appearing cryptic to outsiders not socialised by the culture of skateboarding. Some iterations of ritual appear to be growing in importance, perhaps seeking to signify issues distinct to skateboarding in an era of increased institutionalisation and mainstream commercial popularity.

1. Rites of Passage

The best way to demonstrate the ways that skateboarders have sought to signify rites of passage is through macro and micro life events. I see these divided into the bigger issues of life that are relevant to us all, and smaller specific life events in a skateboarding biography. I began this book with an anecdote about the funeral of a skateboarding friend. This was signified with his skateboards displayed prominently at the altar. There are countless other examples of how skateboarding becomes significant in funerary rites. For example, I have seen coffins of dead skateboarders plastered with skateboard stickers. Following the death of *Thrasher* magazine's long-time chief editor Jake Phelps, owner of the magazine Tony Vitello said that Jake 'would be cremated with his skateboard' (Staley, 2019). A further example is provided by Atencio, Beal, Wright, and ZáNean (2018, pp. 199–200) in their ethnography of skateparks in San Francisco. They report on a memorial following the death of a 20-year-old skateboarder Ronald Diaz who was hit and killed by a car. Instigated by the youth of the local skatepark, the memorial involved hundreds of people revelling in remembrance at the skatepark, skateboarding, drinking, and smoking late into the night. A photo depicts a cross made out of several skateboards tied to the fence of the skatepark with Ronald's photo attached. Visible are candles, beer bottles, a rosary, and scrawled messages of love and respect.

On 12 October 2016, professional skateboarder Dylan Rieder died of leukaemia. The outpouring of sorrow that followed the news of his death was shared millions of times on social media. His sponsor, the board company 'Fucking Awesome,' released a video of his skateboarding set to a solemn dirge. The Los Angeles branch of the Supreme skateshop erected a memorial to Dylan. Thirty of his skateboards, his image on each, were hung with a vase of white lilies placed in front of them. The window of the store replayed his videos while mourning fans laid flowers and left messages. The following weekend when I met up with friends to go skateboarding, Dylan was a topic of conversation. Some had been fortunate enough to meet him. All of us were familiar with his videos and we spoke about them at length. Then, as a homage to Dylan, we all started practising impossibles (an ollie in which the board is scooped vertically wrapping around the back foot in a 360° rotation), a trick he showed particular finesse with.

Death is one distinct example of a rite of passage. Similarly, the birth of a child or marriage can also be signified by including skateboarding. It is perhaps unsurprising that these macro events in life find expression through the ritualised use of skateboards. Sports sociologist Holly Thorpe (2014, p. 100) has highlighted similar practices in other lifestyle sports. She refers to paddle outs, a communal practice to commemorate the death of a surfer. The soulful spirituality of surfing resonates in this example—the ocean is the surfer's hallowed ground. For skateboarding it is concrete and asphalt that becomes the ritual space for commemoration. One example would be the world famous LES skatepark in Manhattan which is commemorated to New York local skateboarder Harold Hunter who died in 2006 at the age of 31. Another example is the 2018 commemorative skateboard competition for acclaimed skateboard videographer Preston P-Stone held at his home DIY skatepark, Lower Bob's.

Moving beyond these macro rites of passage pertaining to standardised notions of life events I propose that there are numerous micro rites of passage in skateboarding. One need only perform a cursory survey of skateboard media interviews to learn of the important landmarks in any skateboarder's biography. One specific rite of passage relates to the moment a skateboarder gets their first board. Then perhaps their first experience in a skateboard shop, and entry into a fraternity of other skateboarders. This is aptly described by David Thornton in his skateboard biography *Nobody*:

So, that night, in the parking lot between the Daranelle post office and what I believe was a Methodist church, I became a member of the skateboard subculture, a full-fledged member of the tribe. … This might sound crazy, but it was like I was hanging out with rocks stars. No, these guys were bigger than rocks stars. It was more of an initiation into a secret religious order. (Thornton, 2016, pp. 35–36)

A life spent skateboarding can include various rites of passage; for example, the moment when a skateboarder learns their first ollie. More potent perhaps is the nerve-wracking experience of dropping in on a transition ramp or bowl for the first time. This requires a leap of faith, the equivalent to a novice swimmer jumping into the deep end of a swimming pool. I have witnessed countless moments when someone achieves this rite. If they are able to do this with others present, a spontaneous celebration will occur. As a ritual act of approval skateboarders will cheer and many will slap the tail of the board on the ground or on the nearest obstacle making a raucous chorus of approval. Other rites of passage might include a first skateboarding trip, often a pilgrimage to some iconic spot; filming a video part; for some this might even escalate to getting photos in a magazine; entering a contest; winning a contest. For skateboarders who achieve some level of success, receiving sponsorship, or more importantly turning professional, is regarded as a prestigious landmark. Professional skateboarders receive their own boards with a custom-made graphic emblazoned with their name. In recent years skateboard companies have gone to elaborate lengths to signify the moment a sponsored skateboarder turns professional. This will often include throwing a surprise party, inviting friends and family, capturing the event on social media, and taking out an advert in a magazine. In the popular podcast *The Nine Club* where skateboarders are interviewed about landmark events in their careers, many of these rites are discussed and reflected upon.

It is significant that a recurring theme in these discussions is the fact that turning professional has become increasingly ritualised as a rite of passage. Veteran skateboarders often remark that they first learned they had turned professional when they saw a board with their name on it in the company warehouse, or when it arrived at their home in the mail. I consider that there are at least three salient dynamics that contribute to the contemporary ritual prominence of turning professional as a celebrated rite of passage. Firstly, skateboard sales mean much less to the industry now than at any other point over the last 30 years. Shoe and energy drink sponsors are able to provide skateboarders with comfortable and sometimes lavish earnings; skateboard companies are not. Skateboard prices have stagnated while the number of board companies has quadrupled. It is now easier than ever for any individual to set up a board company with their own designs and branding. Popular YouTube channels like Revive and Braille show that it is quite simple to make yourself a professional for your own brand (Kerr, 2015). So, the importance of professional skateboards as a career landmark and an integral part of being a sponsored skateboarder has been significantly disrupted. Secondly, social media has facilitated much scrutiny of the day-to-day lives of professional skateboarders. Platforms such as Instagram, YouTube, and to a lesser extent Facebook, all provide a cheap and effective marketing strategy; thus, the opportunity for self and brand promotion on social media and for creating a viral moment with any noteworthy news has become inflated. Thirdly, I believe the growth in significance of the rite of passage of turning professional comes from an understanding that skateboarding has become increasingly institutionalised and skateboarders remain hungry for practices that continue to present the culture as distinct, communal, and connected.

2. Calendrical Rites

The significance of calendrical rituals is their repetitive and cyclical nature. We anticipate their approach and in each celebration there is remembrance and even nostalgia for events that have passed. In Christian traditions Christmas, Easter, and Lent are annual events, and in Hinduism, Diwali and Holi recur each year. In Chinese religion there are important rites surrounding different days of new-year celebrations and Jiao festivals. The most obvious examples of such calendrical rites in skateboarding are skateboarding competitions and jams. Globally recognised events include the annual Go Skateboarding Day founded in 2004 as skateboarding's own holiday by the International Association of Skateboard Companies (IASC). It is annually enacted on June 21 with skateboarders taking to the streets *en masse* each year and engaging in various events sometimes with prizes, food, and frequently with travel between important skateboard spots within any given city. Similarly, competitions like Battle of the Berrics, Street League Skateboarding, Vans Pool Party, and the Vans Park Series attract global attention each year. *Thrasher* magazine's annual Skater of the Year (SOTY) award is anticipated months in advance with professional skateboarders strategically filming video parts in bids to capture the title and the prize of their photo on the cover of the magazine. Calendrical rites also interact with the extant annual rituals of world religions. In Haifa, Israel, the Jewish festival of Yom Kippur has become a festival for local skateboarders precisely because no one is allowed to work on that day, and as a result cars are not driven. The roads become freely available for skateboarders to engage in their own celebrations (Craig, 2018). In many ways this is an appropriated ritual, both in terms of the date of the celebration and the space it inhabits. It is a ritual of festivity, indulged in with communal joy and a hint of political critique as hundreds of Israeli skateboarders descend on Haifa to roll the streets together throughout the day and late into the night. The fact that the Israeli skateboard scene also includes Christian and Arab skateboarders signifies a reorientation of Yom Kippur's meaning and demonstrates that skateboarding remakes not only space but ritual time too.

3. Rites of Exchange and Communion

An informal practice in skateboarding is that of gift exchange. People regularly donate boards, shoes, and clothes to one another. Sometimes such exchanges can be demonstrated by skateboarders filming tricks for one another. In other circumstances promising skateboarders are given free products by companies, often skateboards and shoes. This transaction is termed 'flow' and is symbolically the first step to a career in skateboarding and financial endorsement. The free products are understood as help, reducing the financial burden of skateboarding. The obligation of the skateboarder is not simply to keep skateboarding, but to also progress. The gift exchange of flow is an informal client–patron relationship. Anthropologists recognise that the process of gift exchange is necessitated by its informality, that the reason it means so much is because it is dissimilar to a financial transaction. Drawing on Bourdieu's notion of habitus, Bell (2009, p. 82) suggests that exchange is premised on 'deliberate oversight' and that the misrecognition of a gift as a form of altruistic generosity obscures the ritual itself and thus facilitates its efficacy.

Drawing on the macro rites of passage, calendrical rites, and rites of exchange, the annual Harold Hunter day in New York serves to commemorate the death of the professional skateboarder, and also provides gifts to the local skateboard community. A product toss (effectively the giving away of free skateboards, shoes, and T-shirts) is a common practice. Seen in part as a publicity stunt to encourage skateboarders to endorse a company's products, skateboarders also view these product tosses as a form of community sharing. Skateboarders typically spend lots of money on boards, shoes, and clothing that all take a significant amount of wear and tear. Free product provides a way for companies to also say thanks and demonstrate the ritual significance of gift exchange. So great is the importance of free events and giving back to the community that it becomes difficult to see the skateboard industry as simply a corporate entity. The skateboard industry is also bound by certain codes of cultural gift exchange that skateboarders pay acute attention to. Vans, for instance, organises numerous events to consolidate their authenticity in the skateboard community: competitions, House of Vans art shows, new shoe 'Wear Tests,' and 'Skate Frydays' are all free events and can be read as forms of gift exchange. The Hong Kong House of Vans is a unique concrete skatepark built by California Skateparks on the seventh storey of an old industrial building in the Kwun Tong district of Kowloon. Each Monday evening Vans has given the venue over to women skateboarders, a calendrical event that has become both a skateboarding ritual and a political event. The industry has obligations to skateboarders and skateboarders correspond by continuing to purchase products and in turn validate companies as authentic and cool in the broader culture of skateboarding. Companies that transgress these boundaries may be quickly dismissed by skateboarders and lose their legitimacy in the culture and ultimately suffer commercial losses (Lurper, 2012).

This notion of gift exchange is even more significant at the macro scale with reference to the growth of skateboard philanthropy in the guise of charities and NGOs. The annual Harold Hunter day held every year since 2007 is organised by the Harold Hunter Foundation (HHF, 2019) to help underprivileged youth in New York access skateboarding, 'nurture individual creativity, resourcefulness, and the development of life skills.' Numerous other organisations like the Tony Hawk Foundation, Skateistan, and Skate for Change replicate models of gift exchange. Skateboard philanthropy has become popular largely because skateboarders see it as symbolic of the gift exchange and reciprocity in skateboard culture—it is a macro example of a micro process. As I have previously argued (O'Connor, 2015) and as I explore in more depth in Chap. 11, skateboard philanthropy is underscored by a focus and expectation that the real beneficiaries are skateboarders and the skateboard industry. Similarly, when a skateboarder gives away their board to a novice eager to learn, this is not simply charity. This resonates with the principles of gift exchange in that the skateboard given as a gift is also symbolic of an expectation that the recipient will use it. At a deeper level the exchange also includes a tacit lesson, that 'this is what skateboarding is about,' and it is a responsibility for the recipient to uphold and in time replicate.

Bell (1997, p. 108) includes offerings, sacrifices, and devotionals in this category and thus opens a variety of other avenues for comparison. One of my respondents, Matt from Kansas, provides an anecdote about building a backyard ramp to skate:

> I constantly thought of how the Egyptians built their pyramids to please their gods. When I built my ramp it had to be perfect, it had to like, it had to be nice and square, it had to be the most perfect thing I ever built and when I did make a mistake, boy did it make me mad. It was like, the skate gods are frowning on me.

Matt's example relates to both a devotional service and an offering. The ramp is significant beyond his own instrumental use. The building of it took on ritual significance for Matt, making him feel like he was doing divine work. It is not uncommon to hear of skateboarders making comical remarks that their skateboarding is motivated by a higher calling. They may push themselves further 'for the culture' or to appease the 'skate gods.' Such declarations are often made for comical effect but betray a deeper sentiment held by some in which skateboarding is regarded to be of cosmic consequence.

I believe that a further iteration of exchange demonstrated by sacrifice is particularly prevalent in the thinking of skateboarders. Sacrifice in skateboarding is personal, pertaining to physical injury, bruises, torn skin, and broken bones. Thus, rather than sacrifice being a sadistic act inflicted on others, it is a masochistic act. It can be framed as a catharsis offering a release from anxiety. Falling and injury can be seen as a necessary part of skateboarding and are sometimes greeted with relief, almost as if to get it out of the way. One of my respondents broke his ankle during my research, this came after a number of his friends had experienced their own injuries that had seen them relegated from their boards. In response to his broken ankle he made an Instagram post with a photo of his bandaged ankle in the back of an ambulance simply titled 'guess it's my turn now.' A further example of this comes from Patrick Eisenhauer's blog. Here he muses on the lessons of inevitable injury for older skaters, referring to it as 'paying the piper' (2016). Another respondent, Carl from the USA, who is deeply attuned to the religious aspect of skateboarding, made similar comments, emphasising that injury is the cost of playing:

With many skateboarders, this physical consequence can become somewhat self-flagella[tory]. An idea exists among some of the dedicated that you must 'pay your dues' and take a certain amount of punishment before entering the ranks of the authentic riders. That paying of a physical cost for the ability to clear the mind and focus on [the] present has a … echoes of monastic devotion. There is a certain amount of truth in the concept though, in that you must not be afraid to fall in order to not fall. That courage truly comes from already having taken the fall in the past and surviving it, from pushing personal thresholds of pain tolerance. This monk-like conditioning is not only in the rite of passage by self-abuse, but also in the ritualistic dedication. I have known many skateboarders who rode 'religiously'.

In a more sombre account of injury titled 'I broke my neck, and that's fine,' a middle-aged skateboarder Overfield looks back with gratitude at a host of seminal moments in his skateboard biography. In essence this is a devotional testimony, not bitterness about the possibility that injury has put an end to his skateboarding forever. The author recounts the humble moments of joy on his board. He refers to the time Mike Vallely gave him 'the finger' at a contest, celebrates the fact that he carved (skated round in a surfing fashion) a bench at San Francisco's China Banks and ollied the steps at Hubba Hideout. As a postscript he lists some of his best tricks, including that he did a board slide on a handrail, and kickflipped a set of five steps (Overfield, 2018). In this testimony injury is part of the sacrifice for the 'gifts' of skateboarding. Overfield's skateboard biography touches on various ritualised elements we have surveyed throughout the text. He celebrates his encounters with professional skateboarders (skate gods), he proudly refers to pilgrimages at iconic spots, and lists the tricks he performed at these sites in order to signal the gravitas of such actions.

Injury is thus a type of sacrifice in skateboarding and one that many skateboarders reflect on with pride and humility. In this light, a broken bone is symbolic of a rite of exchange as it appears as though what is derived out of skateboarding for these individuals is so rich and rewarding that the injuries are acts of devotion.

4. Rites of Affliction

Rituals in this category seek to diminish evil, bad spirits, or danger. Lyden (2003, p. 83) suggests that sacrificial acts of penance can manifest as self-affliction. Here the ritualised abuse of Shiite Muslims on the day of Ashura comes to mind. However, Bell argues that the type of ritual depends entirely on the way a culture interprets the problem of evil or danger. In skateboarding we recognise that there is an acceptance of danger and injury. However, in order to navigate the extreme and most unfortunate risks of skateboarding I believe there is macabre symbolic indulgence with danger, pain, and death in skateboarding. We have already treated the iconography of skateboards at length and seen how these court occult symbolism, skeletons, and ghouls. Sean Wilsey writes that skateboarders have superstition towards places where they have fallen and become injured, almost seeing these locations as haunted by bad spirits. Indeed, the only concussion I have ever received has resulted in me assiduously avoiding the very same spot in my local skatepark as a result.

Typically, skateboarders choose to encourage each other while skateboarding, and seldom point out the potential dangers or risks while a skateboarder attempts a trick. Such an intentional focus on danger may translate as simple sympathetic magic (Frazer, 1996, p. 24). Just days before writing this I was chastised by a friend for referring to one of his tricks (a frontside 5.0) as looking comfortable and safe. Invoking safety was seen by contrast to be suggesting the alternative, danger. This relates to superstition about laws of similarity, and laws of contagion—that by mentioning a potential negative you summon it. Such caution about dwelling on the risks and dangers of skateboarding while in the act is then inverted in skateboard media. *Thrasher* magazine has long had a feature called 'Hall of Meat' where readers send in images of their broken limbs or open wounds. In recent years this feature has made its way out of the magazine on to YouTube and Instagram. Video clips on these sites show skateboarders being knocked unconscious as they fall from their boards, being struck by cars, sustaining compound fractures, and frequently injuring their genitals. A regular feature in the now defunct *Skateboarder* magazine titled 'Skate Anatomy' showcased all the major injuries a professional skateboarder had sustained since he/she began skateboarding. Any one of these articles provides a wincing read, but Kyle Leeper's (Skateboarder Magazine, 2012) is a fairly standard account including almost fatal loss of blood, brain bruise, pneumonia, bruised testicles, broken toe, meniscus tear, broken ankle, broken thumb, and broken wrist.

The recounting of these injuries appears to work as rites of affliction in numerous ways. Firstly, they provide a degree of caution for novice skateboarders, reminding them, just as slam sections in videos do, that skateboarding is as much about falling as it is about rolling safely away. Secondly, these testimonies contribute to the community, providing a point of reference in seeing that others have suffered, and more importantly that others have gone on to heal and live to skateboard again. Lastly, they work as an exorcism providing a safe space to deal with the risk and danger without focusing on it while skateboarding. While it might be easy to critique these rites of affliction as hyper-masculine, I would argue that this is a simplified reading of their presentation and meaning. Indeed women skateboarders also embrace the ritual humiliation and catharsis of injuries (Moselle, 2018; The Nine Club, 2017b).

This is demonstrated by Sophie Friedel, who describes her initiation into skateboarding: 'I felt I needed the pain to feel alive and was particularly proud of my wounds. Then, I proudly proclaimed that scars need to be earned—tattoos can be bought' (Friedel, 2015, p. 81).

5. Feasting and Festival

This fifth category is perhaps the most important of all. I do not think the notion of feasting is of specific relevance to skateboarding, but certainly the notion of festival is. If we disregard calendrical festivities, the relevance of spontaneous festivity resides at the heart of skateboarding. Bell's (1997) exploration of festivity corresponds with the catharsis of relaxed social norms, of a liminal space between decorum and chaos. I argue that skateboarding is itself a festival, this is particularly apparent when it is witnessed and analysed in urban settings. The presence of a skateboarder can transform urban space, providing a break with the banality of everyday life. This remaking of space is at the heart of Borden's (2001, 2019) exploration of skateboarding. While it has popularly been framed as a political critique of cities and capitalism, skateboarding can also be understood as a ritual cleansing of mundane non-places in our streets and towns. Sean Wilsey (2014, p. 113) describes skateboarding as 'bringing emotion to emotionless terrain—unloved parking lots, vacant corporate downtowns long after the office workers are home. I remember skating in such places and feeling I was somehow redeeming them from their daily functions, giving them a secret life.' This interpretation is evocative of magic and rites of exchange, that skateboarding is in itself transformative.

The spectacular urban festivity is communicated through skateboard magazines and videos. We constantly see groups of cheering skateboarders, puzzled pedestrians, enthusiastic evening revellers so distracted by the exploits of skateboarders they become waylaid in their night-time sojourns. Countless skateboard videos depict such scenes. One videographer, Greg Hunt (2015), is particularly adept at setting his camera at some distance from the action. As a result, Hunt captures not only the skateboarder in motion, somewhat dwarfed by the surrounding space,

Fig. 8.1 Chris Bradley provides some urban carnival for office workers

but also the candid reaction of pedestrians who stumble upon the impromptu festivity. Dani Bautista captures just such a scene in which skateboarder Chris Bradley nose grinds a 'no parking' sign outside of a Hong Kong office block (Fig. 8.1). In the background, office workers, perhaps on a cigarette break, look on. To the right we see a security guard approaching; we suppose he intends to put an end to the unsanctioned use of that space. This photo provides an insight into the way in which skateboarding can be a festival, with skateboarders pursuing their own interests and yet becoming metropolitan shamans.

Bell's exploration of festival refers to a range of events including the Hindu festival of Holi, Carnival, Mardi Gras, April Fool's, and parades. She highlights that in all of these events there is an opportunity for 'orchestrated anarchy' and 'licentious play' (Bell, 1997, p. 126). One particularly fascinating characteristic of such festivity is the capacity for it to draw dissimilar social groupings together. This is another feature replicated in skateboarding. Participation is often seen to be the most important component of skateboarding, not age, race, class, gender, or ability. Thus, skateboarding is very much a festival in which the taking part is the most significant element. A further point that Bell makes is that festival also facilitates social inversion, when the high becomes the low and the low becomes the high. Festival remakes social relations, creating a ritual space where status is either flipped or elided. Again, in Fig. 8.1, the skateboarder appears to be the hero. He is outside of the typical order of the business world and its pomp of sensible attire, civility, and decorum. Yet at the same time he is part of this world; it is his ritual space and he transforms it, demonstrating the magic overlooked when we confine ourselves to the expected.

Let us not forget that a good many skateboarders are indeed office workers, bankers, frontline service staff in restaurants, engineers, software designers, professors, plumbers, and electricians. All of these occupations similarly occupy various parts of the city. Ocean Howell has reflected on his experience of being an office worker treated deferentially by security guards in daytime San Francisco, and then as an evening skateboarder castigated or dismissed by the very same personnel at night (Pushing Boarders, 2018). Skateboarding thus provides an opportunity for catharsis, remaking these spaces and inverting identity and status in the process. Festival creates a liminal space, moving between social worlds and their associated roles. Lyden (2003, p. 95) argues that festival is partly a process of 'lampooning the status quo' to awaken a spiritual life by subverting the norms and hierarchy. He builds upon the work of Victor and Edith Turner, embracing the way in which ritual creates a liminal space, a portal of sorts, to surrender traditional conventions and touch upon an unstructured and egalitarian community.

The capacity for skateboarding to disrupt social conventions is remarkable. Sophie Friedel's (2015, pp. 61–67) account of working with the Skateistan NGO in Afghanistan provides many rich examples. In one scenario she recalls watching tribal warlords with their AK-47s strapped to their backs attempt to balance on the skateboards they see young children playing on. She observes both their curiosity and joy as they attempt to awkwardly comport themselves on a simple object that has such a capacity for magic. In another anecdote Friedel speaks of skateboarding in an old swimming pool where the Taliban used to execute people. Reflecting on the peculiar feeling of the place and its history, she decides that skateboarding has given the place new life.

My personal experiences with skateboarding help to clarify this point. Most skateboarders are familiar with the way in which their skateboard often makes them a social subject. Holding or riding a skateboard becomes almost an invite for people to speak to you. This is perhaps comparable to the experiences of pregnant women who, simply by the nature of their visible pregnant bulges, are approached with a familiarity from the general public. Parents with newborn children experience this, as do dog owners. It is a break in what Erving Goffman (1963, p. 83) describes as 'civil inattention.' People are more likely to talk to each other in an elevator when there is a break with the norm, perhaps someone dropping an item, the lift spontaneously jerking, or a passenger holding an unusual object. Similarly, the skateboard disrupts social order enough to create new social dynamics. During a summer visit to New York in 2014, I spent a weekend skateboarding solo around Manhattan. That Saturday I was approached numerous times and asked directions, or just informally spoken to about the world cup, street scenes, and of course skateboarding. At the end of Saturday I broke a rib at a skatepark and surrendered my skateboard for the rest of the trip. In stark contrast, on Sunday, when I opted to travel the city by foot, no one approached or spoke to me. Bereft of my board, I was socially invisible.

The skateboard can therefore operate as a portable carnival, and a magic key. In a point that dovetails with the arguments made in the previous chapter, travelling skateboarders experience tourist destinations in distinctly different ways to more conventional tourists. The skateboard provides both access and motivation to visit parts of cities that may very well be off the traditional tourists' map, sequestered in marginal urban locations marked by heavy industry, working-class populations, or high crime. Here skateboarders are able to engage, not in dark tourism (Foley & Lennon, 1996) and not necessarily in pilgrimage, but in a form of ritualised adventure tourism that brings with it festivity and street performance for the local population.

6. Political Rites

Going by the intriguing Yom Kippur Israeli example described earlier and also in part relating to a calendrical rite, skateboarding can also be understood as a political ritual. As Borden (2001, 2019) has so eloquently described, it is both a critique and a reproduction of urban space, capitalism, and modern culture. As a political expression Ferrell (2005) suggests that skateboarding might be the last adventure left in a society that controls and commodifies every experience.

In an evocative take on religion and skateboarding, Chris, a Belfast native born during the late 1960s, discusses growing up skateboarding during the troubles in North Ireland. Despite the sectarian conflict between Protestants and Catholics, he speaks of a context where religion was typically reduced to a volatile political label. Downplaying his personal experiences of the troubles, he emphasised to me how banal the constant tension and military presence were on the streets. Remarkably skateboarding provided a unique escape from the troubles, opening up an organic DIY, depoliticised, space in which the only focus was skateboarding. In carefully listening to Chris and analysing his words, I understand his experience of skateboarding in the mid-1980s and early 1990s as connoting a ritually pure space where, despite its potency, religion was never discussed. He describes the skateboarding community in Belfast prior to the ceasefire and peace process, as largely cut off from the rest of the world. There was no proper skateshop in Belfast and boards were hard to come by. Soldiers stalked the street and ironically because of the emphasis on security, skateboarders were largely left to do as they pleased. Far from criminalised, these youth were able to circumvent the volatile and politically charged status quo in pursuit of a seemingly trivial act of riding their boards. Consequentially skateboarding provided a sense of freedom and mobility that few in Belfast had access to at the time. Chris provides another example of an annual event that provided a ritualised opportunity to reclaim the streets:

> I can remember one time, in particular, where there was a series of protests around a banned march which, for a number of years in a row, meant that there was protests that closed roads and really shut down the entire

province, not just Belfast. That meant that there was a lot of police out and about but they were dealing with everything else. I can remember literally skating down one of the busiest streets in Belfast because there was no traffic, there was no buses. There was nobody about and that was on a Saturday afternoon or at teatime, somewhere that it would have been completely impossible beforehand.

Chris also speaks of a bizarre occasion when the police stopped a car full of skateboarders travelling between sectarian districts. When they explained they were dropping off a friend in a Catholic area, but driving from and then returning to a Protestant area, the police could not comprehend the logic of the situation which defied the times. While sport was used in Northern Ireland to forge bonds across the communities, it was always part of a strategic plan. More commonly, sport was an exclusive domain for the inclusion of specific sectarian identities (Cronin, 2002). In contrast, skateboarding was a self-started cross-community activity that was never about peace, religion, or anti-sectarianism. It was simply about skateboarding and as a result it forged a ritually distinct social space beyond the rigid conservatism of the era. The image of Catholic and Protestant skateboarders negotiating puzzled troops of the Royal Military Police makes much of the contemporary celebration of skateboarding as prosocial appear twee by comparison.

There is a paradox here. In a social context where politics and religion were tightly entwined skateboarding provided a space outside of these considerations. Yet, in being disinterested with these considerations skateboarding became both ritualised and political. Framing skateboarding as a political ritual shows how it is able to tacitly subvert and critique existing social hierarchies and social disparities. Part of what has made skateboarding so important and enduring as a lifestyle and culture has been its capacity to remain meaningful without any explicit politicisation or organisation. Validating Bell's earlier comments, skateboarding as a ritual appears important because it resides in miscommunication. Skateboarders having various identities, not because of an overarching political climate but because of a shared passion for skateboarding, is still considered a radical social expression. However, this dynamic has increasingly been repackaged by NGOs, educators, policy planners, and corporations. I argue that it is precisely the attempt to harness this potent political element in skateboarding that further contributes to individuals seeking to make skateboarding more religious, preserving practices that they see as unique and meaningful beyond the tentacles of institutionalisation and unbridled commercialisation.

In all of these accounts, what skateboarding appears to offer is a space of interaction and expression that transcends typical and uniform codes about sports, hobbies, and subculture. Moreover, it corresponds with the notion that ritual provides a departure from the everyday, a sphere of practice beyond the confines of mundane and profane concerns.

Play

One type of ritual that is of central importance to skateboarding is that of play. This is overlooked in Bell's exploration of ritual. The process of play is something that we often take for granted. Deemed superficial, childish, and yet essential for how the young learn their way in the world. We appear to depart from play as we get older and engage in organised, structured, and meaningful competition with clearly defined objectives. When we play football, the notion of play is elided by the structure that is suggested by the sport of football itself. Literally and figuratively, football has a goal. There is a clear objective to win. Ritual, like play, might be similarly understood as not having an explicit goal in itself; the purpose is its performance alone. One of the most influential explorations of play comes from Johan Huizinga (1949), who sets out to explore the far-reaching impact of play in human culture. His work is remarkable for engaging with both sacred and secular notions of play, but has been criticised for going too far and losing the distinctiveness of play by exploring it as an intrinsic part of contest, war, and legal process (Guttman, 1978, p. 7). For both religious scholars and sociologists of religion, Huizinga's reflection on the sacred status of play is influential. He begins by highlighting a number of qualities that play possesses, being voluntary not obligatory, having an essential 'fun' element, serving as a departure from 'real' life into a sphere entirely of its own being. Along with all of these features, Huizinga (1949, p. 9) declares that 'play has a tendency to be beautiful.' At once play is shown to also be contradictory, it is 'pointless but significant' (1949, p. 19). Most importantly, Huizinga connects play to myth, to the numinous, and also to ritual. Firstly, he engages with the idea of serious play, arguing that seriousness as an idea seeks to exclude play, seeing it as improper and superfluous. Indeed one is encouraged not to play in serious places such as work or while studying. But for Huizinga play is of a higher order because while serious situations seek to exclude play, the norms of play are often very serious in themselves (1949, p. 45). Think how the rules of a make-believe game must be agreed upon and followed despite their futility. Children know the importance of play and the gravitas of following the rules in order for play to be fun. Huizinga (1949, p. 18) also declares that 'ritual is seriousness at its highest and holiest. Can it nevertheless be play?'

These ideas are touched upon by Borden (2001, p. 97), who recognises that skateboarding is in part engaging with the world and relating the body to nature and the cosmos. The skateboard is like a divine object that can connect an individual to conceptions of existence greater than themselves. Borden develops this from the work of Henri Lefebvre (2008, p. 118), who claims that 'toys and games are former magical objects and rituals.' The emphasis here is not on the action as much as on the object. Lefebvre recognises that toys and games have been somewhat stripped of their mystical powers. They have become 'demoted' and 'clothed with new social meaning.' He similarly suggests that this new meaning is confined to expressions such as play, and in the process he signals that play might be superficial. However, he also notes that the potency of these objects lingers on; particularly in games of chance he suggests there is the opportunity to awaken the consciousness to possibility and in turn critique the existing social order in all its banality.

For sociologist of religion Carole Cusack (2013), Huizinga's conception of play helps in the analysis of new or invented religious traditions that tease a path between parody and sincerity. Sports sociologist Allen Guttman (1978) charts a transformation from ritual sport to quantified contemporary sport. He observes that play is autotelic, an activity in which the end is the purpose itself. Sport since the industrial revolution has become somewhat mechanical, ordered, and structured for a specific result. He sees the structuring of sport as a mirror to society. Arguably the growth of lifestyle sports and their popularity might, by the same token, signal that society has become less structured and formal and thus more individualised. Play can therefore be a theme that brings together discussion on both the sociology of lifestyle sports (Thorpe, 2014; Wheaton, 2004, 2013) and the sociology of religion (Clark & Clanton Jr., 2012; Heelas, Woodhead, Seal, Szerszynski, & Tusting, 2005).

From these discussions we can fashion an understanding of skateboarding as a ritual process that is important precisely because it is a separate realm of activity in which there is no clear objective other than that of play. Qualifying skateboarding as fun appears superficial but is, in the light of Huizinga's comments, precisely the quality that makes it so important. Skateboarding appears to be serious fun. I turn to the comments of one of my informants to qualify this point:

> There is a meditative quality to skateboarding that is difficult to articulate. Like many repetitive tasks or skills there can be a calming or focusing effect when one practices the ability consistently. A repeated action refined over time centers the mind and helps the practitioner regain a temporal and moral perspective. Many sports, activities, and hobbies have this meditative quality of calming and refocusing through repetition. ... To ride on a skateboard you are required to have an awareness of the present moment and maintain a certainty in your actions and balance. Failing to do so will have very real consequence: [i]njury, destruction. You find the present moment because you have no choice. If your mind wanders to regrets of the past or worries of the future, you are smacked by the reality of the present. You must have confidence in your actions because your doubts will slam your body into hard concrete.

The conflation of play, ritual, and meditation is a curious development. I refer to another example from a skateboarding blog where the magical tool of the skateboard becomes a portal to connect with a temporal distortion of the self. This blogger reflects on skateboarding as a ritual process that he has been engaged in for 30 years:

> After skating for about 45 minutes, I sat down to take a break. Sitting in the warm night air, with the cicadas droning on in the nearby woods, I suddenly realized how much Salem's Lot physically resembled a night spot

from my distant youth. Maybe that was why this place had that certain sense of magic to it. Then, it seemed as if the fabric of time began to unravel. A distant memory experience came flooding back to me. A hot summer night, when I was about 12-years-old. I was skating in an empty parking lot. I had found some wood, and some bricks, and made a small platform. 12 am. Age 12. Empty Lot and a platform. 12 am. Age 42. Empty Lot and a platform. Suddenly, I was 12, and 42, at the same moment. The continuum of time had collapsed. Generally, we experience our 'now' in terms of our future short and long term goals and possibilities (e.g. take the next left turn in the road, meet a work deadline, retire at 65, find the mounting hardware bolt I just dropped on the floor, etc.). How we comprehend and interpret those goals and possibilities is contextualized in/by our prior experiences. Our 'now' is future orientated, but guided by our past, all of which fuse into a present understanding of our 'now.' Here, in Salem's Lot, all of this was breaking down. The past was guided by the future, 30 years ago was now, and the 'now' was a lived-memory … all at the very same instant. The experience of past, the future, and the now, became a single, seamless, timeless, experience, in which it was difficult to parse apart one from the other. My mind swirled. All I could do was look at my skateboard, and smile, for it … it … alone was the single string which fused the past, present, and future together in this one moment. It alone was the portal. (Sedition, 2016)

In this passage the skateboard is a ritual tool. In its use it creates ritual time, being both in the moment and also in a transcendent place between spheres of existence. Here we can extend that the practice of skateboarding has temporal effects on practitioners, akin to the disruption of time experienced in states of flow where time is slowed in moments of extreme concentration, and sped up as one becomes lost in the concentrated performance of an activity (Abraham, 2017; Csikszentmihalyi, 1997; Kotler, 2006; Lyng, 2005). This is similarly the temporal disruption that is experienced in moments of communitas, in religious rapture. Both of the previous accounts read in this light as spiritual and philosophical reflections on the act of skateboarding.

Ritual time is explored by Mircea Eliade in a variety of his texts. He argues that many calendrical rituals are an attempt to control time, to return to an origin myth, a perfect primordial state in which the world came into existence. In part, this need to replicate the process of creation is part of a broader human anxiety about the inevitability of death; thus ritual repeats what has gone before and pauses time, forestalling the inevitable once more. The ritual and creativity of play have considerable depth in reference to the writings of Eliade. He argues that 'the creation of the world becomes the archetype of every creative human gesture' (Eliade, 1959, p. 45). For as Eliade comments, 'in the festival the sacred dimension of life is recovered' (1963, p. 89).

This notion of sacred ritual time also finds its place in those with existing religious affiliations. Take, for example, the Australian Amar Hadid, a skateboarder of Lebanese descent. She is an observant Muslim who fulfils her five daily prayers and yet finds spiritual fulfilment in the practice of skateboarding. In conversation she states that

> [e]very time I skateboard it is like an escape, like an adventure where you face challenges that push you to your limits and when you overcome those obstacles you feel an incomparable feeling of excitement. For most of us it is not only a sport, it is social as well. There is no better feeling than going out on a sunny day and having a session with friends at the skatepark … Skateboarding is uplifting, challenging and engaging. It uplifts, challenges and engages one's spirit. In itself it is a beautiful sport. It [a]ffects our spirit. It touches our hearts and makes us question our minds, thereby strengthening out mental power. It is habitual and has a deep-rooted effect with a persistent but profound influence on one. Some deem skateboarding spiritual but what skateboarding really does to me is evoke and awaken the spirit.

In Hadid's response skateboarding appears to be an extension of worship touching both the spirit and consolidating communal ties while also being physically and mentally invigorating. Ritually, it 'awakens the spirit.' It is indeed playful and at the same time an activity with serious, earnest, and broad implications. Entwined in all of these accounts is the indivisible notion that skateboarding is performance, something one does. The ritual aspect of skateboarding is about action and there is no greater signifying practice to the identity of a skateboarder than the process of skateboarding (Beal & Weidman, 2003).

Conclusion

In this chapter I have sought to demonstrate how various understandings of ritual resonate with skateboarding. In conclusion it is important to qualify that in arguing that skateboarding can be religious, one need only demonstrate that skateboarding itself manifests as a ritual event. It connects to all of Bell's six categories and in its most distinct rendering is an enactment of urban festivity. Skateboarding can mark the passage of life's most important phases for those who are devotees, and provide a schema to map more nuanced achievements and landmarks. Annual events, exchange, affliction, and sacrifice are all features of what skateboarders recognise as their culture. In our final exploration of play we come to understand how skateboarders see themselves as having access to a special, magical realm of life. In performing ritual some skateboarders consider themselves enlightened, different from the blinkered 'muggles' ignorant of their toy, the true essence of the city, the nearness of freedom and fraternity, and of course the enduring rewards of play.

References

Abraham, I. (2017). *Evangelical Youth Culture: Alternative Music and Extreme Sports Subcultures*. London: Bloomsbury.

Alexander, B. C. (1997). Ritual and Current Studies of Ritual: Overview. In S. D. Glazier (Ed.), *Anthropology of Religion: A Handbook* (pp. 139–160). Westport, CT: Greenwood.

Atencio, M., Beal, B., Wright, M. E., & ZáNean, M. (2018). *Moving Boarders: Skateboarding and the Changing Landscape of Urban Youth Sports*. Fayetteville, AR: University of Arkansas Press.

Beal, B., & Weidman, L. (2003). Authenticity in the Skateboarding World. In R. E. Rinehart & C. Sydnor (Eds.), *To the Extreme: Alternative Sports, Inside and Out* (pp. 337–352). New York: States University of New York Press.

Bell, C. (1997). *Ritual: Perspectives and Dimensions*. Oxford: Oxford University Press.

Bell, C. (2009). *Ritual Theory, Ritual Practice*. Oxford: Oxford University Press.

Borden, I. (2001). *Skateboarding, Space and the City*. Oxford: Berg.

Borden, I. (2019). *Skateboarding and the City: A Complete History*. London: Bloomsbury Visual Arts.

Bowen, J. (2012). *A New Anthropology of Islam*. Cambridge: Cambridge University Press.

Clark, T. R., & Clanton Jr., D. W. (2012). *Understanding Religion and Popular Culture: Theories, Themes, Products and Practices*. London: Routledge.

Craig, A. (Writer). (2018). Episode 2: The Neighbors [Cable Television Show]. *Post Radical*.

Cronin, M. (2002). Catholics and Sport in Northern Ireland: Exclusiveness or Inclusiveness? In T. Magdalinski & T. J. L. Chandler (Eds.), *With God on Their Side: Sport in the Service of Religion* (pp. 20–35). London: Routledge.

Csikszentmihalyi, M. (1997). *Creativity: Flow and the Psychology of Discovery and Invention*. New York: Harper Perennial.

Cusack, C. M. (2010). Sport. In R. D. Hecht & V. F. Biondo (Eds.), *Religion and Everyday Life and Culture* (pp. 915–943). Santa Barbara, CA: Praeger Publishers.

Cusack, C. M. (2013). Play, Narrative and the Creation of Religion: Extending the Theoretical Base of 'Invented Religions'. *Culture and Religion, 14*(4), 362–377. https://doi.org/10.1080/14755610.2013.838797

Cusack, C. M. (2019). Mock Religions. In H. Gooren (Ed.), *Encyclopedia of Latin American Religions*. Berlin: Springer International Publishing.

Eisenhauer, P. (2016). Paying the Piper. *Blog*. Retrieved from http://www.going-homeagain.net/paying-the-piper/

Eliade, M. (1959). *The Sacred and the Profane*. New York: Harcourt.

Eliade, M. (1963). *Myth and Reality*. New York: Harper & Row.

Ferrell, J. (2005). The Only Possible Adventure: Edgework and Anarchy. In S. Lyng (Ed.), *Edgework: The Sociology of Risk Taking* (pp. 75–88). New York: Routledge.

Foley, M., & Lennon, J. J. (1996). JFK and Dark Tourism: A Fascination with Assassination. *International Journal of Heritage Studies, 2*(4), 198–211. https://doi.org/10.1080/13527259608722175

Frazer, J. (1996). *The Golden Bough*. London: Penguin.

Friedel, S. (2015). *The Art of Living Sideways: Skateboarding, Peace and Elicitive Conflict Transformation*. Wiesbaden: Springer.

Geertz, C. (1973). *The Interpretation of Cultures: Selected Essays*. New York: Basic Books.

Goffman, E. (1963). *Behavior in Public Places: Notes on the Social Organization of Gatherings*. New York: The Free Press.

Grimes, R. L. (1985). *Research in Ritual Studies: A Programmatic Essay and Bibliography*. Metuchen, NJ: Scarecrow Press.

Guttman, A. (1978). *From Ritual to Record: The Nature of Modern Sports*. New York: Columbia University Press.

Heelas, P., Woodhead, L., Seal, B., Szerszynski, B., & Tusting, K. (2005). *The Spiritual Revolution: Why Religion Is Giving Way to Spirituality*. Oxford: Blackwell.

HHF. (2019). Harold Hunter Foundation. Retrieved from https://www.harold-hunter.org/

Huizinga, J. (1949). *Homo Ludens: A Study of the Play-Element in Culture*. Kettering, OH: Angelico Press.

Hunt, G. (Writer). (2015). Propeller: A Vans Skateboarding Video [Video]: Vans.

Kerr, C. (2015). Meet the YouTube Stars That Are Disrupting Skateboarding. *Jenkem*. Retrieved from http://www.jenkemmag.com/home/2015/04/24/meet-the-youtube-stars-that-are-disrupting-skateboarding/

Kotler, S. (2006). *West of Jesus: Surfing, Science and the Origins of Beliefs*. New York: Bloomsbury.

Lefebvre, H. (2008). *Critique of Everyday Life: Volume 1* (J. Moore, Trans.). New York: Verso.

Lurper. (2012). How Corporations Are Changing Skateboarding and Why It Matters. *Jenkem*. Retrieved from http://www.jenkemmag.com/home/2012/11/26/how-corporations-are-changing-skateboarding-and-why-it-matters/

Lyden, J. C. (2003). *Film as Religion*. New York: New York University Press.

Lyng, S. (2005). *Edgework: The Sociology of Risk-Taking*. New York: Routledge.

Morissette, J.-F. (2014). The Theatricality of Sport and the Issue of Ideology. *Journal of the Philosophy of Sport, 41*(3), 381–397. https://doi.org/10.1080/00948705.2013.858636

Moselle, C. (Writer). (2018). Skate Kitchen.

O'Connor, P. (2015). Skateboard Philanthropy: Inclusion and Prefigurative Politics. In K. J. Lombard (Ed.), *Skateboarding: Subcultures, Sites and Shifts* (pp. 30–43). London: Routledge.

Overfield, D. (2018, October). I Broke My Neck and That's Fine. *Neverwas*, 16–20.

Pushing Boarders. (2018). University of Skate: A History of Skateboarding in Academia. *YouTube Video*. Retrieved from https://youtu.be/IbFUqkXanbk

Sedition. (2016, August 23). Salem's Lot: A Black Altar, and DIY Worm Holes in Time. *Blog*. Retrieved from http://vatorat.blogspot.hk/2016/08/salems-lot-black-altar-and-diy-worm.html

Skateboarder Magazine. (2012, August). Skate Anatomy: Kyle Leeper. *Skateboarder Magazine*, 34.

Staley, W. (2019, March 20). Jake Phelps Dies at 56; as *Thrasher* Editor, a Skateboarding Guru, Obituary. *The New York Times*. Retrieved from https://www.nytimes.com/2019/03/20/obituaries/jake-phelps-dead.html

The Nine Club. (2017a). Andrew Reynolds | *The Nine Club* with Chris Roberts—Episode 55. *YouTube Video*. Retrieved from https://youtu.be/mU4Y7upvdfg

The Nine Club. (2017b). Nora Vasconcellos | *The Nine Club* with Chris Roberts—Episode 33. *YouTube Video*. Retrieved from https://youtu.be/FnRUzjxnO4s

Thornton, D. (2016). *Nobody: Essays from a Lifer Skater*. UK: Amazon.

Thorpe, H. (2014). *Transnational Mobilities in Action Sport Cultures*. New York: Palgrave Macmillan.

Vice. (2012). Skateboarding with Andrew Reynolds. *YouTube Video*. Retrieved from https://youtu.be/sF_ApPgZCmc

Wheaton, B. (2004). *Understanding Lifestyle Sport: Consumption, Identity, and Difference*. London: Routledge.

Wheaton, B. (2013). *The Cultural Politics of Lifestyle Sports*. New York: Routledge.

Wilsey, S. (2014). *More Curious*. San Francisco: McSweeney's.

Part III

Organisation

9

A Vehicle for Faith

A typical sunny morning in Barcelona sees professional skateboarder Shaun Hover collaborate with local skaters in assisting him filming a series of short video clips for his Instagram feed. Mingling at the legendary Museum for Art Contemporary Barcelona (MACBA) spot and uploading to social media happens to be the fundamentals of the Christian ministry he performs for the group *Calling all Skaters*. Shaun, in his early thirties, is a talented skateboarder and has a gregarious personality. His social media presence includes regular humorous posts about his everyday life, hanging out in Barcelona with his wife and young daughter. In Colorado, a mother, unsettled by the gruesome skateboard graphics of her son's friend, responds by setting up her own Christian skateboard company. While in Ontario, Canada, a small church converts its community hall space to an indoor skatepark and welcomes new members to its congregation. These are all aspects of one of the most overlooked facets of skateboard culture, evangelical skateboard ministry. It is also a vibrant example of the way that religion has become organised into sport. Forming the final part in my polythetic understanding of religion, instances of organisation relate directly to a family of ideas that include worldview, institutions, ideology, and collective action. In Geertz's (1973,

© The Author(s) 2020
P. O'Connor, *Skateboarding and Religion*,
https://doi.org/10.1007/978-3-030-24857-4_9

p. 90) definition of religion this aspect is represented as a conception of a general order of existence. In this chapter I present some examples of how institutionalised religion connects and engages with skateboarding, providing a space of spiritual outreach. I also discuss how these activities can be regarded as forms of appropriation, co-opting the cool and community of skateboarding to present new articulations of religious commitment.

Throughout my research I have found hundreds of Christian skateboard organisations that work to provide a connection between skateboarding and faith. Skateboard ministers are essentially skateboarders who have found Christ and use their culturally specific skills and knowledge to reach unchurched skateboarders. Some are self-taught and others have attended courses, often styled around youth ministry. Much of this evangelical work in 2019 is promoted and sustained through social media. This includes Instagram feeds, Facebook accounts, websites where you can sponsor skaters, help fundraising, and purchase Christian-branded skateboard products. YouTube channels also provide a diverse array of content on young globe-trotting ministers and Christian skateboard tours. Skateboard ministry conforms to, and appears to be transforming, an aspect of 'lifestyle Christianity' (Ostwalt, 2012, p. 202) strongly influenced by modes of consumption and identity politics (Flory & Miller, 2008, p. 74). But it is also apparent in the discussions provided here that skateboard ministers apply earnest effort to lead by example and make a positive impact in the lives of their peers.

This chapter draws on research that I have conducted following the social media accounts of skateboard ministers. I conducted seven interviews, mostly by Skype, with individuals deeply involved in skateboard ministry. These individuals were involved in performing outreach, managing Christian skateboard brands, or working in a skate church. My findings point to a vibrant and connected subculture within the culture of skateboarding. I asked all my informants 'why do skateboarders need Christianity' and most agreed that everybody needs Christ, it is just that the majority of skateboard ministers happen to be both skateboarders and Christian. Yet all of the people I spoke to held assumptions about problematic elements in skateboard culture to which skateboard ministry was able to provide an alternative. Little in the way of research has explored these dynamics, though my findings here are helpful to contrast with the work of Ibrahim Abraham (2017) who has researched evangelical youth culture in alternative music and extreme sports scenes.

I highlight how the issue of social media is important in providing a space where the niche interests of Christian skateboarding can reside. These dynamics are in turn tied to the fact that Christian, Muslim, or openly religious skateboarders are largely overlooked and dismissed by the broader workings of the skateboard industry and their media. This is despite the fact that some Christian skateboard companies have been instrumental in giving numerous professional skateboarders their first step into the industry. Through this chapter we learn that a prejudice towards Christian skateboarders continues to influence the careers of professionals and the ways in which they present themselves. In order to give context to these discussions I begin by providing an outline of skateboard ministry. I then provide a brief overview of the notion of relational ministry and how this theme fits into the development of a commercial version of lifestyle Christianity. I discuss in more detail the findings from my interviews and conclude with a contrasting example of social media skateboard dawah in Indonesia.

Skateboard Ministry

Skateboard ministry refers to the evangelical work and guidance provided by Christian skateboarders, churches, and Christian youth groups. Models of skateboard ministry may include the provision of skateboarding apparatus in a church property, or the outreach of skateboarders in skateparks and skateparks globally. Typically, the aim of this proselytisation is to bring skateboarders to Christ, not to bring skateboarding to Christian youth. There are numerous groups which perform skateboard ministry internationally. Some of these are small projects instigated by local churches and youth groups like the Legacy XS skatepark in Essex, UK. Others are bigger operations like Calling all Skaters, with evangelical activities administered simultaneously in the USA, Europe, Asia, and South America. The St James Church in Ontario, Canada, began opening its doors to skateboarders after finding youth skateboarding on

Church property. Rather than continuing the practice of chasing them away, a young minister suggested welcoming them in. Skateboarders have been provided with a designated space and apparatus to skate and the church has been revitalised with a youthful congregation. One skateboarder reports: 'I gave my life to Jesus. My whole life got transformed. But you know? Skateboarding came with me. There was no way I was dropping skateboarding' (Kalb, 2010). The same pattern has been replicated with the Legacy XS skatepark in the UK which has been funded by a local church group in Chelmsford Essex since 2001. It aims to provide facilities for youth to skateboard and also introduce them to Christianity. The Pastor, Peter Hillman, advocates that the youth who use the skatepark can begin to incorporate their skateboarding as a form of worship. In elaborating what skateboard worship might be, he states that 'rather than landing a trick for the pleasure of me, I am going to land it for the pleasure of you' (Chelmsdio, 2007).

Two of the most well-known skateboard ministry programmes, Calling all Skaters (CAS) and MSSkateMinistry (MSSM), have a very different structure that has emerged through social media promotion. Founded in 2012, CAS is led by American skateboarder Shaun Hover, who, as of 2019, is living in Barcelona. CAS operates the Discipleship Training Schools (DTS), which enrols skateboarders in a self-funded programme of up to six months. A key component of the DTS is outreach, which sees teams of skateboarders travel to a different country and provide skateboard ministry for up to three months. The DTS programme is run in cooperation with Youth with a Mission (YWAM), a global evangelical Christian non-profit group founded in 1960. Between 2012 and 2018, CAS has seen 106 skateboarders complete their DTS. In contrast, MSSM is led by Mike Steinkamp, a talented skateboarder and motivational speaker who looks like the eurocentric vision of Jesus, handsome with long blonde hair and blue eyes. Set up independently by Steinkamp when he was 19, his ministry involves public speaking, skateboard competitions, and social media messages. MSSM produces polished YouTube videos with inspirational life-affirming tales and has a smartphone app *Landing Bolts* that provides a 14-day devotional for skateboarders, to aid them in thinking about and committing to Christ. Both DTS and CAS are led by charismatic and skilled skateboarders who notably ride for the same Christian skateboard company, Untitled Skateboards. Both are also examples of evangelical lifestyle Christianity in the social media age, something I explore in more detail later.

There are a number of Christian skateboard companies such as Manna, Untitled, Reliance, Siren, Wisdom, and Motherboard. Many of these also operate as ministries and provide competitions, and demos (demonstrations of skateboarding by professionals) to promote their brand and their faith. All Christian board companies are small and do most of their trade via their websites or selling boards at events. Jud Heald, owner of Untitled Skateboards, discussed how it was challenging to get skateboard shops to sell his boards, again emphasising the way that Christianity is treated with suspicion within skateboarding.

One of the most fascinating elements of skateboard ministry is that it appears to be a well-developed subculture within the broader culture of skateboarding. Just as the skateboard industry has slowly acknowledged and incorporated female skateboarders (Atencio, Beal, & Wilson, 2009; Kelly, Pomerantz, & Currie, 2006; Kelly, Pomerantz, & Currie, 2007; Pomerantz, Currie, & Kelly, 2004), and just as the impact of YouTube skateboard companies such as Revive and Braille is still only partially understood by the skateboard industry at large (Kerr, 2015), I argue that skateboard ministry is a potential disruptor to the norms of skateboarding as they have evolved over the last 30 years. The thread that ties all of these dynamics (women, YouTubers, Christians) together is that they have all directly benefited from their adoption and use of social media. Indeed, social media has given women skateboarders a platform that niche skateboard media historically refused to do. Skateboard companies and magazines have responded by including women skateboarders as professionals, giving them magazine covers, and increasing the means for them to participate in competitions. Similarly YouTube skater-run channels have been able to provide accessible content and information for new skaters peripheral to skateboard culture (Donnelly, 2006; Dupont, 2014), a group that have long been ignored by skateboard media, or marginalised and humiliated as uninitiated grommets and kooks. The result has been falling board sales by traditional 'core' skateboarding companies and a tier of YouTube skateboard personalities who have turned themselves 'pro' for their own companies. Skateboard ministry presently poses little threat to existing dynamics in skateboarding both social and commercial. However, I argue, that skateboard ministry is a developed aspect of skateboarding that tells us much about Christianity in the twenty-first century, and the various subcultural careers of skateboarders.

The Emergence of Relational Ministry

To foreground this discussion on skateboard ministry it is helpful to provide a cursory sketch of the emergence of contemporary forms of evangelical Christianity that have sought to include the 'unchurched' by relationship building which draws on lifestyle marketing techniques and identity politics. This is the type of evangelical Christianity that has flourished in the USA, where religion has had to compete in the marketplace of ideas, separated as it is from the state (Moore, 1994). It is this intense secularism of the USA, Ostwalt (2012) argues, that has counter-intuitively made the nation so deeply religious. To European sensibilities, this sometimes reads as twee and disingenuous. Europeans are primed for a more officious and less commercial Christianity. America by contrast is the home of mall-sized Mega-Churches, or giant stadiums filled with Christian rock festivals, and Christian-lifestyle stores replete with T-shirts and bumper stickers with slogans like 'Real Men Love Jesus.' In recent years a variety of Christian fashion brands, such as Not of This World (NOTW), Humbled Daily, and Faith Rx'd, have become indicative of the commercial lifestyle branding of religion in the USA. These brands highlight that it is hip to be a Christian who engages in pop culture, keeps fit, and pursues lifestyle sports (Ornella, 2017). There are numerous Christian fashion brands, an annual 'Christian Fashion Week,' and an array of Christian fashion Instagrammers. The rise in Christian marketing and Christians as a sales demographic is an important transformation in North American religious life (Quail, 2009).

This contemporary commercial Christian-lifestyle branding has grown out of the evangelical Christian movement in the USA. During the nineteenth century there were architectural modifications in churches throughout America that began to orient worship towards entertainment (Flory & Miller, 2008, p. 62). This commodification of Christianity is also observable in the early twentieth-century fundamentalism of entrepreneur brothers Milton and Lyman Stewart. These Californian oil millionaire brothers founded a fundamentalist approach to Christianity, arguing a moral position in the modernising world, but also embracing religious work as a commodity. Over three million copies of their publication *The Fundamentals* were published and distributed across the country, all fuelled by their personal wealth (Pietsch, 2013). A trend in evangelism and entertainment grew throughout the century and included the theatrics of Irwin Moore, and preacher Billy Graham who was heavily promoted in the newspapers of Randolph Hirst (Flory & Miller, 2008, pp. 62–63). A new model grew out of Chuck Smith's Cavalry Chapel in California, which sought to accept people as they were, rather than transform them into part of a homogenised congregation—a concession, I would argue, to the growing subjective notions of spirituality (Heelas, Woodhead, Seal, Szerszynski, & Tusting, 2005; Taylor, 1991, p. 26). In Smith's church, unkempt hair and rock music was adopted and embraced by the church as a legitimate expression of worship. The Chapel is regarded as a hub of the subsequent Jesus Movement of the late 1960s and early 1970s (Abraham, 2017). This was further developed by Bill Hybels in the megachurch model at *Willow Creek* in Chicago. Founding the seeker style of evangelism, Hybels adopted market research techniques and pursued a way to make the church relevant and appealing to the unchurched. Flory and Miller (2008) characterise the seeker style of evangelism as a form of appropriation. They argue that while ministry may take on apparently new forms, being consumptive, hip, and lifestyle-oriented, the content remains the same. Thus, Christian rock and Christian fashion brands are effectively shells in which an identical untransformed evangelical technique and message of redemption resides. But for Heelas et al. (2005) this model of Christianity conforms to their argument of the dominance of the subjective turn. Their analysis suggests that in both the UK and the USA, congregations that have worked to provide more subjective expression and reflection by their members have seen less attrition than more rigid Christian congregations that dictate 'life as' a conforming member of a tradition and congregation. In sum, we can bring these themes together and recognise that the secular thread of the USA has facilitated the emergence of the subjective and commercial expressions of Christianity. While individuals may be at ease in constructing an understanding of the sacred that conforms to their lifestyle (tattoos and motorbikes for example) the church has been appropriating practices from popular culture to promote Christianity in an increasingly subjective spiritual context.

The most comprehensive exploration of the new fusion in lifestyle sports and evangelicalism comes from Ibrahim Abraham (2017), who looks at skateboarding, surfing, and rock music subcultures. He finds a host of interrelated themes that are central in this chapter discussing authenticity, flow, relational ministry, serious leisure, and sports for development. Many of Abraham's respondents have successfully fused a subcultural and Christian identity, although they note challenges about the ways they are perceived both by other subcultural participants and Christians. One powerful example relates to the perception that musicians are using Christianity insincerely in order to make money. Abraham (2017, p. 55) notes that for some artists who are moderately talented the church may provide an easier path in their careers. However, he also notes that there are considerable challenges for musicians who decided to be openly Christian, presenting obstacles, or at least a ceiling to the sort of success they might achieve. These findings are echoed in the responses of Jud Heald, who recognises that skateboarders who have been supported by his company have had to downplay or depart from their Christian identity in order to make their name in professional skateboarding. Many of the most well-known professional skateboarders (Christian Hosoi, Steve Caballero, Jamie Thomas, Ray Barbee) became Christian after they were already established skateboarders. Being a committed and public Christian appears to present significant challenges in the cultivation of a skateboard career. However, as Abraham's research suggests, involvement in skateboard ministry may provide an attractive path to those less talented.

Like many of the surfers and musicians Abraham spoke to, there seemed to be a caution about identifying religious elements within skateboarding itself. The experience of flow in skateboarding is likened to religious experience, yet as Abraham (2017, p. 91) notes, it is also problematic as it spills over from religion in the parameters of the profane world. I argue that in light of such caution, skateboard ministry largely, but not entirely, conforms to the appropriation argument that Flory and Miller make. The numerous Christian skateboard organisations I have studied and the individuals I have spoken to tend to embrace skateboarding as a form of ministry in ambiguous terms. This is a critique that I have seen both within the work of Flory and Miller and in religious and evangelical publications. As Stevenson (2007, p. 198) argues, 'I'm sure that the skate ministers are good guys, and they've undoubtedly sacrificed what would be more lucrative gigs from secular sponsors. But it's hard to say what marks this kind of ministry as a Christian activity.' Moreover, I consistently encountered ambivalence about skateboarding and spirituality amongst skateboard ministers. In general, many saw nothing spiritual or enlightening about skateboarding, yet remained enthusiastic about it as a physical outlet. One might argue that skateboarding itself seems simply to be a façade that does not connect to any observable spiritual practice or understanding. That is to say that neither Christianity nor skateboarding seems to have developed any new form in this partnership, and skateboarding could be simply supplanted for any other lifestyle or activity. However, one unique thing is observable in this fusion of skateboarding and Christianity—representation. Time and time again ministers would highlight how skateboarding is a distinct culture, and thus hard for Christians to reach. Being both a Christian and a skateboarder provides a unique position and cultural fluency in what too often are imagined as distinctly different, or even opposed, identities.

One example provides a helpful analogy of how I understand skateboard ministry. The Australian-published 'Skaters Bible' (Bible Society Australia, 2007) is in its essence a straightforward reproduction of the New Testament. It does come with a glossy cover, which depicts an abstract photo of a skateboarder and then includes 20 glossy inserts throughout the Bible which have photos of Christian skateboarders and short testimonials about their calling and commitment to Christ. Invariably the stories confess how great Christ is and the photos speak to the skateboarding. Occasionally skateboarding is mentioned and frequently underlined as only partially fulfilling unlike the truth of Christ. The final glossy inserts of the text provide an overview of the message of the Bible and some key guidelines for living a Christian life relating to abundance, salvation, temptation, drugs, and sex. In sum, there is a distinct division between the elements of the Skaters Bible. Skateboarding is literally inserted and is in almost all of the inserts a visual component where stories of loss and salvation dominate. While I believe that there is no contradiction between being Christian and being a skateboarder, skateboard ministry often appears like an insert, a cut-and-paste combination that is seldom clear about how the two are connected.

A Dark Culture

One recurring theme in my interviews was the fact that skateboarding culture has a tendency to appear subversive, dangerous, and antisocial. In various ways my participants spoke about the Satanic imagery of the skateboard magazine *Thrasher*. Famously one of their logos, the Skategoat, includes a Baphomet with 666 inscribed on its head positioned within a pentagram, part of which is a skateboard truck. This iconic logo has also become a popular tattoo, significant as another ritualised way in which skateboarders fuse media and physical affliction in order to create and sustain community. Figure 9.1 shows a Skategoat tattoo of a 30-year-old woman skateboarder at a Hong Kong skatepark. To her this symbolised membership and commitment to the skateboard community, and was not a religious or Satanic act. However, for Christian skateboarders the logo and the iconography of *Thrasher* was problematic. Three of my participants used the same phrase 'dark culture' to describe skateboarding. For Marco (a pseudonym), a 21-year-old from Florida who now lives in Australia, *Thrasher* represents the worst of skateboarding:

> Look at everything Thrasher puts out. It's six, six, six. It's upside down crosses. It's naked women. It's the world. You know what I mean? My point of view is why wouldn't they act like that? The Bible says you can't blame sinners for their sin.

Shaun Hover recognised this Satanic imagery in *Thrasher* and argued that this corresponded with the anti-religion element in skateboard culture. Much of what he observes is actually mocking Jesus and the crucifixion. Jud Heald also described *Thrasher* as anti-Christ and Satanic and chose to rework the skategoat logo for his brand Untitled skateboards.

Fig. 9.1 *Thrasher* Skategoat tattoo. (Photo by Author)

Instead of using the Satanic goat and pentagram, Jud used a sheep with a cross on its forehead to symbolise Christ as a shepherd and placed it within a Star of David (Fig. 9.2). The reworking of the logo represents how skateboard ministry and Christian skateboard companies provide an alternative to the subversive anti-Christ narrative popular in skateboarding.

Indeed, this was part of the motive behind the establishment of Motherboard, which uses Catholic imagery in their skateboard graphics. The owner of the company was tired of the dark and gruesome images of many skateboard companies. Motherboard is the sister company of Full of Grace USA, which reproduces historic artwork originally appearing in Catholic prayer cards for use in stationery, pendants, and other items. The artwork of Motherboard skateboards is thus influenced by the artwork of Margaret Mary Nealis, a nun from Montreal who was prolific in producing devotional Catholic imagery that has been used throughout

TIE DYE VERSION

Fig. 9.2   Skatesheep Untitled logo courtesy of Jud Heald

the world. Each board includes a hidden image of the Miraculous Medal, a sacramental that is included to provide protection and good luck. These graphics and those of other Christian skateboard companies embody an edgy aesthetic and tease the notion that faith, like skateboarding, is a radical thing.

This was a topic that Jud picked up on. Expressing frustration with the way Christianity was marginalised in the skateboard industry, he emphasised his belief that this was a contradiction. In Jud's argument, skateboarding and religion require faith and commitment. The issue of authenticity is central in both identities. Being a committed Christian is 'punk rock'; Jesus was a rebel, he pushed boundaries and hung out with the most marginal people in society. Jud states that 'skateboarding is not being a poser, being Christian is the same.'

Leading by Example

For Shaun Hover and Mike Steinkamp, skateboard ministry involves marketing themselves. As founder of CAS, Shaun has a strong social media presence with a following of more than 56,000 on Instagram. Originally from Michigan, 32-year-old Shaun lives with his wife and daughter in Barcelona. He has become associated with the MACBA scene, skateboarding with locals and visiting professional skateboarders at this iconic spot. In conversation Shaun presents as sincere, articulate, and intelligent. Like many skateboard ministers Shaun sees a disconnect between skateboarding and religion, emphasising that they are not the same thing:

> For me, I would say skateboarding itself is not a spiritual or religious thing … skateboarding is part of what I believe God has given me and what God has called me to do, the culture that God has called me to represent Christ inside out, and for me, skateboarding is the healthiest thing for my own personal mental health and sanity.

Shaun is passionate about skateboarding; he declares that in his thirties he is more excited and committed to skateboarding than at any other time in his life, and partly this is because he believes that God has willed him to be a representative for Christ in the skateboard community. When I asked Shaun why skateboarders need Jesus, he explained that skateboarding was a powerful culture and identity in its own right, and this formed part of the need to reach this community. He elaborated that 'people who are skateboarders are really skateboarders. That's who we are, more than I'm an American. … My heart is in the skateboarding community. My identity is within that community. That's where I find my values.'

Much of my discussion with Shaun focused on the DTS programmes that CAS runs in collaboration with YWAM. The various strands of CAS are spread out across the USA and globally. They have teams in Los Angeles and Denver and San Francisco where they will hold DTS. From there newly trained skateboard ministers will travel to do outreach in places as diverse as China, Columbia, and Spain. Scrolling through the Instagram page of CAS a variety of posts show skateboarders completing a DTS in Barcelona, skateboarding in the streets of Latvia, Bosnia, Tel Aviv, Berlin, and the UK. Part of this global spread is due to the outreach performed by CAS, but it is also an inheritance from the 106 skateboarders who have completed a DTS. As Shaun highlights, many of these individuals have gone on to travel and perform skateboard ministry, set up their own skateboard companies, or have become more deeply involved in church work.

With regard to how all of this is financed, Shaun is candid: everyone is self-funded. A student signing up for a DTS pays to join and as a result gets housing, food, travel, and teaching materials covered.

> Everyone is in charge of their own fundraising, basically no one gets paid. We're part of Youth With A Mission (YAWM), which is a massive Christian organisation with over 20,000 full-time workers worldwide and nobody gets paid.

Despite this declaration, both YAWM and CAS survive through various sponsorships and corporate support. But much of Shaun's support comes from donations of people who are encouraged by his message and his lifestyle. Being very active and visible on Instagram as both an accomplished and committed skateboarder, but also a devoted husband and father, carries with it a cachet of wholesome coolness. The importance of social media for Shaun cannot be understated. This is where he provides the crucial insights into his everyday life and leads through example. Unlike many skateboard ministers, Shaun Hover's Instagram feed provides little insight into his faith and work as a skateboard minister. His feed is similar to many other well-known professional skateboarders.

> The reason I have a following on Instagram isn't because I'm such a famous skater that people follow me, it's because I've been posting cool stuff on Instagram for a long time ... what I felt from the Holy Spirit was, don't make your Instagram just pictures showing your daily life. Make your Instagram sick skateboarding clips.

Many of Shaun's friends and colleagues have challenged him on why his Instagram is not a more authentic representation of his life and ministry. He responds that his account is purely a skateboarding platform and need not be anything else. However, he is also conscious that this following feeds into part of his broader mission.

> I show up to MACBA with my kid. People see me with my child, the way that I love her, the way we hang out. I want people to be able to maybe see something that they haven't seen in skateboarding, or see something that they have never seen before, which maybe is a dad loving his little girl, or me and my wife having a healthy lasting marriage.

Shaun is thus living life before his followers just as one of Abraham's surf ministers describes (2017, p. 106). This includes setting an example for others and circumventing the need to preach. In many ways Mike Steinkamp has a similar experience. He has produced a number of beautifully edited YouTube videos that contain evocative scenes of skateboarding alongside messages about the richness of a life committed to Christ. Mike's ministry is much smaller than Shaun's and involves him talking at Christian camps and conferences and organising skateboard competitions. Both Mike and Shaun recognise how central social media has been in developing their ministry. In the early 2000s when Untitled skateboards first established itself as a company, ministry involved touring around the country and providing demos at skateparks. Increasingly this style of ministry has become less popular because in many locations throughout the USA people have become blasé about professional skateboarders and are much more attuned to the constant feed of information on their phone than the antics of a touring Christian skateboard company.

Skateboarding is the key ingredient of Mike's skateboard ministry. He stated respectfully that it is hard to take someone seriously who does not belong in skateboarding. Emphasising that the notion of authenticity is key in skateboard culture, Mike asserts that skateboard ministry requires the specific skills of skateboarders. He provided an analogy by discussing prison ministry that normally includes former convicts. I questioned Mike on the issue of appropriation, and he responded sympathetically about the problem that this posed for skateboard ministry:

> I think what you are kind of addressing is authenticity at some point. Like people look at it and they go, well this looks fake or cheesy, because you're just saying, I am a Christian motorcycle rider, or I am a Christian graffiti

artist. I kind of get that. I think it even feels fake in skateboarding sometimes when you talk to a skateboard minister who isn't sold out, completely
in love with skateboarding. To be honest with you, I even have a hard
time with it.

Of all the ministers I spoke to, Mike appeared most at ease in accepting the tensions between skateboarding and religion. He was balanced in
his criticism of the skateboard industry and the ways in which skateboard
ministry was sometimes organised and presented. Indeed, this was a feature Jud also acknowledged. Being a Christian skateboard company
required leading by example, and some companies have historically been
inauthentic in their work and commitment to religious principles. For
Mike this meant not profiting from his ministry. In order to pay the bills
he works on producing promotional videos in the film industry and flips
houses to make extra cash. He, like many others, does not take a salary
from his ministry and while he does not publicise this fact, he believes it
is part of the authenticity that ministry requires.

Precarity appears to be a feature of skateboard ministry. Jud stated that
'you need multiple streams of income' to survive in skateboard ministry.
Beyond the running of a company or marketing oneself on social media,
all skateboard ministers need to be entrepreneurial in order to pay their
bills. Some like Marco and Shawn are reliant on fundraising and donations, setting up GoFundMe pages, and relying on their Christian network often for housing, skateboards, and travel expenses. Others fund
their ministry activities through their own work.

A Tool

While Shaun, Jud, and Mike all place skateboarding as a central feature
of what they do, they all also see that their faith is the most important
thing. While Mike is passionate about skateboarding he also regards it as
ephemeral and a distraction from the bigger questions. His point being
that while skateboarding is good while you are young and healthy, what
happens when you become injured or too old to skate? Skateboard ministry is important for them because it communicates this need to connect
with something bigger than skateboarding.

However, for two of my informants skateboarding was simply regarded as a tool. Marco underlined that skateboarding was nothing more than a way to establish rapport:

It's never been and will never be about skateboarding. I'm not preaching to kids about skateboarding. I actually hate it when all dudes want to talk about is skateboarding.

These same themes were echoed by Dave Tinker from Florida who established Wisdom skateboards, a Christian-focused board company, and is also Director of Services at Skaters for Christ (SFC). The Jericho skatepark is owned by SFC and provides some free sessions for skateboarders if they participate in Bible study. Previously involved in ministry through Christian rock music, Dave explains in a YouTube video that he was motivated to get involved with skateboarding because of its 'dark culture' (Backstage with Tinker, 2017). Dave is clear that he has surfed but never skateboarded and is therefore 'outside' of the culture. Dave explained to me that skateboarding is solely a tool to reach out to youth, and that skateboarding itself is not really a necessary focus. In seeking to provide an inclusive community at the Jericho skatepark Dave explains that SFC has been open to scooters. But as a result, skateboarders have largely stopped visiting the skatepark and SFC is considering rebranding itself as Scooters for Christ.

Such comments add considerable fuel to the argument that skateboard ministers are appropriators as Flory and Miller suggest (2008), in essence using skateboarding for an evangelical agenda by exploiting skateboard culture. This in many ways is remarkable as it contrasts starkly with the creative spiritual talk of many skateboarders who find both meaning and solace in the rituals and community of skateboarding. What I have observed in skateboard ministry is a disengagement with the subjective spirituality described by many of my respondents. This becomes even more distinct when Marco describes the practice of relational evangelism. This practice is not about going out and preaching, it is about learning who young people are, taking an interest in their daily life, asking them about their day, going to the cinema together, hanging out and cooking pancakes. Marco says 'being relational, it's not standing on a pedestal going, you're going to burn … it's just about relationships. About honouring the person and seeing the potential in them. Just being their friend.' Despite this rhetoric, Marco remained focused on the fact that his ultimate goal is to share the Lord's message and he even reflected on the fact that he might be holding himself back by focusing too much on skateboarders and skatepark ministry.

A further contrast to this dynamic is provided by the St James skate church in Ontario. I spoke to Eric, an outreach worker and former social worker connected to the Church. He explained how around 2010 the church experienced a problem during the harsh weather with skateboarders breaking into the church hall and skateboarding inside. Initially the youths were all chased away and banned from the church until discussion in the congregation suggested that they should be welcoming the skateboarders in. Several years later the church has been transformed by the infusion of youth in the church and the swelling attendance. Eric highlights that the process is not one way; this is not about skateboarders simply coming to Christ, it is also about a Church and congregation relearning their Christian values. In a very different way Eric recognises skateboarding as a tool, but importantly one to develop community and communication between groups of people. He describes skateboarding as a 'unique community' that truly care for and 'help each other.' This is again similar to an account provided by Abraham (2017, p. 99) in which skateboarder's sense of community appears like a religious congregation without the paraphernalia of organised religion. Ironically a number of skateparks have been built in older churches no longer used by a religious community. Take, for example, Skatehal Arhmen (Skatehal, 2017) in the Netherlands and the ornate Skate Church in Coruño, Spain, painted by artist Okuda (Inkandmovement, 2017).

Critiquing Skateboard Ministry

Skateboard ministry is an overlooked and little understood phenomenon within skateboard culture. Indeed, many skateboarders are suspicious of Christian programmes connected to skateboarding, particularly if they involve a skatepark with mandatory prayer time. One skatepark in

Chattanooga Tennessee was only built after the local government made skateboarding in Chattanooga illegal. I interviewed one local skateboarder from the area who was deeply critical of the skatepark and the fees they levied on skateboarders that he then believed to be directed back to the church. While he was deeply suspicious of this scenario my further investigations also suggested that he was at least partially misled and that the skatepark did charge for sessions but also had free access for those that attended a prayer meeting. In the end the skatepark closed to the disappointment of many who regularly attended. In another example a skateboarder takes to YouTube in criticism of the Legacy X skatepark's Christian 'brainwashing' (Broomfield, 2012). As common as these critiques are, many churches are doing no more than providing one weekly evening of prayer and free skateboarding. They are able to help skateboarders in providing facilities, stepping in where there are not local resources or funds available to support a burgeoning local scene. Abraham argues that unless a ministry 'is willing to invest in a skate park, and maintain a church presence in a religiously neutral space, there is no obvious material benefits a church can offer local skateboarders' (2017, p. 100).

Of greater interest is the larger network of Christian non-profits and their methods of relational evangelism. This model was used by both Marco and Shaun, and it is also part of the structure and focus of Skate Life, a Christian skateboard non-profit under the Umbrella of Canadian parachurch Young Life. More generally it appears to be the model of all skateboard ministry I have observed: Relational evangelism. YWAM, for example, which CAS is affiliated with, has come under various forms of criticism for a range of 'cult-like' practices. Critics have warned that the shepherding of relational ministry can be coercive, deceitful, and contribute what some have phrased as 'spiritual abuse.' More readily apparent in my conversations with both Marco and Shaun is the financial burden that skateboard ministry involves. Individuals fund themselves and often pay rent to an organisation like YWAM. Furthermore, they are living and socialising within the group almost exclusively. In effect, young people are paying the organisation to participate and the organisation provides full-time workers or volunteers with no wages. This leads to a Ponzi-type situation where the youth ministers who are most famous, who possess the largest social networks, end up acquiring many more funds than a cook volunteering in the organisation. Reflecting on this situation with regard to social media skateboard ministry, it is clear that there is a distinct thread of entrepreneurialism involved. While this is nothing new in skateboarding, it is arguably an issue in conflict with the mission and sincerity of religious work and spiritual guidance, especially in a context that focuses explicitly on youth. The commercial interests of Christian-branded skateboard companies like Untitled, Reliance, Siren, and Motherboards often go hand in hand with evangelical work. Untitled skateboards spent years travelling their skaters to skateparks across the USA and performing 'demos,' essentially putting on a show of great tricks for spectators and thus promoting their brand and the gospel. This type of evangelism has become increasingly less successful as skateboarders have now become indifferent to such teams unless they include notable and famous professional skateboarders. Christian-themed skateboards are thus appealing to Christian skateboarders and their parents, providing an alternative to images and themes on boards that may be unsavoury and against their religious and spiritual orientation. Yet, while they are fundamentally brands, Christian skateboard companies provide some connection between skateboarding and Christianity, typically religiously inspired graphics and endorsement by Christian skateboarders. This connection is consistently less apparent in skateboard ministry, which too often uses skateboarding simply as a tool to direct people to Christ.

Future Organisation

As skateboarding continues to grow as a legitimate inclusive global sport, so too do the avenues for religious expression and organisation. The social media potency of this is clear. While skateboard media is reluctant or simply unwilling to represent Christian skateboard brands, Instagram, YouTube, and Facebook are open. Similarly, Instagram is a vibrant resource for Muslim skateboarders in South East Asia to promote their lifestyle and beliefs. Dinia, a 24-year-old woman skateboarder from Indonesia, posts a mix of evocative religiously themed images and videos on her Instagram feed alongside posts about skateboarding. Often her posts combine the two, and on some occasions she posts her own original artwork that fuses Islam and skateboarding. In one of her pieces of art she depicts a female skateboarder dressed in an abaya, pushing along on her board whilst holding an Islamic flag with the Shahada written in ornate Arabic (see Fig. 9.3). The Shahada forms the first of the five pillars of Islam; it is a creed, the profession of faith. It translates as 'There is no god but God. Muhammad is the messenger of God.' Written above this image is the word Tauhid, which is the principle of unity, the affirmation of one universal God. Other posts on Dinia's Instagram are similar, one depicts a simple image of a girl skateboarding in an abaya with the words 'pushing to Janah,' which can be translated as skateboarding to heaven. Another image, this time a photo taken at Istiqlal Mosque in Jakarta, shows a card with a written slogan stating 'I love skateboarding, but first I love Allah, Islam, Qur'an.' Speaking with Dinia I learned that there are some parallels to skateboarding ministry in Indonesia. In Islam the process of pro-

Fig. 9.3   Tauhid by Dinia Sahana (from 2018)

moting or inviting people to religion is called *dawah*. Browsing through Instagram feeds shows an emerging organisation of skateboarding dawah, where efforts to infuse youth with a commitment to religion draw upon lifestyle sports, philanthropic works, and rock music. One group based in Bandung called Shift focuses on youth dawah and has the collaboration of some notable Indonesian skateboarders. The Shift Instagram account is vibrant and active, promoting frequent events and has over 1 million followers (@pemudahijrah, 2018).

Dinia's artwork and the Shift youth organisation show how it is not just Christianity that is using skateboarding to bring young people closer to religion. These activities and organisations also connect to forms of philanthropy that have become very visible not just in skateboarding (Skateistan, Be the Change, the Tony Hawk Foundation) but more broadly in lifestyle sports (Action Sports for Development and Peace, 2018). Many skateboard charities have religious foundations or motivations and those that do not still occupy a moral and ethical space that links them to religious activities. However, the focus in this chapter has been to highlight how religion has organised itself around skateboarding.

Dinia is also an example of some of the new articulations of Islamic feminine identity that are being accessed and performed on social media. Williams and Kamaludeen (2017) have discussed this through the fusion of fashionista and hipsters social media identities with hijab-wearing Muslim young women and the development of hijabista and hijabster subjectivities. Both of these portmanteau neologisms are popular hashtags on social media platforms. Another term, hijabcore (Pasbani, 2017), also relates to hijab-wearing metal enthusiasts, many of which have gained a platform and exposure through YouTube. Dinia reinforces her own ideas about the role of religion and the hijabista and hijabster movements. She is critical that these are not modest or pious practices. While makeup and glamorous fashion goes against Dinia's principles, she understands that skateboarding is a sport and is thus acceptable under Islam. It is significant that religion, and religious dress, becomes important for Muslim women skateboarders in Islamic countries in South East Asia. Malaysian skateboarder Fatin Syahirah Roszizi participated in the street skateboarding component of the 2018 Asian Games. She competed with her headscarf and wore a helmet on top. She was also subject to widespread criticism on social media for her performance. Some of this criticism conflated her poor scoring as representing not just Malaysia badly but also her religion of Islam. In contrast, Fatin received wide support from the skateboarding community, even receiving messages of support from professional skateboarders Tony Hawk and Daewon Song (Malaysiakini, 2018).

Most strikingly, while this chapter deals explicitly with organised and institutionalised religion, the notion that skateboarding is, or can be regarded as, religious is fairly weak in the accounts of my respondents. It appears that in linking skateboarding to organised religion the practice and device become de-mythologised. What is clear in the accounts of all the individuals I spoke to about skateboard ministry is that skateboarding is transient, and religious truth is eternal. As much as skateboarding can be fun, exhilarating, social, and even an integral part of one's identity, skateboard ministry ultimately approaches the activity as a tool to connect with Christianity. The charge of appropriation is potent here; it can appear as though Christian groups want to feed off the community and cool of skateboarding. There seems little that is authentic in the marriage of the two; these are not examples of a new niche Church of Christianity. Take, for example, the Church of John Coltrane, which infuses Christian worship with a liturgy in which the music of Coltrane is central (Bahan, 2015). My research was unable to uncover any instance in which skateboarding became an acknowledged part of the spiritual practice of my Christian informants. However, as my discussion in the following chapter indicates, this does not mean that this is not already taking place or unlikely to occur beyond Christianity. What is most apparent about skateboard ministry is that skateboarders can, and often are religious, and that the organisations and groups provide a means for them to share their worldview and to work and worship collectively with others. Mike Steinkamp was both sensitive and critical of the way in which non-skateboarders became involved in skateboard ministry, and Jud Heald argued the case that both Christianity and skateboarding are radical acts of commitment and bravery. This resonates with Abraham's findings from other research on evangelism in youth cultures where one respondents argues that 'if you're a born-again Christian, you're already quite radical' (2017, p. 52). In Jud's and Mike's articulations there appears no contradiction or inauthenticity about the meeting of skateboarding and Christianity. In contrast, the example of Dave Tinker feeds to some of the greater criticisms of evangelical work in skateboarding. The fact that the Jericho skatepark is considering giving up on skateboarders in order to focus on scooters instead will validate the scepticism many skateboarders have about the involvement of Christianity in skateboarding. For other critics the involvement of any Christian group or church in skateboarding is disingenuous, ultimately being a covert way to get young people into Christianity (Broomfield, 2012). This alone is not a reason to be cynical about skateboard ministry as there is no shortage of venal and insincere business practices in the skateboard industry unconnected to religion. In this chapter I have only scratched the surface of what is a distinct and growing trend. Much more can be explored on the subject of skateboard ministry, especially as other religions begin to engage with similar models. Abraham (2017, p. 19), for instance, discusses Hindu-oriented Krishnacore punk and Ostwalt (2012, p. 219) refers to the King David Bikers, a Jewish motorcycle gang that find religious reinforcement through their bikes. It is distinct that the dynamics that have fuelled the growth in the institutional organisation of religion and skateboarding are both the growth in skateboarding's mainstream popularity and the democratic nature of social media. In part, skateboard ministry is both part of the increased mainstream popularity of skateboarding and also a response to it.

References

@pemudahijrah. (2018). Shift—Pemuda Hijrah. *Instagram Account.* Retrieved from https://www.instagram.com/pemudahijrah/

Abraham, I. (2017). *Evangelical Youth Culture: Alternative Music and Extreme Sports Subcultures.* London: Bloomsbury.

Action Sports for Development and Peace. (2018). ASDP. Retrieved from http://www.actionsportsfordev.org/

Atencio, M., Beal, B., & Wilson, C. (2009). The Distinction of Risk: Urban Skateboarding, Street Habitus and the Construction of Hierarchical Gender Relations. *Qualitative Research in Sport and Exercise, 1*(1), 3–20. https://doi.org/10.1080/19398440802567907

Backstage with Tinker. (2017). Why I Started a Skateboard Company—Episode 1. *YouTube Video*. Retrieved from https://youtu.be/O1j3Z_AbZFQ

Bahan, N. L. (2015). *The Coltrane Church: Apostles of Sound, Agents of Social Justice*. Jefferson, NC: McFarland & Co Inc.

Bible Society Australia. (2007). *The Skaters Bible*. Minto, NSW: Bible Society Australia.

Broomfield, M. (2012). Religious Brainwashing at Legacy Xs Skate Park in Benfleet? *YouTube Video*. Retrieved from https://youtu.be/Rw5i3p7mlbA

Chelmsdio. (2007). Legacyxs—Fresh Expressions. *YouTube Video*. Retrieved from https://youtu.be/qHOYhCPHz20

Donnelly, M. (2006). Studying Extreme Sports: Beyond the Core Participants. *Journal of Sports and Social Issues, 30*(2), 219–224.

Dupont, T. (2014). From Core to Consumer: The Informal Hierarchy of the Skateboard Scene. *Journal of Contemporary Ethnography, 43*(5), 556–581.

Flory, R., & Miller, D. E. (2008). *Finding Faith: The Spiritual Quest of the Post-boomer Generation*. London: Rutgers University Press.

Geertz, C. (1973). *The Interpretation of Cultures: Selected Essays*. New York: Basic Books.

Heelas, P., Woodhead, L., Seal, B., Szerszynski, B., & Tusting, K. (2005). *The Spiritual Revolution: Why Religion Is Giving Way to Spirituality*. Oxford: Blackwell.

Inkandmovement. (2017). Kaos Temple by Okuda. Retrieved from http://ink-andmovement.com/project/kaos-temple-by-okuda/

Kalb, A. (2010). Skater Church.Mov. *YouTube Video*. Retrieved from https://youtu.be/3K20scK-eWE

Kelly, D. M., Pomerantz, S., & Currie, D. (2006). Skater Girlhood and Emphasized Femininity: 'You Can't Land an Ollie Properly in Heels'. *Gender and Education, 17*(3), 229–248. https://doi.org/10.1080/09540250500 145163

Kelly, D. M., Pomerantz, S., & Currie, D. H. (2007). "You Can Break So Many More Rules": The Identity Work and Play of Becoming Skater Girls. In M. D. Giardina & M. K. Donnelly (Eds.), *Youth Culture and Sport* (pp. 113–125). London: Routledge.

Kerr, C. (2015). Meet the YouTube Stars That Are Disrupting Skateboarding. *Jenkem*. Retrieved from http://www.jenkemmag.com/home/2015/04/24/meet-the-youtube-stars-that-are-disrupting-skateboarding/

Malaysiakini. (2018). 'Ignore the Haters': Tony Hawk, Daewon Back under Fire National Skater. *Malaysiakini*. Retrieved from https://www.malaysiakini.com/news/441237

Moore, R. L. (1994). *Selling God: American Religion in the Marketplace of Culture*. Oxford: Oxford University Press.

Ornella, A. D. (2017). 'Jesus Saves' and 'Clothed in Christ': Athletic Religious Apparel in the Christian Crossfit Community. *Sport in Society*, 1–15. https://doi.org/10.1080/17430437.2017.1360580

Ostwalt, C. (2012). *Secular Steeples: Popular Culture and the Religious Imagination* (2nd ed.). London: Bloomsbury.

Pasbani, R. (2017). Hijab-Core! Meet the Indonesian All-Girl Muslim Metal Band, Voice of Baceprot. Retrieved from http://www.metalinjection.net/latest-news/yes/hijab-core-meet-the-indonesian-all-girl-muslim-metal-band-voice-of-baceprot

Pietsch, B. M. (2013). Lyman Stewart and Early Fundamentalism. *Church History, 82*(3), 617–646. https://doi.org/10.1017/S0009640713000656

Pomerantz, S., Currie, D. H., & Kelly, D. M. (2004). Sk8er Girls: Skateboarders, Girlhood and Feminism in Motion. *Women's Studies International Forum, 27*(5–6), 547–557. https://doi.org/10.1016/j.wsif.2004.09.009

Quail, C. M. (2009). "The Battle for the Toy Box": Christogimmicks and Christian Consumer Culture. In S. R. Steinberg & J. L. Kincheloe (Eds.), *Christotainment: Selling Jesus Through Popular Culture* (pp. 153–201). Boulder, CO: Westview Press.

Skatehal. (2017). Skatehal Arnhem. Retrieved from https://www.skatehalarnhem.nl/

Stevenson, T. W. (2007). *Brand Jesus: Christianity in a Consumerist Age*. New York: Seabury Books.

Taylor, C. (1991). *The Malaise of Modernity*. Concord, ON: Anansi.

Williams, J. P., & Kamaludeen, M. N. (2017). Muslim Girl Culture and Social Control in Southeast Asia: Exploring the Hijabista and Hijabster Phenomena. *Crime, Media, Culture*. https://doi.org/10.1177/1741659016687346.

10

DIY Religion

Early skateboard culture embodied the notion of DIY. Young children typically built their boards independently, sourcing parts from roller skates and cutting a board out of whatever available wood they could find. This ethic of self-reliance has continued to be part of the skateboarding identity, whether it is connected to setting up your own board or your own board company. The DIY element of skateboarding is tightly connected to the explorative creativity of certain aspects of the culture. It therefore makes a certain amount of sense that some skateboarders deem it fit to organise their own DIY religions. In most cases these consciously created religions eschew the label of religion, yet embrace a host of ethics, rituals, and communalism that parallel both organised religion and contemporary invented, fictive, or mock religions (Cowan & Bromley, 2015; Cusack, 2010, 2013; Sutcliffe & Cusack, 2013; Taira, 2013). In other examples these are personal constructs, akin to new-age spiritual practices (Bellah, Madsen, Sullivan, Swidler, & Tipton, 2008; Heelas, 2006) and attempts by individuals to make sense of what they find meaningful and instructive in their lives. While representing very different levels of organisation and self-identification as religions, these practices all conform to attempts in establishing a repertoire of meaning in skateboarding that has

© The Author(s) 2020
P. O'Connor, *Skateboarding and Religion*,
https://doi.org/10.1007/978-3-030-24857-4_10

received little attention. I read these expressions of DIY religion as examples of organisation, particularly with regard to how they attempt to reify a worldview or cosmology of skateboarding.

This chapter draws heavily from the influential work of Carole Cusack, who has explored a variety of iterations of invented religions. These have typically emerged from popular culture, been influenced by films, and found in literature. She describes these as 'exercises of the imagination that have developed in a creative (though sometimes oppositional) partnership with the influential popular cultural narratives' (Cusack, 2010, p. 7). Invented religions such as *Discordianism*, *Jediism*, *Matrixism*, and *The Church of the Flying Spaghetti* are all united in presenting a critique of religion while conforming to the fundamental tenets of a host of academic definitions of religion. By being reflexively self-aware of their own fictitious nature, these movements challenge us to consider what is really important about religion. In Cusack's (2013) research a focus on invented, intentionally and self-consciously fictive religions is shown to also engage with the importance of joyful play. She states that these religions view 'the ludic and play as legitimate sources of ultimate meaning; in no sense inferior materials upon which to base a religion than factual accounts, attested experiences or historical events' (2013, p. 371). Taking this notion of play seriously seems to be a key tenet of skateboarding. Lefebvre's (1991, p. 118) argument that 'toys and games are former magical objects and rituals' is applied in Borden's (2001, p. 97) analysis of skateboarding. In various ways Borden shows that skateboarders, and their media, experiment with notions of spirituality, joy, and play. Thus, I suggest, in a scaled down version of Cusack's invented religions, that skateboarders are both parodying religion and fostering a space of community and spirituality in invoking religious language and symbolism.

But I also argue that examples of DIY religion in skateboarding are part of a negotiation of rights and recognition. As skateboarding has become a legitimised sport, a fashion, and a referent in popular culture, it has also fragmented. The various cultural worlds of skateboarding all serve to disrupt not just the practices and organisation of skateboarding, but also the identities of its veterans. Thus, DIY skateboard religion can also be seen as a way to preserve and sanctify parts of the culture held to be meaningful to some individuals. It can also be argued that DIY religion, as Taira (2013) has claimed, is a means to access recognition, rights, and power. It may in turn be feasible to imagine that skateboarders could one day champion cultural and religious rights to claim entitlement to freely skateboard city streets, particularly at a time of festivity such as the annual 'Go Skateboarding Day.' With reference to the Barrier Kult (Ba. Ku.) group, it is evident that their ritual practice is also a mode of resistance to the commercialisation and celebrity of contemporary skateboarding. Their religion is one of defiance personified in their commitment to only skate one type of apparatus and claiming it as the archetype of skateboarding objects. Ba. Ku. may also be understood as a response to the organised Christian involvement in skateboarding, particularly in establishing their own dogma, ritual, and satanic imagery.

In the examples of individualised religious practice I also see connections to the work Heelas, Woodhead, Seal, Szerszynski, and Tusting (2005) have performed on the spiritual revolution. My informants speak of their subjective well-being and spiritual experiences. Skateboarding is something that keeps them happy, gives them focus, clears their mind, and puts life into perspective. It is clear that skateboarding, as part of their practice and identity, contributes to their broader worldview. These practices connect to the processes of pilgrimage observed in Chap. 5, but go one step further in seeking to connect to imaginative and experiential elements of skateboarding that are not physically tangible. Skateboarding operates as a way for these people to make sense of the world in ways that are culturally appropriate for them. Some examples clearly conform to what has also been described as 'religious individualism' (Bellah et al., 2008, pp. 232–233). In turn, they represent ethics that are either derived or connected to skateboard culture, highlighting once more skateboarding as a cultural field of communication.

Skateboard Cults

The season finale of the 2018 Viceland television show *Post Radical* features a variety of skateboarders who are described as 'fetishists': individuals who have a quaint fascination with some part of skateboard culture. One segment explores the Ba. Ku. group. They take their name from the ubiquitous modular concrete Jersey Barriers that line roads and highways throughout the world. Common as these elements are, the name of the concrete object is little known beyond highway construction workers and skateboarders. A Jersey Barrier stands at a metre in height with slanted sides that make it an appealing object to street skateboarders. Yet it is also an object notoriously difficult to skate. Established in Vancouver in 2003, the Ba. Ku. invoke a variety of ritualised practices. They are committed to only skating Jersey Barriers and protecting their anonymity with balaclavas while doing so (Fig. 10.1). They have produced zines, videos, branded skateboards, and maintain a blog in which all writing is presented in block capital letters (Nieratko, 2015). The Jersey Barrier is used to replicate the tight transitions of ramp and pool skateboarding from the 1980s. Focusing on this one form of obstacle, they declare, is an act of militancy to the ethos of skateboarding fostered by the elliptical transition of the barrier. The Ba. Ku. skateboard videos are also peppered with pentagrams, inverted crosses, and the occult. Photos of the Kult and some of their skateboard graphics include the use of long knives. These are a symbol of stabbing and again relate to the way skateboards interact with the Jersey Barrier. The front nose of the skateboard tends to stab into the concrete as the board is ridden into the tight transition.

More fascinating is the underlying doctrine of Ba. Ku. which is oppositional to the celebrity and commercialisation of skateboarding. In various accounts, Ba. Ku. members express distaste in the way skateboarding has become a celebrated aspect of popular culture. They emphasise that professional skateboarders are not idols or heroes, and cannot be regarded as role models (Craig, 2018). One Kult member claims that they believe skateboarding should be anti-notoriety, glorifying the act of skateboarding, not the professional doing it. Curiously this mirrors the principles of some Christian skateboarders who skate not for their own triumphs but for the glory of Christ. It is a central motif represented by Ba. Ku. members donning balaclavas—these symbolise the belief that skateboarding should be an anonymous act and skateboarders *per se* should not be celebrated. Ba. Ku. has a global reach and has become a celebrated brand in its own way. Kult members refer to this as plague spreading, more readily understood as the growth in recognition and support of Ba. Ku.'s ethics and aesthetics. Ba. Ku. has released its own skateboards in collaboration

Fig. 10.1 Barrier Kult member ritually skating a Jersey Barrier. (Photo: Anthony Tafuro)

with brands such as Skull Skates and Heroin Skateboards, sold its own DVDs, T-Shirts, and knife-shaped plastic rails. They have even collaborated with Emerica shoes and Gullwing trucks and released Ba. Ku. branded products. Clearly, they are not against the commercial aspects of skateboard culture, but instead resistant to certain forms of mainstream celebration.

Yet, despite the efforts of Ba. Ku. to preserve their anonymity, as their movement has grown in popularity, so has interest in the real identities of their members. One post on their blog urges followers to stop trying to figure out who they are (The Barrier Kult, 2013). My contact with the Kult was strictly anonymous and maintained a form of ritual purity with all communications being in capitals and using Ba. Ku. ritual language such as 'plague,' 'stabbing,' and 'militancy.' Browsing through their blog emphasises these elements and the reader has to attune themselves to the style of Ba. Ku. communications, typically termed 'attacks.' Skateboards are referred to as 'knives,' and 'hordes' are groups or sects of Ba. Ku. spread across the globe. Each Kult member takes on a ritualised name and the list of members sounds dark and arcane with monikers such as *Deer Man of Dark Woods, Vlad Mountain Impaler, The Black Glove of Internal Combustion, Beast of Gevaudan, Muskellunge of Dark Island,* and *Rotting Dog in Black River.* Each name is chosen by the putative leader of the group Depth Leviathan Dweller and caters to the interests and style of each member. The dark tone of the Kult is evident in their videos, the first of which, *Horde,* was released in 2004. Throughout the 17-minute video, barrier skateboarding is interspersed with excerpts from satanic horror movies and demonic imagery. The music to all of their videos is black metal, a genre which lyrically emphasises the bleakness of the natural world, paganism, and morbid mythology. During the video candles are occasionally placed on barriers that are being skated and a Church of Satan flag is used intermittently. In one segment between skateboarding, we see wolves feasting on a carcass in the wild. I read this imagery as being both oppositional to the popular tone of contemporary skateboarding and also a means to invoke the danger and risk inherent in skateboarding. Ba. Ku. rituals and paraphernalia play on sociophobics in a similar way to horror movies, using satanic imagery and music to unsettle and unnerve. While these images may be cool in their own way, they are indeed a departure from the clean-cut, Nike–Adidas/energy drinks face of skateboarding.

In framing the doctrine and ideology of Ba. Ku. it is readily apparent that there is a political aspect to what they are doing. In one interview their purpose is framed as the desire to 'protect the integrity of skateboarding' (urbanrushshawtv4, 2010). Fundamentally they wish to unsettle the mainstream popularity of skateboarding and are invested in a creative form of culture jamming. The Blackspot shoe from Adbusters (2018) is a corresponding example. This was designed as part of the alter-globalisation movement to challenge the commercial clout of Nike and their use of sweatshop labour. The Blackspot evolved out of the debate surrounding Naomi Klein's (2010) influential *No Logo* book. The shoe ultimately moves the focus away from the fetish of the brand, label, or logo, and its surrounding celebrity endorsements and suggests that shoes should be simply 'shoes' and not a contributor to inequality. Similarly, Ba. Ku. attempts to reorient people's understanding of skateboarding and in so doing invokes religious symbolism and ritual.

The Kult provides a curious example of an invented or DIY religion. All of their activities are deeply ritualised; they venerate the Jersey Barrier and have their own doctrine. Yet while adopting religious elements they intentionally refute the label of religion. When interviewed in *Post Radical* (Craig, 2018), Depth Leviathan Dweller invokes religion and then stops short of adopting the label.

> Depth Leviathan Dweller: We don't need to skate anything else all we need is these altars.
>> Rick McCrank: So, there is sort of a religious aspect to it?
>> Depth Leviathan Dweller: I would say more of a code.

The deference to code rather than religion is one that Cusack (2010, p. 127) notes with regard to *Jediism*. In one example a Jedi temple in Texas registered as a non-profit group and adopted a stipulated code, creed, and oath. In my own communications with Depth Leviathan Dweller a similar position is adopted. I challenged him on the fact that Ba. Ku. has a following and is similar to a variety of movements that Cusack has identified as new religions. He acknowledged (writing only in capitals) a 'belief structure' but again stopped short of using the word religion.

THE BARRIER KULT DEFINITELY HAS A FANATICAL FOLLOWING DUE TO [ITS] UNWRITTEN VARIOUS 'RULES' AND MANDATES THAT OTHERS WHO TRULY UNDERSTAND LIKE TO EMULATE. SO YES, A BELIEF STRUCTURE FROM REPEATED INTERVIEWS AND VIDEOS THAT GRIND INTO PEOPLE THE DECONSTRUCTION OF SKATEBOARDING ITSELF.

Depth Leviathan Dweller explained to me that skateboarding is a sport that 'accidentally' has its roots in punk rock and deviance. He argues that skateboarding is at an 'apocalyptical moment' where 'brand hype' and 'pro worship' has become destructive. The goal of Ba. Ku. is to strip 'skateboarding back to its purity' in pursuing physical manoeuvres that invoke the essence of the sport.

The success of Ba. Ku. can be measured in various ways. Firstly, in terms of duration, this rather arcane group has managed to acquire a global reach. Nearly 15 years after their first video, they continue to produce merchandise and release new videos. Various smaller Ba. Ku. 'hordes' have emerged across North America, Asia, and Europe. There have also been at least two movements which, influenced by Ba. Ku., have turned their focus to the parking block. This object is akin to a pavement or sidewalk curb but constructed to be placed in parking lots to demarcate where cars should park, preventing them from rolling away. Two different Parking Block Kults have existed: one Canadian, which released a video in 2011 and then largely disappeared; and another more recent group in the USA which began in 2016 and maintains an Instagram account (@ parkingblockkult, 2017). Images on their feed show members skating parking blocks, but also include various designs of parking blocks, and Satanic imagery in which parking blocks have been inserted. In an interview on their blog they adopt a similar aesthetic to Ba. Ku., writing only in capitals and referring to parking blocks as 'low-lying altars' (Parking Block Kult, 2016). They similarly are an anonymous group who take a critical stance of the celebrity and sportification of skateboarding, stating that 'televised contest stunts are poison.' Interest in these practices indicates that some skateboarders are invested in preserving some form of meaning that they derive from skateboarding. Turning attention to social media one may find a variety of skateboard communities that are on the periphery of the skateboard cult movement. Facebook groups such as 'The Jeff Grosso Kult' and 'The Lance Mountain Cult' along with other curb fraternities on Instagram such as 'Fellows Union Curb Club' and 'Curb Crushers Grand Order' are some examples which are not yet discernible as quasi-religious beyond their adulation for either specific professional skateboarders or a skateboarding object. The Fellows Union Instagram has over 6000 followers and its own website which sells merchandise such as stickers and T-shirts. The focus of this group is the skating of a long sliding curb in a parking lot and the development of a community around it (@fellowsunioncurbclub, 2019). Devotion for curbs and other objects is, however, not particularly unusual. In an issue of one skateboarding zine a writer states that 'a simple curb is a church. A ditch is a cathedral' (Czarski, 2016, p. 7).

Beyond Ba. Ku. there are other nascent forms of religious organisation. The Worble skateboard collective hailing from Vermont have emphasised a connection to the wild and Nature in their often innovative skateboarding. In their 2018 video *Toxic Planet*, a character referred to as a skate monk bequeaths aphorisms between segments of skateboarding. Dave Mull of The Worble suggests that their group is less of a religion and more of a spiritual collective. He states that in The Worble 'everything is about adventure and experiencing the world around us as wild and free, testing our physical capabilities and, really, overcoming fear with a kind of faith' (Glenney, 2018). Mull claims that skateboarding is a humiliating act where the practitioner is always failing in some form. This in itself becomes a motivation, providing a burst of adrenalin that allows you to achieve the 'impossible.' In *Toxic Planet* the skate monk declares that '[w]e mistake our flying for falling. We mistake our falling for flying.' These statements in the video are juxtaposed with footage of various members of The Worble falling off their boards and injuring themselves: a slam section. It is a peculiar feature of skateboard videos that failures are not entirely erased during production. Painful falls, or slams, are represented not just as entertainment, but also as an act of honesty and authenticity. Everyone falls off their skateboard at some point.

Building on a previous discussion of ritual in Chap. 8, I propose that this is another instance of the 'lowly' that Turner (1977) identifies as a feature of the liminal status of communitas. In the ritual act of humiliation, we supposedly achieve parity with all others and experience a catharsis that has a community enhancing and liberating effect. Unlike Ba. Ku., the focus of The Worble is on freedom and being wild in the wild, yet they also appear to be pursuing some kind of 'essence' to skateboarding and constructing a doctrine, or lifestyle religion through it.

Another example is the Cardinal Sins Skate Cult based in the USA. Initially founded by a dozen skateboarders who collaborated to rent a warehouse space in which they could build an indoor ramp. One of the members explains that the title of the group has multiple meanings:

> The idea of referring to ourselves as a cult was partially in sarcasm, but it also had two intentional effects. First, it acted as a bit of a buffer to outsiders. The local community was quick to shutdown these type of spaces so we had to be somewhat wary of who was allowed to come skate. Calling it a cult made strangers reluctant to assume they could skate without an invite. Second, it made most of us treat the place with a little more reverence than just another warehouse to skate in. We jokingly referred to weekly sessions as "going to church" and members as "sinners". I think that this buffer from outsiders, respect for the bowl, and ritual sessions are all part of why it not only still exists, but has doubled in size - both in square footage and number of members.

Cardinal Sins play with the title of cult in both a humorous way and in an instrumental fashion as a form of boundary construction. They have invested time and money into creating a place to skate, and they do not want it abused and put in jeopardy. Strikingly one member informed me that skateboarding was a serious pursuit that required practitioners to engage in cosmological reflection—the practice necessitates people being involved in the moment, present, and aware. Echoing the comments made in the Worble video he also stated that 'you must not be afraid to fall in order to not fall,' highlighting that Cardinal Sins is more than a sports club, a collaboration of like-minded skateboarders in a ritual process. In fact, the moniker of cult was adopted intentionally to distance the group from sports groups and clubs. As my informant reports 'club' has connotations of bowling and softball which 'leaned too hard towards the middle-aged suburbanization they spent their lives rebelling against.' Similarly, pushing back on the sporting notion of a club, the cult was constructed to ward off casual skaters and the uncommitted. Members of the cult signal their inclusion by wearing patches, diacritic marks to the initiated about their participation and piety in skateboarding (Fig. 10.2).

In organising these cults, members are seeking to move beyond some form of spiritual identification and make distinct ritual and ideology. This has broader implications about claims to an authenticity and essence in skateboarding that they appear to be seeking to preserve. While there is much about Ba. Ku. that is gauche and absurd, there is also reflexivity

Fig. 10.2 Patch for Cardinal Sins Skate Cult members

in acknowledging this. By establishing a militant skateboard faith, they also parody what skateboarding has become. Professional skateboarders are cast as false idols, and the hero worship and adulation of them is revealed to be as absurd as the practice of skating a vertical piece of concrete adorned with candles while wearing a balaclava. Thus, Ba. Ku. and Cardinal Sins Skate Cult are engaged in serious parody (Mäkelä & Petsche, 2013), which clearly has an ideological and political edge. The satirical power of invented religions should not be dismissed as it is instructive not only on the passions of popular culture but also on the boundaries of our spiritual lives.

Ba. Ku. also urges us to address the tension between new religions and cults. In refuting the label of religion but adopting the mantle of 'kult' Ba. Ku. is arguably constructing an invented cult. Yet this is a paradox, as typically the notion of cult is used as a way to challenge and discredit new religious movements. As Cowan and Bromley identify, cult is for many people 'just a four-letter word for any religion someone doesn't like' (2015, p. 11). Indeed, Ba. Ku. appears to have constructed a deliberately oppositional movement as a form of boundary construction around skateboarding. In using black metal and Satanism it plays directly into the rhetoric of anti-cultists who claim that all cults are evil in some form, exploiting their adherents financially, emotionally, or sexually. Yet in truth, many of the new religious movements that crop up every year are no more pernicious than established and traditional religions; it just happens to be that most people only learn of them when there is a scandal like the Heavens Gate suicide pact or the Branch Davidian crisis in Waco (Cowan & Bromley, 2015). For all its posturing Ba. Ku. seems indifferent to exploitation and only really cares about its message, rather than exponential growth. On reflection, the issues that Ba. Ku. is resisting in skateboarding culture, that is, celebrity and commercialisation, may just as easily also be understood as cults, particularly for Ba. Ku., which feels as though skateboarding is being desecrated in its contemporary transformations. The issue of 'cult' may have further significance in the compelling nature of skateboarding, itself a tight-knit and often arcane community. Moreover, skateboarding can be a socially exclusive bubble to some people. One of my respondents in his fifties spoke about how, despite his love for skateboarding, it might have held him back from doing other things. He stated that 'I was a bit of a skateboard fundamentalist when I was in my late teens and twenties. And I think that I did it to the exclusion of everything else.' While this may be a typical trait of youth, it does additionally indicate that skateboarding can become all-enveloping. This resonates with the argument that skateboarding is in itself a cultural world, that it is a lifestyle (Wheaton, 2013), and that in some manifestations it can be regarded as a cult-like unhealthy obsession.

These cults may not be solely male expressions of community and spirituality. Recent years have seen the development of a number of women-only skate crews that are visible on social media, many having their own zines, and merchandise. The Skate Kitchen hailing from New York is arguably the most well known of these women skate crews. Members of the Skate Kitchen became the subject and stars of a full-length dramatic feature film (Moselle, 2018) highlighting the popular interest in women skateboarding subjectivities. Another group, the Seattle-based Skate Witches, formed in 2014 as entrants in a skateboard competition. They have subsequently grown in popularity and organise an annual scavenger hunt, similar to the Thrasher King of the Road event, in which teams of women skateboarders must perform a series of tasks, many of which are zany and absurd. Founding member Kristin Ebeling chose the name of the group in reference to a film skit from the 1980s that she came across on YouTube (Plotnick, 1986). This short comical film depicts a group of three skater girls dressed in punk attire who harass male skateboarders. It concludes with a call for more skater girls and stipulates that they must all have pet rats. The twenty-first-century Skate Witches have no such requirements, but do have a savvy website where you can buy shirts, videos, and zines that document the activities of women skaters associated with the crew (Skate Witches, 2019). The term witch, although used in jest, similarly plays on occult ideas of subversive and arcane ritual practices, while also being evocative of esoteric feminine spiritual and sexual powers. Similarly, the term skate kitchen subverts the sexist assumption that women 'should be in the kitchen.' In a similar critique, the logo of the Jerusalem Skater Girls is that of a stiletto heel shoe on a skateboard. Harnessing the symbols of femininity and recasting them in satirical ways is in part a process of claiming power. It is similar to how skateboard graphics have played with religious and political iconography. Despite the fact that groups like the Skate Witches and the Skate Kitchen are focal on providing spaces for women skaters, these groupings as a by-product can also facilitate spiritual reflection. As we have seen through this text, the religious side of skateboarding is not simply a male preoccupation. Sophie Friedel (2015) writes a searchingly honest account of the impact skateboarding has had on her soul, and refers to the joy, community, and freedom of skateboarding as 'gifts.' Various women respondents in my research have spoken about bodily affect, how skateboarding gives them somatic freedom. Some liken this to yoga, others talk of bliss and self-expression that women often feel socially restricted from openly engaging in. Perhaps most powerfully women skate crews offer a space of friendship beyond typical notions of femininity surrounding competition for male attention and approval (Kelly, Pomerantz, & Currie, 2006; Pomerantz, Currie, & Kelly, 2004).

A further tangent that does not quite fit with previous discussions on religious organisation is the way in which some professional skateboarders have courted what is perhaps the most famous of modern cults, the Church of Scientology. Most noteworthy is professional skateboarder and owner of the Berrics skatepark and website, Steve Berra. He explains how Scientology has helped him with his career and life, providing a way to check his emotions and mental state. He also confesses that when he was first introduced to Scientology via a girlfriend, he saw it as bad, but having explored it and finding it helpful he now thinks people are naive to dismiss it as some peculiar cult or networking group (Ware, 2013). Rumours have circulated that other professional skateboarders such as Eric Koston and Jim Greco have also dabbled in Scientology. Founder of the popular YouTube channel and skateboard company Braille Skateboarding, Aaron Kyro is also reportedly involved in Scientology (Scientology, 2009). He appears in one video talking about how Scientology actually helped him learn skateboard tricks quicker and faster. Scientology is interesting to note because it may be one of the most widely recognised and acknowledged invented religions that has assumed some level of popular legitimacy and institutional recognition. It is a registered faith in the USA and exempt from paying taxes. It is also widely recognised as a cult and has received a vast amount of criticism for bullying and pressuring members who have left the church (Cowan & Bromley, 2015; Urban, 2006).

It may also be prudent here to consider that skateboarding may simply be regarded as a cult. This fact was relayed to me during one skateboarding event that I held at Lingnan University in which professional skateboarders Candy Jacobs and Margeilyn Didal participated. One of my colleagues commented that 'when I hear people very enthusiastic about skateboarding, it sounds like a cult to me … that it has some mystical quality that you can't define, you can't describe it.' She went on to ask more generally whether it is possible to be only half a skater, to not be committed, to not be passionate. I think a response to this question is the prevalence of religious notions of skateboarding and the development of niche cult-like groupings. If anything, these affiliations appear to be shielding themselves against the 'partial' or non-committed skateboarder who represents an existential threat to the lifestyle and culture of skateboarding that is cherished by so many. The half a skater is arguably a product of the mainstream popularity and sportification of skateboarding.

I recognise Ba. Ku. and its derivatives as conforming to the features of the invented religions that Cusack (2010) discusses. Ba. Ku. does not attempt to identify itself as a religion as that would involve it in the messy process of seeking some form of recognition and legitimacy. Presently it has no interest in pursuing the rights that Taira (2013) sees many new religious movements as desiring. Its battle for recognition and rights is within the world of skateboarding itself. Yet what it has constructed is clearly conforming to the blueprint of religion, involving doctrine, ritual, and community. Skateboarders have mobilised for cultural heritage (Blayney, 2014; Borden, 2015; Brown, 2014; Pratt, 2015; Ruiz, Snelson, Madgin, & Webb, 2019; Skateboarding Heritage Foundation, 2016; Trotter, 2017); it is feasible that they may at some stage begin to pursue cultural rights that attend to their ritualism, identity, and self-expression. At the heart of all these practices are individuals who, as skateboarders and consumers of skateboard products, are involved in the discursive practice (or corresponding culture) of reifying skateboarding. We must also be mindful that movements like Ba. Ku. emerge from personal practice. Religious movements begin with individuals and this is our next focus.

Personal Practices

In reflecting on the idea of where new religions come from, we can identify charismatic personalities as being instrumental. At the same time, I would argue that a new religion also needs individuals primed and receptive to these incipient ideologies and movements. My following examples look at a collection of individuals who are already open and receptive to the idea of skateboard religion and spirituality. To begin with, I return to the notion of *skate gods* that I explored in Chap. 3 with regard to venerated professionals; I now explore how the term is recast as a notion of benevolent luck or guidance. God is used here as a notion of both power and fate that orchestrates fortunes in the skateboarding world. This can be read as suggesting a skateboarding worldview or cosmology, an ordering of reality and its constitutive elements. This phrase is often reproduced in offhand remarks, with no elaboration. As a result, the notion is fraught with ambiguity. It is, however, significant that the phrase is used at all.

My first example of the phrase comes from professional skateboarder Anthony Shetler who produces his own podcast on skateboarding. In one episode he provides commentary on a series of short skateboard videos from the Helaclips website. Referring to one clip, he reports that the skateboarder is having a battle landing a trick down a triple set (three flights of stairs). Shetler explains:

> The whole time he is talking there's just slam after slam and some are sketchier than others. And some he's like bolts, like I was saying, he just can't ride away. It's like the skate gods won't give it to him. (Shelter, 2016)

We might infer that Shetler is referring to a notion of luck, that despite the best efforts of the skateboarder in question, he is being denied his prize. Thus, when individuals are lucky in skateboarding, it is not due to their own skill and agility, but perhaps also some larger divine providence. This is of course only a turn of phrase, but mixed in with other elements of skateboarding vernacular I recognise it as part of DIY religion. Early on in my research I diligently recorded such phrases, noting down every time they occurred, but due to the frequency of their use in everyday exchanges, magazines, and videos I stopped keeping notations simply due to data saturation. The popularity of such phraseology may also be indicative of emerging religious identification and should not be dismissed as simply superficial.

A very distinct example of the imagining of skate gods comes from an artistic feature in the March 2013 issue of *Thrasher* skateboard magazine. Four deities are depicted sophisticatedly blending elements of skateboard culture and religious iconography (see Fig. 10.3). These are invented hybrid gods and each has a name provided and a brief explanation of their divine powers (Callahan, 2013). The four gods *Space Viking*, *Poser Annihilator*, *Shred Possessor*, and *Our Lady of the Follow Through* draw on Norse mythology, Hindu polytheism, and the Catholic cult of *Our Lady of Guadalupe*. What can be made of such a feature? In conversation with

Fig. 10.3   The Skate Gods, James Callahan

the artist James Callahan, he confesses a deep interest in skateboarding and the religious imagination. Originally, he created these images due to his fascination with polytheistic religion and folklore. He states:

> For me personally, skateboarding has always had a meditative quality, and for many others it inspires a devotion and sacrifices that can be difficult, if not impossible, to articulate. It seemed like an excellent arena to create some characters that represent some of these indescribable sensations, fears, and urges.

Each of the deities has a variety of symbolic detail. The character named Space Viking has a sword in his left hand which has a hilt constructed out of a 'skate tool.' Other motifs include wheels, trucks, and a tattoo of an iconic skateboard logo. It would not be difficult to write at length about each character and the meanings they personify. Callahan's fascination with religion and skateboarding has led him to do a variety of different works that fuse the two. In another feature for *Thrasher* magazine's website, he illustrated a webcomic *Ditch Diablo* (Callahan & Creagan, 2017) in which a skateboarder had to make a series of decisions as they skated obstacles in a drainage ditch. The 'choose your own adventure' style of the webcomic plays heavily on the danger and sociophobics of skateboarding, eliciting the notion that skateboarding courts not only injury, but deviant spectres. In order to triumph in the story, you must choose a path that relies on good judgement, skateboard knowledge, and intellect. This conforms to Callahan's opinion that 'skateboarding has a punitive aspect when the focus on meditation is lost'; thus it is not simply a sport or hobby, but a ritual enactment of focus and concentration. Here we can link Callahan's understandings to both the sociological notion of edgework and the concept of flow. What is teased out in his artwork is the fear and danger associated with the commitment to skateboard, and this in turn connects to both a way of life and philosophical outlook.

In another interview focused on the topic of being an 'older skateboarder,' Matt from Kansas brought up the subject of religion at various times in our conversation. When I asked him if he was religious, he gave the following response:

> Like, if I'm religious, I'm religious about skateboarding. And if I were to refer to a God I'm referring to like, the skate god[s] and they don't really

have a name, I consider them like preachers guiding me along my journey. And as far as all the other religions go, [i]t doesn't bother me if you're religious, I just don't want to be preached to. Skateboarding kind of showed me that religion is needed and that all those atheists telling people that religion is stupid are kind of wrong because … Christian Hosoi, [i]f he can quit doing drugs because of the Word of God, then yes we need religion because it made him change his ways and even though he's a little different now and he's not as good as he used to be, he's off drugs and he's still skating.

For another one of my respondents, Archie from the UK, there was a very clear association that Mark Gonzales is a living quasi-god whom he proudly idolises. We got on to the subject of his admiration for Gonzales by discussing social media and skateboarding message boards. Archie dismissed online trolls and asserted that as a mature skateboarder, he was comfortable with his own preferences and choices.

I'm 41 years old now and I can't afford to waste anymore of my life worrying about this little prick from fucking Sheffield. You know, telling me that Mark Gonzales is an overrated hack, it's like well you know, that's your opinion, you know. I personally think the man is as close to a divine being as I'll ever experience in my life … he's kind of like the skateboarding equivalent of Yoda. So yes, he's just one of my inspirations in life non-stop and I wish he was my dad.

Archie's comments are worthy of reflection at a variety of levels. Firstly, it is evocative that a mature man places such admiration towards another man who has found fame simply through the practice of riding a skateboard. This would clearly be antithetical to the Ba. Ku. ideology. Secondly, by invoking Yoda and the Star Wars universe, Archie aligns his spiritual and philosophical understanding of skateboarding firmly within popular culture (McDowell, 2012). Thirdly, in wishing that Gonzales, a man only seven years older than Archie, was his father, he echoes the paternalism of monotheistic religion. In contrasting this account with the concept of invented religions, it is worth noting the manufactured faith of *Iglesia Maradoniana*. With its origins in Argentina, but claiming a following of more than 120,000, it is a devotional religion to the footballer Diego Maradona (Cusack, 2019). In a further elaboration of Archie's devotion to Gonzales a ritual practice emerged. Referring to one short video available on YouTube called 'Weekend with the Gonz' (GetmeoutofVA, 2011), Archie confessed that he liked to watch this video at least once or twice a week. Repetitively viewing this enabled Archie to be mindful of the playfulness and creativity that Gonzales applies in his skateboarding and life in general. Archie can also be understood as performing a calendrical media ritual, observing what to him has become a religious text on a weekly basis. This emphasises once more that media aids in suturing the divide between personal practices and communitas.

Moving beyond the notion of gods, some individuals have sought to reify such notions into ritual practice. One of my informants, Gavin in his early forties, has a shrine to a parking curb in his bedroom. He places candles around this in an act that is both satirical of religion and evocative of his emotional engagement with skateboarding. He elaborates on the circumstance surrounding the shrine by referring to an evening skateboarding with friends:

> We were getting a couple parking blocks to put together at this one spot, and one of them broke. And it broke off into this like little, I don't know, nine-inch piece, and I was like, 'that needs to go in my bedroom.' … My room is filled with, you know, things that I'm passionate about and I thought it would be kind of a kitschy, kind of a fun, kind of 'not an entire thing.' And then when I got it back in the house I was like, well, I'm obviously going to put a candle on it and make it into a little altar. So, it's something I'm serious about, but at the same time there's an element of fun and play and, you know, a bit of sarcasm in it as well.

Gavin is in no way alone in such activities and attitudes to skateboarding. I have come across skateboarders who have held on to old boards, a perished set of wheels, or a cracked pair of Independent trucks. These items become fetishes, a way to celebrate skateboarding experiences, and keep them near. Fun and play are also central in Gavin's account, recognising something serious in the way he feels about the parking block and something absurd at the same time.

The theme of fetish is also adopted in the *Post Radical* television show when professional skateboarder Frank Gerwer is interviewed. Frank keeps a collection of mundane chunks of concrete at his apartment. These, however, are tokens from iconic San Francisco skateboard spots such as the Hubba Hideout and EMB. One of Frank's mementos is a chunk of a handrail from an office plaza that was adjacent to the city's Union Square. The handrail is known as *Cardiel's Rail* due to the fact that John Cardiel was known to be the only skateboarder to land a trick on the object. Rick McCrank holds the chunk of handrail in his hand, looks into the camera, and states that to skateboarders it is 'like holding a holy thing, the energy of that moment in time is still in these objects' (Craig, 2018).

Nascent and Furtive

In concluding this chapter, I wish to focus on the way in which these DIY skateboard religions are both nascent and furtive. These qualities, the emergent and the secretive, seem to be particularly prevalent in the previous examples. A popular trope is that of the cult which signifies both a small arcane group and also something deviant that others should be cautious of. The use of the phrase cult in many of the examples mentioned resonates with the sociological practice of boundary construction, signalling difference and the cultivation of a distinct 'in-group.' Some skateboarders are organising religious activities for themselves replete with doctrines, rituals, and community. Yet they consistently stop short of recognising or labelling what they do as religious. More typically these activities might be framed as spiritual and personally meaningful. Thus, these DIY religions conform to the subjective spiritual milieu that Heelas et al. (2005) address in their research on the spiritual revolution occurring in the West. The reticence to be recognised as religious is furtive, wanting to be disassociated with what religion means, while continuing to replicate it. In part, this connects to an earlier attraction to skateboarding in that it was not organised, controlled, or even approved of. Thus, embracing a religion of skateboarding is an ambivalent activity, with individuals wanting at once to express and share the depth of meaning they get in their practice and similarly wanting to distance themselves from activities they feel excluded from or distaste for.

In being both nascent and furtive we return to the issue of creative play. The bond between religion and sport begins with the recognition of play as an important creative and spiritual process, one to be taken seriously precisely because it provides a space to throw off inhibition and social mores. Some of my respondents enjoyed Ba. Ku. because they believed the group was simply being sarcastic and making fun of skateboarding. This is indeed one legitimate reading of the Ba. Ku., and a reading that resonates with the idea of playfulness. This reading also presents as a further example of resistance to the 'religious' within skateboarding, seeing such connections as purely comical parodies rather than serious social movements or commentary.

Thus, the question that becomes apparent in this discussion is why skateboarders are so resistant to religion. Broaching this issue with my respondents inevitably comes back to the same motifs. *Religion is organised and skateboarding is not.* Veteran skateboarder and artist Pete from California states:

> Religion has a lot of sets of rules. Skateboarding thrives because it's very anti-authoritarian in and of itself. Once you start to attach rules to it, it'll just kind of like phase out. I don't think that skateboarding can be a religion. I mean you can have religious experiences with it. But I don't think it'll ever be a religion because it's always breaking off from itself and like reinventing itself at the same time.

I argue it is precisely these dynamics of rules, control, and order that are increasingly being imposed and adopted in skateboarding as it professionalises. I believe that these instigate nascent forms of religious identification as a form of resistance, and an example of how little institutional control skateboarders have over their pastime, culture, way of life, and identity. At the root of all the practices we have explored in this chapter is an attempt to capture and represent something that is unique and meaningful in skateboarding, and to arguably raise it above other representations. In response to commercialisation and sportification movements Ba. Ku. is making a space for the practice of skateboarding as it understands it. The fact that, as Pete claims earlier, skateboarding is moving and fluid, that it reinvents itself, is all the more reason to establish practices that seek to capture what is poignant about skateboarding. While some might pursue this in terms of religion, it may also be the case that the ethics and principles of skateboarding become a focus around which to organise activities that come to personify what skateboarding 'is all about.' This, as the following chapter explores, dovetails with the cultural notion of religion and can be seen as a further attempt to exercise some form of control over the continued development of skateboarding.

References

@fellowsunioncurbclub. (2019). Fellowsunioncurbclub. *Instagram Account*. Retrieved from https://www.instagram.com/fellowsunioncurbclub/

@parkingblockkult. (2017, June 19). Twilight of the Gods Is the Dawn of a New Crust. Retrieved from https://www.instagram.com/p/BVfoVnyj1l5/

Adbusters. (2018). The Blackspot Unswoosher. Retrieved from https://subscribe.adbusters.org/products/blackspot

Bellah, R. N., Madsen, R., Sullivan, W. M., Swidler, A., & Tipton, S. M. (2008). *Habits of the Heart: Individualism and Commitment in American Life*. Los Angeles: University of California Press.

Blayney, S. (2014). *Long Live South Bank*. London: Long Live Southbank.

Borden, I. (2001). *Skateboarding, Space and the City*. Oxford: Berg.

Borden, I. (2015). Southbank Skateboarding, London and Urban Culture: The Undercroft, Hungerford Bridge and House of Vans. In K. J. Lombard (Ed.), *Skateboarding: Subculture, Sites and Shifts* (pp. 91–107). London: Routledge.

Brown, M. (2014, October 29). The Rom, Hornchurch, Becomes First Skatepark in Europe to Get Listed Status. *The Guardian*. Retrieved from https://www.theguardian.com/culture/2014/oct/29/the-rom-hornchurch-first-skatepark-europe-listed-status

Callahan, J. (2013, March). Skate Gods. *Thrasher*, pp. 32–33.

Callahan, J., & Creagan, A. (2017). The Ditch Diablo Comic Book. *Thrasher*. Retrieved from http://www.thrashermagazine.com/articles/the-ditch-diablo-comic-book/

Cowan, D. E., & Bromley, D. G. (2015). *Cults and New Religions: A Brief History*. Chichester: Wiley-Blackwell.

Craig, A. (Writer). (2018). Episode 6: A Rolling Obsession [Cable Television Show]. *Post Radical*.

Cusack, C. M. (2010). *Invented Religions: Imagination, Fiction and Faith*. Farnham: Ashgate.

Cusack, C. M. (2013). Play, Narrative and the Creation of Religion: Extending the Theoretical Base of 'Invented Religions'. *Culture and Religion, 14*(4), 362–377. https://doi.org/10.1080/14755610.2013.838797

Cusack, C. M. (2019). Mock Religions. In H. Gooren (Ed.), *Encyclopedia of Latin American Religions*. Berlin: Springer International Publishing.

Czarski, B. (2016). Those Who Wander Can Still Get Lost. *Luchaskate Magazine*.

Friedel, S. (2015). *The Art of Living Sideways: Skateboarding, Peace and Elicitive Conflict Transformation*. Wiesbaden: Springer.

GetmeoutofVA. (2011). Mark Gonzales—Weekend with the Gonz. *YouTube Video*. Retrieved from https://youtu.be/ixSpr_ZB7rw

Glenney, B. (2018, August 31). Dave Mull Interview. Retrieved from http://www.thrashermagazine.com/articles/dave-mull-interview/

Heelas, P. (2006, Spring–Summer). Challenging Secularization Theory: The Growth of "New Age" Spiritualities of Life. *The Hedgehog Review, 8*(1–2), 46–58.

Heelas, P., Woodhead, L., Seal, B., Szerszynski, B., & Tusting, K. (2005). *The Spiritual Revolution: Why Religion Is Giving Way to Spirituality*. Oxford: Blackwell.

Kelly, D. M., Pomerantz, S., & Currie, D. (2006). Skater Girlhood and Emphasized Femininity: 'You Can't Land an Ollie Properly in Heels'. *Gender and Education, 17*(3), 229–248. https://doi.org/10.1080/09540250500145163

Klein, N. (2010). *No Logo: No Space, No Choice, No Job* (10th Anniversary ed.). New York: Picador.

Lefebvre, H. (1991). *The Production of Space*. Malden, MA: Blackwell.

Mäkelä, E., & Petsche, J. J. M. (2013). Serious Parody: Discordianism as Liquid Religion. *Culture and Religion, 14*(4), 411–423. https://doi.org/10.1080/14755610.2013.841269

McDowell, J. C. (2012). "Unlearn What You Have Learned" (Yoda): The Critical Study of the Myth of Star Wars. In T. R. Clark & D. W. Clanton Jr. (Eds.), *Understanding Religion and Popular Culture: Theories, Themes, Products and Practices* (pp. 104–117). London: Routledge.

Moselle, C. (Writer). (2018). Skate Kitchen.

Nieratko, C. (2015). Barrier Kult Is the Anonymous Elite Black Warrior Metal Skate Crew Here to Jack Your Shit. Retrieved from https://www.vice.com/en_us/article/ppxb87/vancouvers-barrier-kult-are-the-anonymous-elite-black-war-metal-skate-crew-here-to-jack-your-shit

Parking Block Kult. (2016). Parking Block Kult Interview. Retrieved from http://blockkult.blogspot.hk/2016/05/parking-block-kult-interview.html

Plotnick, D. (Writer). (1986). Skate Witches.

Pomerantz, S., Currie, D. H., & Kelly, D. M. (2004). Sk8er Girls: Skateboarders, Girlhood and Feminism in Motion. *Women's Studies International Forum, 27*(5–6), 547–557. https://doi.org/10.1016/j.wsif.2004.09.009

Pratt, D. (2015, June 16). Demolition of Historic Bro Bowl Skateboard Park Begins. *Tampa Bay Times.* Retrieved from http://www.tbo.com/news/politics/demolition-of-historic-bro-bowl-begins-in-downtown-tampa-20150616/

Ruiz, P., Snelson, T., Madgin, R., & Webb, D. (2019). 'Look at What We Made': Communicating Subcultural Value on London's Southbank. *Cultural Studies,* 1–26. https://doi.org/10.1080/09502386.2019.1621916

Scientology. (2009). I Am a Scientologist: Aaron, Skateboarder. *YouTube Video.* Retrieved from https://www.youtube.com/watch?v=clBtEd631i0

Shelter, A. (2016). Hellaclips #1. In A. Shelter (Ed.), *The Shelter Show.* Retrieved from http://theshetlershow.podomatic.com/entry/2016-06-08T09_12_01-07_00

Skate Witches. (2019). The Skate Witches Zine. Retrieved from https://www.theskatewitches.com/

Skateboarding Heritage Foundation. (2016, March). Save the Bro Bowl. *Skateboarding Heritage Foundation.* Retrieved from http://www.skateboardingheritage.org/programsmenu/brobowl/

Sutcliffe, S. J., & Cusack, C. M. (2013). Introduction: Making It (All?) Up—'Invented Religions' and the Study of 'Religion'. *Culture and Religion, 14*(4), 353–361. https://doi.org/10.1080/14755610.2013.839952

Taira, T. (2013). The Category of 'Invented Religion': A New Opportunity for Studying Discourses on 'Religion'. *Culture and Religion, 14*(4), 477–493. https://doi.org/10.1080/14755610.2013.838799

The Barrier Kult. (2013). False Claims of Ba. Ku. 'Identity'. Retrieved from http://thebarrierkult.blogspot.com/2013/08/the-identities-of-barrier-kult-titled.html

Trotter, L. (2017). Walking with Skateboarders: The Southbank Struggle (Short Version of LSE Argonaut Magazine). *Academia.edu.* Retrieved from https://www.academia.edu/12748160\Walking_with_skateboarders_the_Southbank_struggle_short_version_for_LSE_Argonaut_magazine_

Turner, V. (1977). *The Ritual Process: Structure and Anti-structure.* Ithaca, NY: Cornell University Press.

Urban, H. B. (2006). Fair Game: Secrecy, Security, and the Church of Scientology in Cold War America. *Journal of the American Academy of Religion, 74*(2), 356–389. https://doi.org/10.1093/jaarel/lfj084

urbanrushshawtv4. (2010). Skull Skates on Urban Rush. *YouTube Video*. Retrieved from https://youtu.be/cHGtpp6vWrs

Ware, L. (2013). Steve Berra. *48Blocks*. Retrieved from http://48blocks.com/steveberra/

Wheaton, B. (2013). *The Cultural Politics of Lifestyle Sports*. New York: Routledge.

11

Self–help

Skateboarding saved my life is a popular refrain. This is the phrase used in the opening to Mike Vallely's *Drive* video which documents his philosophy with montages of him skateboarding and travelling around the USA (Jeremias, 2003). He goes on to clarify that skateboarding 'gave me a creative outlet and in turn self-respect and hope … empowering me with a very physical but productive form of self-expression.' Fundamentally *Drive* is a skateboard video, but it is also an important document championing the prosocial positivity of skateboarding. The video is unique in that it is only about Vallely; it emphasises the individual and with it self-reliance, commitment, and discipline. In the years since its release the recognition of skateboarding as a positive pastime has boomed. A series of high-profile NGOs and charities, the visibility of female skateboarders, ethnic diversity, a range of sexual identities, have all contributed to the popular appeal and greater acceptance of skateboarding. *Drive* is by no means antecedent to this movement, but merely a distinct example of its growth.

In the video Vallely celebrates skateboarding but makes a pointed criticism of the way the skateboard industry is changing, and the big business enterprise skateboarding has become. In no small part this video responds

P. O'Connor, *Skateboarding and Religion*,
https://doi.org/10.1007/978-3-030-24857-4_11

to the growth in popularity of skateboarding, the post X-Games moment of ESPN coverage and sports drinks endorsements, and the popularity of the Tony Hawk Pro Skater (THPS) video game. These transformations are noted by Lombard (2010) as bringing new opportunities to skateboarders, while also being issues of contestation and conflict over ownership. For example, Vallely critiques the changing industry, but also profits from being included as a playable character in the fourth instalment of the THPS video game. Skateboarders increasingly have to navigate an ambiguous commercial world, making choices about paying bills and remaining authentic. Many skateboarders have responded by choosing to do good works which they see as communicating the essence of skateboarding in response to its potent commercial and corporate clout.

In no small part mobile technologies and social media have further facilitated the dispersal and sharing of prosocial (Gilchrist & Wheaton, 2017) messages and afforded new opportunities for skateboarders to activate democratic and inclusive projects. The ascent of skateboarding as a uniquely malleable tool for personal development and social inclusion is poignant. Skateboarding appears to have codes, ethics, and rituals that transcend many social obstacles of class, ethnicity, gender, and age. At an organisational level there has been a tremendous amount of work surrounding philanthropic endeavours associated with skateboarding. These represent a form of religious work that fit our third typology of *organisation* and are demonstrated in institutions providing a worldview, collective action, and ideology. I read Mike Vallely's *Drive* as an attempt to preserve skateboarding as he understands it—to assert a worldview and set of ethics as a form of cultural conservation in an era of rapid transformation.

In this chapter I explore how skateboarding can be understood as self-help. I recognise that this has a religious component in that, in a rather secular way, skateboarding has been used to do the developmental and philanthropic work that has traditionally been the role of religion, or the state. The fact that skateboarding NGOs now engage in activities as diverse as clothing the homeless, bringing fresh water to communities, or educating youth in a war-ravaged nation says something bold about economic liberalisation, globalisation, and neo-liberal politics. It also says something subtler about the role of religion and morality in the twenty-first century. Responding to this complexity, my argument about self-help is layered. I begin by addressing what I call skateboard philanthropy, which demonstrates various forms of self-help. Take, for example, the message that skateboarding contains: 'get up and try again,' or the fact that NGOs are often skater-started grass-roots initiatives, or more cynically the argument that philanthropy is self-interested and ultimately glorifies and promotes skateboarding (O'Connor, 2015). All these are distinct instances of self-help. Skateboard philanthropy is, I argue, quasi-religious and tied to broader movements of Sports for Development and Peace building (SDP) and Action Sports for Development and Peace (ASDP) initiatives. I move beyond skateboard philanthropy and explore self-help literature and its religious and spiritual connections. I show how a variety of books, videos, biographies, and blogs further promote skateboarding in a self-help ethos. While covering a diverse array of approaches, like philanthropic organisations, the texts are similarly infused with the recognition that skateboarding is prosocial. The texts are often confessional and spiritual, or even new-age in content. They provide philosophy, aphorisms, and guidance to initiates. Moreover, they appear to be more tacit examples of the DIY religiosity explored in the previous chapter, underlining once more that skateboarding has a set of beliefs, ethics, rituals, or, more simply, a worldview.

While occupying very different spaces and roles in skateboard culture, I see both philanthropy and the prosocial literature on skateboarding as ideologically connected. More worrying is the way such ideology has been embraced by the machinations of rapacious neo-liberal capitalism. This is astutely described by Gregory Mitchell (2016, p. 91), who argues that 'the excruciating elegance of neoliberalism is that the system appears so natural and inevitable that we seldom notice when late capitalism is at work in our lives.' Indeed, the fact that Mitchell's comment is so fitting, and yet lifted from a context in which he explores gay tourism in Brazil, only serves to highlight the insidious workings and reach of the market. Fundamentally, the social benefits of skateboarding deliver the best economic rewards for those who promote and recycle such images. Under the neo-liberal schema these translate as board sales, funding, sponsorship, subscribers, retweets, and likes. By promoting skateboarding, either for your brand, community, YouTube channel, university, or book, you can be seen to be helping yourself.

Skateboard Philanthropy

Skateboard philanthropy comes in a variety of incarnations. My first involvement with it was in the UK in 1998 when I worked with my local skateshop in Exeter to raise money and obtain land to build the city's first skatepark. The grass--roots initiative involved a mix of 'older' skateboarders pooling their knowledge, resources, and social capital to raise awareness and organise events. At its foundation there was a self-help sentiment. We wanted our own place to skateboard. At the same time, we promoted the benefits of skateboarding: 'it keeps youth occupied,' 'it is exercise,' and, perhaps more dishonestly, 'a skatepark would keep us out of the city centre.' In many ways, fundraising and campaigning for skateparks was one of the first instances of organised philanthropy that skateboarders got involved in. It is no surprise that these movements began in the 1990s as this was the era of the criminalisation of skateboarding and the development of architectures of exclusion, or skatestoppers to move skateboarders out of urban centres. Another very distinct example of skateparks and self-help is the DIY movement of funding and building your own skatepark. The most well-known and earliest example of this is the Burnside project in Portland, Oregon (Borden, 2001). Subsequently the DIY movement has spread across the globe (Gilligan, 2014) and has been embraced in some settings as a social good bringing with it gentrifying consequences (Howell, 2005; SOLO Skateboard Magazine, 2017). The DIY initiative is seen to be so central to skateboarding culture that the skateboard company Deluxe distribution provides small grants for DIY projects of US$200 up to three times a week (DLXSF, 2018). Operating at a much larger level is the Tony Hawk Foundation which has helped fund more than 609 skateparks in the USA and provided guidance and advocacy for thousands of skatepark projects globally. The Tony Hawk Foundation champions the self-help ethos because it only engages in projects which have been activated by local skateboard communities. It collaborates with grass-roots movements and provides co-funding with the local government and organisations in dialogue with the needs and requirements of skateboarders (The Nine Club, 2018).

Since the early 2000s skateboard philanthropy has manifested in Skatepark Builds (Tony Hawk Foundation), funding boards for under-privileged youth (Board Rescue), helping youth with autism (A Skate Foundation), raising involvement of girls and women in skateboarding (Skate Like a Girl), educating youth in Afghanistan (Skateistan), and helping young people in Palestine (SkatePal). Generally, these organisa-tions are secular, but the non-profit One Love is the work of a Christian family that has built the first skatepark in Tonga after emigrating from the USA to follow the call of Christ (One Love, 2018). A comprehensive list of organisations can be found on the ASDP website, which also pro-vides filters to differentiate the type of work they are involved in (Action Sports for Development and Peace, 2018). The ASDP categorises initia-tives as working in areas relevant to youth, education, empowerment, justice, community, environment, health, and recovery. Similarly, Atencio, Beal, Wright, and ZáNean (2018) explore the relevance of ASDP in skateboarding and the relationship such initiates have to neo-liberal ideology and practice. More broadly, academic work on skate-board philanthropy stems from the sociology of sport where a robust discussion on SDP has emerged.

The United Nations Office on Sports for Development and Peace building is an initiative introduced by then UN secretary general Kofi Anan in 2001 (Thorpe, 2014, p. 3). Further connections have been noted during the early 2000s by Giulianotti (2004), with sports programmes being used by the likes of the International Commission for the Red Cross (ICRC), International Labour Organisation (ILO), and the United Nations High Commissioner Refugees (UNHCR). The timeline of these activities highlights that skateboard philanthropy has been developing in concert with broader social movements surrounding development and sport. It is also relevant that this era coincides with the growth in collabo-ration between religious organisations and development initiatives (Haynes, 2007). In no small way these connections are part of a broader movement of self-help development characteristic of the neo-liberal age. Indeed, Thorpe and Rinehart (2013) link their critique of action sport NGOs to the global processes of neo-liberalism. They importantly highlight that the legitimacy of such work often rests on cooperation and collaboration with governments and commercial enterprises. This is a broader process that can be seen across a range of NGOs and grass-roots organisations seeking to make change. Take, for example, the work of Kohl-Arenas (2015), who argues in an ethnography of farmworkers in California that many self-help initiatives ultimately end up reinforcing dominant power mechanisms and disguising power differentials when focusing philanthropy towards those who are marginal and with least agency. Within the SDP movement there is an extant critique that sport is seen to be a saviour in itself, and that the groups targeted by SDP programmes are somewhat helpless when it comes to manifesting their own versions of sport. Here the critique is on the 'deficit' model, that youth in war-torn areas, for example, are helpless victims passively waiting to be rescued by football, parkour, or skateboarding (Spaaij, 2011; Thorpe & Ahmad, 2013). Critique is also levelled at the way certain groups and individuals promote sports in 'evangelical' terms, as a quick-fix remedy to a range of social ills (Giulianotti, 2004). This approach is deconstructed by Coakley (2011), who argues that too often SDP programmes are adopted, funded, and facilitated despite the absence of evidence of their benefits. He identifies that when programmes fail to succeed, they can still receive funding with the assumption that sport is always good. Most interestingly, failures to engage, rehabilitate, or improve the life of young people through sports programmes 'has led scholars to conclude that the relationship is contingent,' that sport is not some magical tool for development (2011, p. 309).

These assumptions are interesting to contrast with regard to skateboarding. Many skateboarders are still starkly aware that their pastime has and continues to be associated with criminality and deviance despite the recent mainstream and Olympic acceptance of skateboarding. Similarly, our exploration of skateboard ministers with their critique of the 'dark culture' highlights that the 'sport' of skateboarding is not universally regarded as a social good. The litany of professional skateboarders that have served time in prison, that are recovering alcoholics, or substance abusers, and their sometimes violent crimes, raises the question of the blanket prosocial benefits of skateboarding and other sports. The life-saving qualities of skateboarding are also increasingly questioned as a number of notable professional skateboarders have committed suicide in recent years. Mental health is becoming more widely discussed and was a key focus in the 2019 Pushing Boarders conference (Pushing Boarders,

2019). Yet Gilchrist and Wheaton (2017, pp. 4–5) recognise that the tide has turned; popular imaginings of skateboarders as antisocial and rebellious appear to be outweighed by the positive examples and their benefits.

This critical edge of sports sociology recognises that SDP and ASDP initiatives must work with local knowledge, existing sports interests, and grass-roots initiatives in order to carry on the work that they do (Coakley, 2011; Spaaij, 2011; Thorpe, 2014; Thorpe & Ahmad, 2013; Thorpe & Rinehart, 2013). This fundamentally returns to the theme of self-help. Philanthropy, in order to be successful with sports initiatives, needs to be hands off in certain demands and impositions. Yet, at the same time, philanthropists must also navigate a problematic relationship with neo-liberal and commercial interests for public and private levels of funding. One would not be cynical in assuming that the greatest beneficiaries of skateboard philanthropy end up being the skateboard industry, and increasingly the multinational companies that own large swathes of skateboarding brands. This fits with the arguments of Kohl-Arenas and suggests that skateboard philanthropy ends up being self-help for skateboarding above and beyond any other result. The fact that self-help is an apposite metaphor for neo-liberalism, ontological individualism, and the DIY ethos of skateboarding is not lost. Self-help is part of what Heelas, Woodhead, Seal, Szerszynski, and Tusting (2005) recognise in the 'supposed' spiritual revolution of individuals pursuing their own philosophies and therapeutic lifestyles.

Sophie Friedel's work in this area is particularly important. As a passionate skateboarder she enrolled as a volunteer in Skateistan and also pursued a Master's degree in Peace. Her book *The Art of Living Sideways* (2015) is a love song to skateboarding, an academic treatise on peace studies, and also a thoughtful and informed critique of SDP. She argues that SDP is imposing institutional control over skateboarding, and that there is a thin line between providing space for youth to engage with sports and cultural imperialism. Indeed, it is not hard to see promotional material about skateboarding in Afghanistan, Nepal, and Ethiopia as part of an unfolding neo-orientalism narrative. These new SDP initiatives are not Christian missionaries, but they do possess ethics and politics that they are clearly transmitting and importing into new cultural contexts. Friedel (2015, p. 71) interprets the work of Richard Giulianotti in identifying four tendencies of SDP as neo-liberal, development interventionist, strategic developmentalist, and social justice–oriented. In a similar way to skateboard ministry, SDP and ASDP appropriate skateboarding for their own political narratives. Arguably it is skateboarding's inherent creativity and flexibility that make it so open to such differing political positions. As Weyland (2004, p. xiv) states, 'skating can be anything.' It is precisely this quality which appeals in the current political and social climate. Skateboarding represents an almost entirely open cultural system welcoming with only one ardent demand and concern: you must participate. But participation can be a challenging path for many volunteers who travel like missionaries to work in foreign countries for skateboard charities. They can be exposed to traumatic experiences and end up working closely with vulnerable, disturbed, and abused youth. These skateboard volunteers become pulled, sometimes haplessly, into a world where their time, effort, and mental health are made vulnerable by larger systems of power and oppression.

In June 2018, Oliver Percovich, the founder of the NGO Skateistan, launched the Goodpush Alliance (Skateistan & Rhianon, 2018), which is aimed at helping groups involved in skateboard philanthropy be successful and sustainable. The reason for this initiative is that a variety of skateboard philanthropy projects have had short-lived success, or encountered challenging and frustrating obstacles. Take, for example, the original Holystoked Bangalore skatepark that was a collaboration between the NGO 'Make Life Skate Life' and the jeans company offshoot Levi's Skateboarding (Smith, 2013). Instrumental in the project was local skateboarder Abhishek who resigned from his office job to pursue his love of skateboarding. The skatepark received the support of a group of professional skateboarders who helped build the park and documented the process for a Levi's promotional video. Local children from a variety of different backgrounds were able to transcend social and gender divisions in the skatepark. Children were getting an education, exercise, and building a community. Yet within a year a neighbour unhappy with the skatepark pushed for it to be closed and destroyed (TEDx Talks, 2014). Subsequently, a second Bangalore skatepark has been built through a new collaboration with Adidas (Holystoked, 2018). However, the full story of the first Holystoked skatepark is not as well promoted or as easily accessible as the initial Levi's-funded promotional video on the skatepark build. Levi's have removed the 17-minute documentary of the skatepark project from YouTube and their website, though copied versions are still available for access (Millivanilton, 2013). Of even more interest is the fact that the Make Life Skate Life website continues to have photos promoting the work they have done at the Holystoked skatepark despite the fact it no longer exists (MakeLifeSkateLife, 2018). Another example of the opaque work of skateboard philanthropy can be observed in the 'Skate for Change' initiative which advocates skateboarders making a positive impact in their community. The Skate for Change project has sought to bring water, clothing, and food to homeless people in Lincoln Nebraska, USA. Working with the principle that skateboarders traverse the city and often share space with homeless people, founder Mike Smith has influenced a movement to make this a positive encounter. Skate for Change has chapters in a variety of cities in the USA and beyond. In late 2014 a group of teenagers set up their own version of Skate for Change in Hong Kong as part of a final-year project for their high school examinations. They were able to complete a series of outings to provide goods for the homeless across the city, but after their graduation the group disbanded as various members left the city to attend university in other locations. Similarly, the superb work of Skateistan, which often promotes its work through images of young women skateboarding, is ambiguous in its ultimate impact on the fate of these youth. Many girls who attend the Skateistan school eventually leave and get married, often while still young. Their new roles as wives and mothers typically bring an end to their skateboarding and education. These examples are not provided in order to be cynical about the benefits produced, but to highlight that the social media buzz surrounding some optics provide only a shallow image of the real processes at work. It often appears that the greatest beneficiaries are those sponsoring these philanthropic activities rather than the people and communities they are focused upon. This is a point also suggested by Atencio et al. (2018) in that the boom in skatepark builds in the Bay area of San Francisco has resulted in a host of private public spaces. Built on the pretext of engaging and providing for young people, these spaces often obscure the neo-liberal machinations and values at work in them, ranging from the companies that profit from these spaces and the philosophies of child-rearing that accompany them.

A more balanced response may be that skateboarding in itself embraces such transience and impermanence. For example, an informant who received one of the Deluxe grants to make DIY spots in his/her local town found that within two years all four of the small sites that were worked on were removed, destroyed, or obstructed in some way. Perhaps, then, it would be better to highlight that skateboard philanthropy is best attuned to helping skateboarders rather than being developmental and educational. This is not to deny the benefit of skateboarding to commercial enterprises, neo-liberal models of governance and education, and developmental agendas. Rather, some skateboarders seem willing to allow aspects of their culture to be co-opted if it provides them with more opportunity to skate, more facilities, along with better health care and remuneration. Some are arguably naive about the processes at work, others are fully aware and see it as a 'them or us' scenario where the necessity to pay bills and fend for themselves becomes a primary concern.

This last point is one that I have previously made (O'Connor, 2015). I have argued that skateboard philanthropy, while often inspirational, and undoubtedly beneficial to tens of thousands if not millions globally, is fundamentally self-help. This I have suggested is a type of prefigurative politics, by which skateboarders ensure the continuation and preservation of their culture by placing it as a central component in the good works they initiate and support. A strong feature of ASDP organisations is their tendency to embrace the cultural politics of lifestyle sports. Skateboarding can be radically inclusive, fostering cooperation and participation regardless of ability, age, gender, and ethnicity. Skateboard philanthropy promotes these same ethics and as a result promotes or, to use Giulianotti's term, 'evangelises' skateboarding itself. The point in critiquing this is to provide some form of redress to the way skateboard philanthropy has become something of an echo chamber, perhaps even a cult, or an exquisite example of lifestyle religion in itself.

'Skateboarding Saved My Life'

The phrase that began this chapter can be found in the title to more than 40 YouTube videos. Countless others describe how skateboarding 'changed my life' or 'saved me from despair.' These videos discuss youth who have been made homeless, individuals who have struggled with ADHD, dyslexia, dyspraxia, and autism, or those who have experienced abuse, imprisonment, or suffered the tolls of horrific tragedies such as murder and suicide within their families. Consistently skateboarding is described as a way out, a path for personal growth, and a release from the sometimes insurmountable challenges of everyday life. In no small measure the features we have explored through this text come to be significant. Skateboarding provides a meditation, a sense of community, a feeling of power and self-determination. A body of biographical literature on skateboarding echoes these stories and offers more context. Rodney Mullen's memoir *Mutt* details the strained relationship he had with his father, his battles with loneliness, and even suicidal thoughts. Skateboarding is described throughout as a saviour.

Interested in these themes, I have sought to contrast a variety of books on skateboarding with self-help literature. In what ways are they similar? How do they provide a guide to weather personal challenges, and ultimately what do they tell us about skateboarding? At a fundamental level I see these texts as attempts to organise skateboarding around a set of ethics and principles. The implication is that although skateboarding is celebrated as having no rules, and is inclusive and open, there exists a set of principles and behaviours which one should adhere to nevertheless. In no small way the proliferation of these texts serves as a secular form of skateboard ministry. They are invested with the self-help ethos of self-cultivation and ontologies of the self, typical of contemporary explorations of religion and spirituality (Bellah, Madsen, Sullivan, Swidler, & Tipton, 2008; Heelas et al., 2005; Ostwalt, 2012; Palmer, 2017). I read these as responses to the growth in popularity of skateboarding, mainstream support, increased sportification, and Olympic validation.

Firstly, what do I mean by self-help texts? Broadly speaking, I am referring to a body of popular non-fiction work which aims to help people structure and order their lives more productively and harmoniously. These books tend to include plain-speaking language, provide personal anecdotes by authors, and include a mix of popular psychology and spiritual advice. McGee (2005, p. 11) has identified that self-help books doubled in popularity between the 1970s and the year 2000, and Bergsma (2008) notes that in 2000 Americans spent more than US$563 million on self-help books. Woodstock (2005) reaches further back and provides a content analysis of self-help literature from the 1880s to the 1990s. She argues that early self-help books embraced religious themes, scientific reason from the 1940s onwards, and by the 1980s they 'incorporated popular psychology approaches into a hybrid "Spirituality"' (2005, p. 155). She also notes that throughout the last century self-help books have remained 'perennially popular' and perhaps part and parcel of the tremendous social change that has unfolded during this era (2005, p. 156). However, despite this popularity, self-help books have been the subject of a great deal of criticism and popular derision. These titles are criticised for being poorly written, fraudulent, ineffective, offering false hope, and at worse destroying relationships (Bergsma, 2008, p. 349).

Self-help literature is described by Lichterman (1992) as a 'thin culture,' a term he develops borrowing from Geertz's (1973) notion of thick description. 'Thin' is representative of self-help because such books provide a schema for self-improvement without requiring any deep commitment from readers. Lichterman frames this as part of their appeal, recognising that self-help books are part of the radical individualisation explored by Bellah et al. (2008), and also a response to disenchantment with religion. Thus, self-help books that provide a secular religious form of instruction, support, and guidance, are in part popular because they do not require the commitment or suspension of disbelief that many see as central features in religious ideology. This interesting argument must also be understood in contrast with Bergsma's (2008, p. 437) claim that self-help books are popular because they are affordable, provide a popular and accessible way to disseminate psychological theories, present private forms of therapy, and include exciting possibilities regarding relationships, wealth, and sex.

How then does skateboarding interact with this literature? Firstly, I see a number of ways in which skateboarding and self-help books are fused. The most obvious example is the litany of 'how to' guides about skateboarding. These provide an introduction to the basics of skateboarding and detail trick tips, explanations about equipment, and even guides on how to build ramps. Yet, even in these essentially descriptive books there can be a series of broad instructions that inform readers on the ethics and worldviews of skateboarding. Take, for example, Per Welinder and Peter

Whitley's book *Mastering Skateboarding* (2012). This provides advice on how to fit in with other skateboarders which can be summarised as (1) 'Don't whine or Bragg'; (2) 'Have fun'; and (3) 'Be safe' (2012, p. 6). The book is mostly devoted to describing tricks and how to perform them, yet throughout the words 'fear' and 'stoked' are often used, connecting to the embodied experience of risk and transcendence. Many books provide trick tips for young children new to skateboarding, and adults seeking to hone their skills (Badillo, 2007; Beal, 2013; Becker, 2009; Gifford, 2006; Goodfellow, 2006; Morgan, 2005; Stock & Powell, 2010). My previous arguments about mythology, skate gods, sacred places, and iconic videos all have purchase in these types of texts. Typically, a potted history of skateboarding is provided in the introduction to these texts. This history resonates with the origin myth of California. Similarly, some instruction on the icons of skateboarding is included, identifying a selection of pioneers or legends. Patty Segovia's children's book on girl skaters provides an account of women pioneers and humorously inverts gender dynamics by asserting that skateboarding is not just for girls: 'guys are great skateboarders, too!' (2007, p. 22). Goodfellow's 176-page book explores 36 tricks with more than 500 photos. It is essentially a step-by-step guide to performing ramp tricks, yet it provides space to discuss *The Search for Animal Chin* and its Confucian connections (2006, p. 13).

Moving past these texts, biographies by skateboarders tend to also provide some form of self-help reflection. I have already mentioned Rodney Mullen's (Mullen & Mortimer 2004) biography, and similarly Christian Hosoi's (Hosoi & Ahrens 2012) and Tony Hawk's (Hawk & Mortimer 2001), all contain self-help elements. Beyond the big names of iconic professionals, the everyman memoirs about skateboarding are also worthy of attention. Take, for example, Jocko Weyland's *The Answer Is Never* (2002) or Sean Wilsey's *More Curious* (2014), both engaging books that speak of the emotional and spiritual meaning of skateboarding, but neither framed as self-help or instruction. David Thornton's self-published work *Nobody: Essays from a Lifer Skater* (2016) is autobiographical but focuses strictly on a skateboarding biography. We learn little about the man off the board. At times through the text he provides advice; this becomes most instructional in the final chapter where he shares his experience of skateboarding and parenting. He guides readers in the delicate balance between pursuing places to skate and remaining respectful and considerate of those we encounter whilst skateboarding. It is no surprise that Thornton has been involved in blogging and making zines for some years. In the skateboard blogosphere of middle-aged men there is a subtle interplay between biographical content and motivational posts aimed to inspire people to get out and skate more. The blog *Concrete Existence* provides an evocative mix of these elements, including reviews on the best hardware supplies to make rough curb stones skateable, a skateboarders take on Gay Pride, and a reworking of the *Tao Te Ching* for skateboarding (Sedition, 2017). A more explicit exploration of religion is provided by Rabbi Dovid Tsap (2014), who blogs about skateboarding's connections to the Kabbalah. In blogs, and other social media, we see the opportunity for skateboarders to explore their own interests, and as a collection they provide numerous philosophical detours about skateboarding, religion, and the experiences of older skateboarders (Eisenhauer, 2016; Neverwas, 2018; Sedition, 2017; Tsap, 2014).

Beyond the 'veteran blogs,' 'core biographies,' and 'how to' texts are a few 'my philosophy' books which appear to take on more of the features of self-help books. Firstly, the self-published work of Neal Unger (Unger & Earhart, 2018) requires some context. Unger is a skateboarder who has achieved a cult following as a 'senior' skateboarder and has also risen to prominence via social media. Although well known he is not a professional skateboarder and is lauded mostly as an evocative example of a skateboarder in his sixties. He has a striking appearance with long white hair and a tall slim physique. He has pioneered his own skateboard trick the 'Sissy Bounce, Finger Flip,' which he developed in frustration of his inability to perform a kickflip. One YouTube video in which Unger talks about his desire to continue skateboarding regardless of his age has more than 1.8 million views at the time of writing (Juiceaya, 2014). Unger has also appeared in numerous videos and websites, and collaborated with various companies (Old Skateboards, 2015); he even appears in the *We Are Blood* (Evans, 2015) video that was discussed at length in Chap. 6. His book has the rather long title *Dude Logic: Skateboarding philosopher Neal A Unger shares his thoughts on being human, the meaning of life and whatever else he can think of … Grab your best tricks and go for a ride with The Dude*. While it leverages his skateboard celebrity, the book is a series of anecdotes in which Unger shares his philosophy on life which extends to advice on how to be a considerate lover and to recognising the validity of religion in all aspects of life. Much of the text discusses Christian religion, god, and spirituality but always through anecdotal reflections and never in a sustained manner. Skateboarding is a rather shallow element in Unger's book while guidance and advice are the most prominent features of the text.

Similar to Unger is Doug Brown, who is also considered to be peripheral to the world of professional skateboarding, yet has achieved some notoriety and success through a partnership with the Gravity Games competition in 2002. Brown has promoted himself as a professional skateboarder, rock musician, and motivational speaker. He has even endorsed a brand of extreme sports deodorant called 'X-Air.' Brown has written books about his life that seek to provide a guide and inspiration for his readers. His book *The Bliss of the Unwind* (2014) conforms to the 'thin culture' argument of Lichterman in that it is just a series of anecdotes about his life and how he became a professional skateboarder through commitment and belief in himself. Brown declares that 'my skateboard has led me to unbelievable places, but I've always been more than just a skateboarder in my career.' Speaking about how he helps young people he goes on to explain that 'I encourage them to find in themselves what will lead them to connect with others, in turn making a difference in people's lives' (2014, p. 168). The book reads not as an evangelical treatise about skateboarding, but about the author himself and his pop-culture passions. In my analysis I came to the conclusion that this was a self-help book without any method or ideology. Its primary frame is to inspire through personal stories of adversity and determination. Skateboarding, although referred to and pictured on the front cover, is again a superficial part of the text.

What appears to be emerging is the adoption of skateboarding as an adjunct part of new-age philosophy and self-help, buoyed and propelled by the visibility of skateboarding in prosocial and philanthropic programmes and SDP/ASDP philosophy. Take, for example, Chris Grosso's self-help text *The Indie Spiritualist* (2014), which includes on its front cover an endorsement from Tony Hawk. The text picks up a selection of themes in which the author talks about his battle with substance abuse and depression. His argument can be summarised as an affirmation that you can be spiritual while also having tattoos, piercings, enjoying pop culture, and listening to heavy metal and hip hop. Grosso sees spiritual lessons in rock music, Donnie Darko, and skateboarding. He speaks about the philosophy of professional skateboarder Mike Vallely, celebrating individuality and having the strength to walk one's own path (2014, p. 63). Grosso describes how skateboarding changed his worldview as a youth: 'Growing up, things like punk, movies, art, and skateboarding touched my heart, they were my spiritual teachings, and continue to be a large part of my spiritual growth to this very day' (2014, p. 35). His book guides his readers with references and weblinks to his own music. The final parts of the book also give readers a guide on mediation techniques and suggestions for films and music that the author loves and finds spiritually uplifting. Grosso is an example of the hybrid mix of religion, spirituality, and pop culture. His marketing of spirituality and pop culture can be regarded as analogous to commercialised Christianity (Steinberg & Joe, 2018; Twitchell, 2007). Once more the book has a wholly superficial engagement with skateboarding; it is used almost in a decorative manner to flag the points Grosso wishes to make. In his most recent book *Dead Set on Living* (2018) with Alice Peck, this time endorsed by Bam Margera and reviewed in *Thrasher* magazine, Grosso peppers his spiritual talk with references to his skateboarding identity. Just as Christians have appropriated rock music (Flory & Miller, 2008) and skateboarding for their own ends, new-age spirituality is doing the same. In doing so, it provides an alternative understanding of self-help, in that these appropriations ultimately appear to be self-centred, pleasing, and serving themselves.

While Grosso's works are clearly both self-help and spiritual explorations, they are the most superficially involved with skateboarding, with Doug Brown and Neal Unger appearing somewhere in the middle. However, Grosso's writing can be framed with a distinct genre of self-help and spirituality books which focus on 'alternative' lifestyles and 'punk spirituality.' Buddhist Noah Levine makes numerous mentions to his time skateboarding in his book *Dharma Punx: A Memoir* (2003). His follow-up book *Against the Stream: A Buddhist Manual for Spiritual Revolutionaries* (2007) makes no mention of skateboarding, but engages with the theme of alternative spirituality. Similar texts have been written by Brad Warner with titles such as *Don't Be a Jerk: And Other Practical Advice from Dogen, Japan's Greatest Zen Master* (2016), and *Hardcore Zen: Punk Rock, Monster Movies and the Truth about Reality* (2003). Both Warner and Levine speak of Buddhist spirituality through a pop-culture frame. Their works are relevant to our discussion not because they touch upon skateboarding, but because they are examples of an expanding and fluid relationship between pop culture and religion (Clark & Clanton Jr, 2012; Cowan, 2008; Cusack, 2010). Just as there has long been an association between sport and religion, I predict we shall see more associations not just between skateboarding and religion, but also amongst other lifestyle sports as they become more entrenched in popular culture, commercial life, and everyday activities. These patterns complement the discussions of Heelas et al. (2005) that chart a rise in alternative spiritual practices, and also of Ostwalt (2012), who argues that the secular is becoming more sacred and the sacred more secular (Table 11.1).

Table 11.1 Skateboarding and self-help literature

			Representation of	
Genre	Examples	Self-help	Skateboarding	Religion/ spirituality
How to	Becker (2009) Badillo (2007) Goodfellow (2006) Gifford (2006) Stock and Powell (2010)	Strong	Strong	Weak
Core biography	Hawk & Mortimer (2001) Mullen & Mortimer (2004) Hosoi & Ahrens (2012) Weyland (2004)	Weak	Strong	Mild
Veteran blogs	Sedition (2017) Eisenhauer (2016) Neverwas (2018) Tsap (2014)	Mild	Strong	Mild/ Strong
My philosophy	Unger and Earhart (2018) Brown (2014)	Strong	Weak	Mild
New age	Grosso (2014) Levine (2003)	Strong	Weak	Strong

Skateboarding as Self-help

This chapter has focused on two seemingly divergent themes: one skateboard philanthropy and the other self-help texts. My argument is that these themes dovetail in that they are all responses to the changing cultural world of skateboarding. Skateboard philanthropy seeks to promote the prosocial benefits of skateboarding in a myriad of ways. A variety of books on skateboarding similarly represent how skateboarding is being preserved in its ethics and worldview, and also co-opted in the wide-ranging new-age philosophy of spiritual growth. Both celebrate skateboarding as a prosocial activity. I see these developments, like increased religious identification surrounding skateboarding, as efforts to preserve and control skateboard culture in the face of rapid change within the social world, industry, and sport of skateboarding.

I view skateboard philanthropy organisations as crypto-religious, embedding and activating a series of moral codes and ethics in their mission statements. These in turn conflate skateboarding with a particular worldview, attitude, and disposition regarding inclusion, discipline, and hard work. While seldom being religious programmes, skateboarding charities and NGOs can be seen as secular religions, or lifestyle religions. They have organisation, funding, mission statements, personnel, and merchandise. Some, like the *Tony Hawk Foundation* and *Be the Change—The Sheckler Foundation*, draw on the celebrity status of their founders. At their core these philanthropic endeavours reproduce a worldview and ideology surrounding skateboarding and its positive effects. Indivisible from the good works these activities perform is the fact that they also promote skateboarding. Skateboard philanthropy initiatives are organised secular self-help. As we have seen, some SDP and ASDP programmes are open to critique as imperialist ventures, co-opting skateboarding for an alternative agenda and politics. This can be juxtaposed with skateboard ministry, which ultimately uses skateboarding as an evangelical tool for the church, not for skateboarding itself.

In contrast, the notion that skateboarding is able to save lives is explored in a variety of videos, literature, and blogs. I have shown how a collection of books can be understood as a body of self-help literature on skateboarding. This is a diverse field where works range from 'how to' perform tricks to new-age explorations of Buddhist philosophy. These are not a cogent collection of work; some appear to be focused on skateboarding, others purely on self-help spirituality. I argue that these books are in no way unrelated to skateboard philanthropy, but are direct responses to the new social climate in which skateboarding is deemed prosocial and a positive influence on individual well-being. Moreover, I believe that there will be further integration of skateboarding self-help philosophies. These are not unrelated to the field of skateboarding and religion, but they do appear to lean towards secular organisation. Like many self-help books they are written to be accessible, 'thin' in the necessity of commitment by their readers, and aligned with the primacy of the individual as the arbiter of spiritual development.

As the final chapter dealing with *organisation*, self-help can be contrasted with the earlier themes which deal with invented religions and skateboard ministry or dawah. All three topics demonstrate an ambivalent relationship between skateboarding and religion. Religious organisation stresses the importance of faith above and beyond any real spiritual connection to skateboarding. This in itself elides the embodied spiritual experience of skateboarding. Invented or personalised religions demonstrate both a political project and a radically individualised spiritual approach. Skateboard philanthropy engages in good works stripped of spirituality, in sum being an exquisite vehicle for neo-liberal ideology.

I feel uneasy making these points as I feel so much of skateboard philanthropy makes a positive impact. But I am all too aware that skateboarding is for me a rewarding and enjoyable activity in itself. What I am sceptical of is the capacity for skateboard philanthropy to overturn the ideological architecture which it is subsumed and promoted under: neo-liberal capitalism. Take, for instance, the notion that failure is an acceptable part of skateboarding. In neo-liberal thinking this is valid, but only under the rubric that some final success or triumph is achieved. Many skateboarders deal mostly with failure and I would argue that the ethic of accepting and tolerating failures, both ours and those of others, is currently lost in the promotion of skateboarding. Failure is seen too often as only a step in a final process of triumph. While I do believe skateboarding can manifest change, it is rapidly becoming aligned with a form of liberal politics that is increasingly exclusive. I am also critical of the way in which the purported positivity of skateboarding can be myopically read as an endorsement of all activities and personnel involved in skateboarding. To be more explicitly blunt, the promotion and syphoning of skateboarding into a prosocial inclusive activity runs the risk of alienating those whom it may hold the most potential for.

References

Action Sports for Development and Peace. (2018). ASDP. Retrieved from http://www.actionsportsfordev.org/

Atencio, M., Beal, B., Wright, M. E., & ZáNean, M. (2018). *Moving Boarders: Skateboarding and the Changing Landscape of Urban Youth Sports*. Fayetteville, AR: University of Arkansas Press.

Badillo, S. (2007). *Skateboarding: Legendary Tricks*. Chula Vista, CA: Tracks Publishing.

Beal, B. (2013). *Skateboarding: The Ultimate Guide*. Santa Barbara, CA: Greenwood.

Becker, H. (2009). *Skateboarding Science*. New York: Crabtree Publishing Company.

Bellah, R. N., Madsen, R., Sullivan, W. M., Swidler, A., & Tipton, S. M. (2008). *Habits of the Heart: Individualism and Commitment in American Life*. Los Angeles: University of California Press.

Bergsma, A. (2008). Do Self-help Books Help? *Journal of Happiness Studies, 9*. https://doi.org/10.1007/s10902-006-9041-2

Borden, I. (2001). *Skateboarding, Space and the City*. Oxford: Berg.

Brown, D. (2014). *Bliss of the Unwind: My Life Beyond the Board*. USA: Nikazone.

Clark, T. R., & Clanton Jr., D. W. (2012). *Understanding Religion and Popular Culture: Theories, Themes, Products and Practices*. London: Routledge.

Coakley, J. (2011). Youth Sports: What Counts as "Positive Development". *Journal of Sport and Social Issues, 35*(3), 306–324.

Cowan, D. E. (2008). *Sacred Terror: Religion and Horror on the Silver Screen*. Waco, TX: Baylor University Press.

Cusack, C. M. (2010). *Invented Religions: Imagination, Fiction and Faith*. Farnham, UK: Ashgate.

DLXSF. (2018). Deluxe Distribution—The Grants Fund. Retrieved from http://www.dlxsf.com/thegrantsfund/

Eisenhauer, P. (2016). Paying the Piper. *Blog*. Retrieved from http://www.going-homeagain.net/paying-the-piper/

Evans, T. (Writer). (2015). We Are Blood [DVD].

Flory, R., & Miller, D. E. (2008). *Finding Faith: The Spiritual Quest of the Post-Boomer Generation*. London: Rutgers University Press.

Friedel, S. (2015). *The Art of Living Sideways: Skateboarding, Peace and Elicitive Conflict Transformation*. Wiesbaden: Springer.

Geertz, C. (1973). *The Interpretation of Cultures: Selected Essays*. New York: Basic Books.

Gifford, C. (2006). *Skateboarding: Learn to Skate Like a Pro*. London: DK.

Gilchrist, P., & Wheaton, B. (2017). The Social Benefits of Informal and Lifestyle Sports: A Research Agenda. *International Journal of Sport Policy and Politics, 9*(1), 1–10. https://doi.org/10.1080/19406940.2017.1293132

Gilligan, R. (2014). *DIY/Underground Skateparks*. Munich: Prestel Verlag.

Giulianotti, R. (2004). Human Rights, Globalization and Sentimental Education: The Case of Sport. *Sport in Society, 7*(3), 355–369. https://doi.org/10.1080/17430430042000291686

Goodfellow, E. (2006). *Skateboarding: Ramp Tricks*. Chula Vista, CA: Tracks Publishing.

Grosso, C. (2014). *The Indie Spiritualist*. New York: Atria Paperback.

Grosso, C., & Peck, A. (2018). *Dead Set on Living: Making the Difficult Journey from F**Cking up to Waking Up*. New York: Gallery Books.

Hawk, T., & Mortimer, S. (2001). *Hawk: Occupation: Skateboarder*. New York: Regan Books.

Haynes, J. (2007). *Religion and Development: Conflict or Cooperation?* London: Palgrave Macmillan.

Heelas, P., Woodhead, L., Seal, B., Szerszynski, B., & Tusting, K. (2005). *The Spiritual Revolution: Why Religion Is Giving Way to Spirituality*. Oxford: Blackwell.

Holystoked. (2018). Skateparks. Retrieved from https://www.holystoked.com/pages/skateparks

Hosoi, C., & Ahrens, C. (2012). *Hosoi: My Life as a Skateboarder Junkie Inmate Pastor*. New York: HarperOne.

Howell, O. (2005). The "Creative Class" and the Gentrifying City. *Journal of Architectural Education, 59*(2), 32–42. https://doi.org/10.1111/j.1531-314X.2005.00014.x

Jeremias, M. (Writer). (2003). Drive: My Life in Skateboarding [DVD]. In B. Worldwide (Producer): Move Collective.

Juiceaya. (2014). Neal Unger—60 Year Old Skateboarder. *YouTube Video*. Retrieved from https://youtu.be/lM4FQ_FqEhQ

Kohl-Arenas, E. (2015). *The Self-Help Myth: How Philanthropy Fails to Alleviate Poverty*. Oakland, CA: University of California Press.

Levine, N. (2003). *Dharma Punx: A Memoir*. New York: Harper Collins.

Levine, N. (2007). *Against the Stream: A Buddhist Manual for Spiritual Revolutionaries*. New York: HarperCollins.

Lichterman, P. (1992). Self-Help Reading as a Thin Culture. *Media, Culture and Society, 14*(3), 421–447. https://doi.org/10.1177/016344392014003005

Lombard, K.-J. (2010). Skate and Create/Skate and Destroy: The Commercial and Governmental Incorporation of Skateboarding. *Continuum, 24*(4), 475–488. https://doi.org/10.1080/10304310903294713

MakeLifeSkateLife. (2018). Holystoked Skatepark. Retrieved from https://makelifeskatelife.org/projects/india/

McGee, M. (2005). *Self-Help, Inc.: Makeover Culture in American Life*. Oxford: Oxford University Press.

Millivanilton. (2013). Make Life Skate Life Y Levi's—Construcción De Skatepark En Bangalore, India (Subtitulado). *YouTube Video*. Retrieved from https://youtu.be/LTi-_Pp5Bzg

Mitchell, G. (2016). *Tourist Attractions: Performing Race and Masculinity in Brazil's Sexual Economy*. Chicago: University of Chicago Press.

Morgan, J. (2005). *No Limits: Skateboarding*. Minnesota: Smart Apple Media.

Mullen, R., & Mortimer, S. (2004). *The Mutt: How to Skateboard and Not Kill Yourself*. New York: Reagan Books.

Neverwas, B. (2018). Stupidfest 2018—The Whole Story Part 5: Day Two Part One. *Blog Entry*. Retrieved from https://neverwasskateboarding.com/stupidfest-2018-the-whole-story-part-5-day-two-part-one/

O'Connor, P. (2015). Skateboard Philanthropy: Inclusion and Prefigurative Politics. In K. J. Lombard (Ed.), *Skateboarding: Subcultures, Sites and Shifts* (pp. 30–43). London: Routledge.

Old Skateboards. (2015). From Pines to Palms with 58 Year Old Skateboarder Neal. A. Unger. *Video File*. Retrieved from https://www.youtube.com/watch?v=wDbQQWruAWs

One Love. (2018). One Love—Living One Love for God. Retrieved from https://liveonelove.org/

Ostwalt, C. (2012). *Secular Steeples: Popular Culture and the Religious Imagination* (2nd ed.). London: Bloomsbury.

Palmer, D. A. (2017). *Dream Trippers: Global Daoism and the Predicament of Modern Spirituality*. Chicago: University of Chicago Press.

Pushing Boarders. (2019, August 15). *Pushing Boarders Opening: You Can Talk to Me*. Malmö: Bryggeriet Skatepark.

Sedition. (2017). The Tao Te Chin(G) of Skateboarding: A Guide to Stoke (Part 1). *Blog*. Retrieved from http://vatorat.blogspot.com/2017/01/the-tao-te-ching-of-skateboarding-guide.html

Segovia, P. (2007). *Skate Girls*. Chanhassen, MN: The Child's World.

Skateistan & Rhianon. (2018). Global Update: Sharing Knowledge, One Push at a Time. Retrieved from https://medium.com/@Skateistan/global-update-sharing-knowledge-one-push-at-a-time-397927f38959

Smith, J. (2013). The Trials and Tribulations of Building a Skatepark in India. *Vice*. Retrieved from https://www.vice.com/sv/article/vdy574/the-trials-and-tribulations-of-building-a-skatepark-in-india

SOLO Skateboard Magazine. (2017). Pontus Alv—Absolute Event Horizon. *YouTube Video*. Retrieved from https://youtu.be/zvHjdKSbJ-I

Spaaij, R. (2011). *Sport and Social Mobility: Crossing Boundaries*. London: Routledge.

Steinberg, S. R., & Joe, L. (2018). *Christotainment: Selling Jesus Through Popular Culture*. Routledge.

Stock, C., & Powell, B. (2010). *Skateboarding Step-by-Step*. New York: Rosen Publishing Group.

TEDx Talks. (2014). What I Learned from Building a Skatepark | Abhishek | Tedxbangalore. *YouTube Video*. Retrieved from https://youtu.be/KxOAa6_St7Y

The Nine Club. (2018). Tony Hawk | *The Nine Club* with Chris Roberts—Episode 100. *YouTube Video*. Retrieved from https://youtu.be/z4pwm37EVyw

Thornton, D. (2016). *Nobody: Essays from a Lifer Skater*. UK: Amazon.

Thorpe, H. (2014). Action Sports for Youth Development: Critical Insights for the SDP Community. *International Journal of Sport Policy and Politics, 8*(1), 91–116. https://doi.org/10.1080/19406940.2014.925952

Thorpe, H., & Ahmad, N. (2013). Youth, Action Sports and Political Agency in the Middle East: Lessons from a Grassroots Parkour Group in Gaza. *International Review for the Sociology of Sport, 50*(6), 678–704. https://doi.org/10.1177/1012690213490521

Thorpe, H., & Rinehart, R. (2013). Action Sport NGOs in a Neo-Liberal Context: The Cases of Skateistan and Surf Aid International. *Journal of Sport & Social Issues, 37*(2), 115–141. https://doi.org/10.1177/0193723512455923

Tsap, D. (2014). Skateboarding: What's Love Got to Do with It? *Blog*. Retrieved from http://spiritualskating.blogspot.com/2014/01/skateboarding-whats-love-got-to-do-with.html

Twitchell, J. B. (2007). *Shopping for God: How Christianity Went from in Your Heart to in Your Face*. New York: Simon & Schuster.

Unger, N., & Earhart, M. (2018). *Dude Logic: Skateboarding Philosopher Neal a Unger Shares His Thoughts on Being Human, the Meaning of Life and Whatever Else He Can Think of…Grab Your Best Tricks and Go for a Ride with the Dude*. Online Publishing: CreateSpace Independent Publishing Platform.

Warner, B. (2003). *Hardcore Zen: Punk Rock, Monster Movies and the Truth About Reality*. Somerville, MA: Wisdom Publications.

Warner, B. (2016). *Don't Be a Jerk: And Other Practical Advice from Dogen, Japan's Greatest Zen Master*. Novato, CA: New World Library.

Welinder, P., & Whitley, P. (2012). *Mastering Skateboarding*. Champaign: Human Kinetics.

Weyland, J. (2002). *The Answer Is Never: A Skateboarder's History of the World*. New York: Grove Press.

Weyland, J. (2004). Attractive to the Unattractive. In J. Hocking, J. Knutson, J. Maher, & J. Weyland (Eds.), *Life and Limb: Skateboarders Write from the Deep End* (pp. ix–xiv). Brooklyn, NY: Soft Skull Press.

Wilsey, S. (2014). *More Curious*. San Francisco: McSweeney's.

Woodstock, L. (2005). Vying Constructions of Reality: Religion, Science, and "Positive Thinking" in Self-Help Literature. *Journal of Media and Religion, 4*(3), 155–178.

12

Conclusion

I began skateboarding at the age of 11, but by the age of 17 I had all but stopped. A convergence of changes resulted in a few weeks off my board slowly turning into months. Basically, my skateboard crew split up, I moved to a new school, my local skateshop shut down, I became short-sighted, and I contracted glandular fever. But my identity was still that of a skateboarder. I remember, when I was 17, coming across a zany individual at the Glastonbury festival who would sell you a postcard of your tribe. He stopped me and a friend and identified us as 'Indie Kids.' I was horrified. I was wearing Skate Rags, a Krux T-Shirt, and scuffed Vans Half-Cabs. How could I be misread? Over the next two years I faced some personal challenges and started to pursue ways to gain spiritual fulfilment. I practised Kung Fu, Tai Chi, and Chi Kung. I studied philosophy, experimented with self-help books, and meditated. I pined for skateboarding but forgot why I had stopped. One day my girlfriend bemused at my melancholy when observing a group of skaters suggested I buy a board. At age 20, anxious that I was already far too old, I began skateboarding again. A gaping void had been filled in my life and I started to wonder if the previous years would have been simpler and less full of angst if I had never ceased to skateboard. Despite all of my enquiries into

© The Author(s) 2020
P. O'Connor, *Skateboarding and Religion*,
https://doi.org/10.1007/978-3-030-24857-4_12

religion and new-age lifestyles, for me, this was the most therapeutic. I was content and happy, and the answer was so very simple: a skateboard.

Skateboarding is the most religious of all contemporary sports and yet hardly anyone notices. It is a perfect example of the concept of lifestyle religion. It is a ritual practice, political, playful, and open to all manner of articulations and interpretations. Skateboarders worldwide recognise an origin myth to their craft, and their boards regularly pay homage to sacred symbols and also create them anew. I have argued that skateboarding makes holy places out of overlooked street corners, while skateboarders praise a host of icons that liken their culture to a polytheistic cosmology. I have demonstrated how skateboarding religions are emerging, and how organised religion seeks to harness and work with the community of skateboarders. I have also put forth the argument that charitable works have sought to make skateboarding a secular faith, replete with a philosophy complementary to neo-liberalism, underpinning a motive of self-help and personal accountability. I have structured the text in a manner that facilitated discussion of practices that were both nuanced and explicit in religious terms. I have shown how skateboarding can be both hostile to and wary of organised religion while also being a vehicle for its promotion and the articulation of alternative religious subjectivities. In this final chapter I make a closing argument that religious identification in skateboarding is part of a broader social process in which, as Ostwalt (2012) has argued, the sacred becomes secular and the secular becomes sacred. Moreover, the religious identification that skateboarders find in their activities can be likened to what Heelas, Woodhead, Seal, Szerszynski, and Tusting (2005) have observed in increased spiritual exploration premised on subjective well-being. My analysis indicates that skateboarding has been swept up in these transformations. Here, I argue in conclusion that there will be increased religious identification in skateboarding in coming years and this will similarly be observable in other lifestyle sports which have developed vibrant and discernible cultural politics in their practice. Furthermore, I see a continued engagement and growth in lifestyle religion, attending to both strong notions of individualism central in contemporary globalised mediated society and the deep-seated need for human bonds and recognition fostered via communitas. Before exploring these arguments in more depth, I shall begin by summarising the arguments and terrain we have covered up to this point.

Observation, Performance, Organisation

The sections of the text, observation, performance, and organisation, all speak of different ways in which the connections between skateboarding and religion can be explored. Firstly, we observed the origin myth of skateboarding, recognising how a globally reproduced narrative has emerged, placing California as the homeland of skateboarding. Through the celebrity of skateboarding we saw how certain individuals had been attributed superhuman, sage-like, and godly status. Then addressing the iconography of skateboard art I demonstrated how skateboarding has a fascination with religion and indeed how the physical, material space of the board provides a canvas for expressing and critiquing notions of the divine. Here I also argued that skateboarding's visual culture disturbs and undermines a clear distinction between the profane and the sacred. I also suggested that religion was observable in skateboarding in ways that simply do not translate to other sports. In this first part religious motifs are distinctly observable; religion surrounds skateboarding even if at first glance it is seen to be superficial.

The performance of skateboarding became the second focus of the text and encompassed the way skateboarding has been captured and reproduced in media. In the analysis of two skateboard videos filmed 30 years apart the journey of skateboarding was likened to a spiritual path. Each of the videos suggested a meaning or ethic to skateboarding, one being the pursuit of fun, the other being community. While not distinctly religious, these features pertain to how skateboarding is performed, consumed, and understood. The factors were all shown to contribute to feelings of communitas, transcendence, and an engagement with a notion of ritual quest, or skateboarding as a life journey in itself. The relevance of video became much of the foundation for my discussion on pilgrimage. Here I explored how skateboarders have engaged with space to fulfil and complete meaningful sojourns often propelled by skateboard media. In the testimonies of various skateboarders these trips were shown to have emotional and spiritual significance, building on the experience of communitas, and also being a ritual expression. The final chapter to address performance explored the vibrancy of ritual process in skateboarding. It detailed a variety of instances where rites of passage, festivity, and politics are all invoked in skateboarding to communicate meaning and sustain community. It was here that I argued more completely that skateboarding is playful, and perhaps best understood as a performance of ritual play.

The final part of the book took the topic of religion in its most recognisable form and addressed the various ways in which religion and skateboarding have been organised. The first of these explorations came in the form of evangelical skateboard ministry which I argued appropriated skateboarding to further religious outreach. I also demonstrated how skateboard ministry was a distinct and overlooked element of skateboard culture that has seen considerable growth and promotion via social media. The second treatment of organisation adopted the paradigm of invented religions to address how some groups and individuals had sought to construct their own self-made religious cults and practices centred on skateboarding. I argued that these were in part a response to the popularity of skateboarding and were for many attempts, both tacit and overt, to keep skateboarding special and meaningful. The final chapter of organisation explored philanthropy and self-help literature to argue that the celebrated ethics of skateboarding are prefigurative methods to help and sustain skateboarding, highlighting that it is both more than a sport and an activity to be entrusted and managed by skateboarders. Here I argued that the promotion of skateboarding as a prosocial activity is actually a further form of religious organisation in which skateboarding has become a secular faith.

In order to tie these disparate threads together I committed to a polythetic definition of religion and structured this in response to Clifford Geertz's (1973) understanding of religion as a cultural system. From this foundation I proposed a concept of lifestyle religion which was open and malleable to popular culture, heterodox ideas, consumption, and subcultural practices. This allowed me to suggest that sometimes religion can simply be observed and at other times it can be practised even when practitioners do not readily recognise what they are doing as religious, and in other scenarios religion is organised around institutions, extant traditions, objects, and ethics. By looking at skateboarding through a polythetic understanding of religion I have attempted to provide a rubric to address all manner of connections between skateboarding and religion. This I hope has given scholars and enthusiasts new ways to conceive of and consider skateboarding, and also some alternative examples of religion, sport, and popular culture. It is my hope that this schema, along with the concept of lifestyle religion, will also be helpful in delineating the relevance of religion in other lifestyle sports.

Lifestyle Religion

I have proposed that lifestyle religions can be understood as physical expressions that are subcultural, consumptive, and individualised. Accordingly, a lifestyle religion includes ritual practice and action that facilitate community. This is clearly visible in skateboarding and other lifestyle sports, but it could also be analogous to video game enthusiasts, airsoft practitioners, vegans, and perhaps fashion bloggers. A central motif in lifestyle religion would be the capacity to demonstrate commitment while never really having to become dedicated to a theology, dogma, or sacred text. Lifestyle religions do not demand exclusivity or the rigid moral and ritual strictures that can be found in traditional religions. But their most salient features would be an orientation around some pop-culture elements that have been captured and disseminated on mass media. Indeed, Taylor (2007) argues that the increased spiritual identification in surfing in recent years is propelled by media. As we have seen throughout this book, media is of central importance in skateboard culture, providing rich text to build community and understanding, to construct and maintain identities. The salience of social media in new cultural articulations of skateboarding—be that women skateboarders, alternative sexualities, social justice pioneers, health gurus, middle-aged and senior participants, the disabled, or the religious—serves only to underline the power of media.

It is the fusion of these components with an individualised philosophy, the values, freedom, and autonomy that distinguish the importance of both lifestyle and identity. Countless skateboarders reminded me that skateboarding could never really become a religion because it rejected organisation. A key component, they affirmed, was that skateboarding was about freedom. As skateboarding debuts as an Olympic sport it is no longer simple to dismiss the charge that skateboarding refutes organisation. This is a fallacy. But much like the alternative philosophies explored by Heelas et al. (2005), skateboarding is malleable for articulation—an empty vessel in which to project notions of the sacred. It is precisely because skateboarding is considered free that it is so accessible as a lifestyle component on which to graft ideas about identity, spirituality, and therapeutic fulfilment.

Lifestyle religion is thus one way to understand the meaningful way people engage with pop-culture practices in individualised ways significant to their own identities and foster connections and communities with like-minded others. The attraction of lifestyle religion is that it is non-committal, and holds no control over individuals to conform to a set of rigid social structures and moral obligations. At most there are subcultural codes and contracts which can be rescinded upon with ease. I argue that lifestyle religion is a nascent development which can be observed in elements of skateboard culture, and in other lifestyle sports. Moreover, it relates broadly to the religious and spiritual identification people have been exploring in popular culture, through film, literature, music, and a host of alternative lifestyles (Clark & Clanton Jr, 2012; Cowan, 2012a, 2012b; Cusack, 2010, 2013, 2019; Cusack & Digance, 2009; Digance & Cusack, 2008; Scholes, 2012; Wilder & Rehwaldt, 2012).

Looking Beyond Skateboarding

I believe in skateboarding scholarship precisely because it provides a rich context by which we can understand more about society, space, and culture. Skateboarding is not a niche concern; it presents valuable lessons to us in its multiple forms. The insights from this research are thus relevant to the sociology of religion and the growth of lifestyle sports.

Transformation in religious practice is largely noted to be taking place in the Global North (Heelas et al., 2005, p. 49). These are similarly the same parts of the world in which lifestyle sports have emerged, and despite rapid global growth continue to have their largest impact (Wheaton, 2015, p. 636). The draw of new forms of spiritual practice as subjective life projects also mirrors the attraction that many have to hedonistic, informal, and risky lifestyle sports. Activities like surfing, snowboarding, and parkour require no formal membership and have no national affiliation, in contrast to traditional sports like baseball and football that developed in concert with national identity (Thorpe, 2014b, p. 4). While spiritual practice and lifestyle sports in their new forms are often imagined to be individual pursuits that resist control, rules, and organisation, both have become highly integrated into the new (post-Fordist) economy and thrive in 'niche markets' (Wheaton, 2015, p. 635), often propelled by 'New Media' (Dart, 2012) and user-generated content (MacKay & Dallaire, 2014; Thorpe, 2014b, p. 70). New spiritual practices and lifestyle sports are seen to be attractive to policymakers and governments because they replicate a set of values that promote individual responsibility, healthy lifestyles, and consumption (Gilchrist & Wheaton, 2011; Lombard, 2010; Thorpe, 2014a; Wheaton, 2015).

A connection between lifestyle sports and the values of the neo-liberal economy has been identified by a variety of scholars (Howell, 2008; Thorpe & Rinehart, 2013; Wheaton, 2013). Individual responsibility, entrepreneurial ethos, and responsible risk-taking are all seen to be values central to success in lifestyle sports and the post-Fordist economy. Gilchrist and Wheaton (2011, p. 121) speak of a 'political shift' in which 'risky, counter-cultural, deviant lifestyles' are recast as 'inclusive' and 'anti-competitive,' and become tools for social and urban development. Their research speaks of the training regimes and healthy eating of parkour practitioners. In a similar way skateboarding, long associated with rebellion and anarchy, has incorporated an embrace of healthy lifestyles. In one of the leading skateboard magazines professional skateboarder Manny Santiago speaks of his vegan diet as a way to maintain and prolong his career (Transworld Skateboarding, 2015, p. 88). Santiago explains that he changed his diet after being influenced by other skateboarders and speaks of the ills of chemically altered food, yet stops short of criticising the energy drinks that sponsor him and other skateboarders. With this interplay between healthy pursuits, commercial interests, and neo-liberal ideology in lifestyle sports, it is relevant to ask how new spiritual and new sporting practices interact. My discussions in various chapters foreground this. Take, for example, Bayer Pharmaceuticals' appropriation of the Lyon 25, skateboard philanthropy, and its connection to new-age self-help philosophy, or the emergence of skate cults. The key argument here is not simply the connection between skateboarding and religion. More centrally this discussion highlights how skateboarding has become an increasingly appealing vehicle for religious and spiritual ideologies. This replicates the general features of lifestyle sports as activities that are both inclusive and flexible.

What Comes Next?

Although the scope of this work is broad, it is by no means exhaustive. Readers will note that many topics have been omitted. I have not, for instance, explored the religious biographies of certain professionals such as Lance Mountain and his quasi-religious skateboard team, The Firm. Or the more contemporary example of Beatrice Domond's Christian faith and study of Hebrew. I have also not discussed the professionals who have become born-again Christians such as Steve Caballero, Ryan Sheckler, Lennie Kirk, and Salman Agah. There is room for a treatment of other religions in professional skateboarding such as Jordan Richter's conversion to Islam, Guru Khalsa's Sikh heritage and increasing religiosity, Steve Olson's psychedelic travels, Josh Stewart's conspiracy-oriented Theories of Atlantis, and a host of professionals connected to Rastafarianism such as Jef Hartsel, Lewis Marnell, and Nyjah Huston.

I have similarly not explored numerous threads in religious studies, such as the psychology of religion, sexual practices, conversion, heresy or, for instance, theology. More than anything else this has been a first step in opening a space for academic discussion on skateboarding and religion, and more generally lifestyle sports. I do hope that this work is complimentary to other works on religion and popular culture and contemporary transformations in new and alternative religious practices.

I am particularly interested in exploring how religion and skateboarding interact in non-Western contexts. I have touched on skateboarding and Islam in Malaysia and Indonesia. These are areas ripe for further and focused enquiry. Similarly, the emerging skateboard culture in the Indian subcontinent is already showing signs both of incorporating religious symbolism and importantly transgressing longstanding barriers of faith, caste, and gender. In all of these scenarios the online world stands out as an important space where skateboarding and religion are combined, juxtaposed, and explored. Again, I anticipate similar developments in other lifestyle sports while remaining mindful that skateboarding's versatility makes it arguably more potent for reimagining than other sports.

A Sense of Meaning

Professor Iain Borden concludes his 2019 work 'Skateboarding and the City' by reflecting on how skateboarding can provide practitioners access to 'a magnificent life.' My observations throughout this research and the testimonies I have collected all point to the fact that skateboarding is incredibly meaningful to many of the people who practise it. I have witnessed people overcome heartbreak, fight addiction, combat loneliness, and get in shape via their skateboards. I have spoken to grown men who have tried to communicate with tears in their eyes just how important skateboarding has been to them. It has provided ritual process, text, and community to so many individuals; it has acted like a religion.

I have tried to delineate the reasons why this has taken place. Skateboarding is not like other sports. I cannot think of another sport that emphasises fun in the same way, or values critical art as part of its culture, or one that has such a comparable romance with mundane architecture. But I do see parallels in other lifestyle sports, and I believe that surfing, snowboarding, and parkour are moving in a similar direction. Heelas et al. (2005) argue that those who derive meaning from new-age spiritual, health, and well-being philosophies are part of a holistic milieu. These individuals believe that truth can be found in a variety of practices. Most importantly, these individuals are hesitant to obey some external authority. They prioritise finding their own tools for spiritual guidance, and preferably ones that appeal to their values, interests, and feelings. They also argue that the holistic milieu is growing.

It is clear to me that skateboarding offers much to those who are in the holistic milieu. The appeal has also been recognised by various religious organisations who seek to harness the enthusiasm for skateboarding and other lifestyle sports onto evangelical programmes. Skateboarding and religion are connected, and to many people skateboarding is a religion. I am emphatic that these same dynamics are observable and emerging in other lifestyle sports. I close with a final quote that captures much of the present tension in skateboarding. Many of the people I spoke to recognised something magical or spiritual in their activity, and they were anxious that this evocative quality was somehow being lost in the current popularity of the sport. Here are the words of climber Kevin Kelly recounted by Edith Turner (2012, p. 20) on the subject of how the unique feeling of communitas, its joys, and camaraderie should be nurtured and respected:

> The best you can do is *not kill it*. When it pops up, don't crush it. When it starts rolling, don't formalize it. When it sparks, fan it. But don't move it to better quarters. Try to keep accountants and architects and police and do-gooders away from it. Let it remain inefficient, wasteful, edgy, marginal, in the basement, downtown, in the 'burbs, in the hotel ballroom, on the fringes, out back, in Camp 4. When it happens, honor and protect it.

References

Clark, T. R., & Clanton Jr., D. W. (2012). *Understanding Religion and Popular Culture: Theories, Themes, Products and Practices*. London: Routledge.

Cowan, D. E. (2012a). Religion in Cinema Horror. In T. R. Clark & D. W. Clanton Jr. (Eds.), *Understanding Religion and Popular Culture: Theories, Themes, Products and Practices* (pp. 56–71). London: Routledge.

Cowan, D. E. (2012b). Religion in Science Fiction Film and Television. In T. R. Clark & D. W. Clanton Jr. (Eds.), *Understanding Religion and Popular Culture: Theories, Themes, Products and Practices* (pp. 41–55). London: Routledge.

Cusack, C. M. (2010). *Invented Religions: Imagination, Fiction and Faith*. Farnham, UK: Ashgate.

Cusack, C. M. (2013). Play, Narrative and the Creation of Religion: Extending the Theoretical Base of 'Invented Religions'. *Culture and Religion, 14*(4), 362–377. https://doi.org/10.1080/14755610.2013.838797

Cusack, C. M. (2019). Mock Religions. In H. Gooren (Ed.), *Encyclopedia of Latin American Religions*. Berlin: Springer International Publishing.

Cusack, C. M., & Digance, J. (2009). The Melbourne Cup: Australian Identity and Secular Pilgrimage. *Sport in Society, 12*(7), 876–889. https://doi.org/10.1080/17430430903053109

Dart, J. (2012). New Media, Professional Sport and Political Economy. *Journal of Sport and Social Issues, 38*(6), 528–547. https://doi.org/10.1177/0193723512467356

Digance, J., & Cusack, C. M. (2008). Secular Pilgrimage Events: Druid Gorsedd and Stargate Alignments. In C. M. Cusack & P. Oldmeadow (Eds.), *The End of Religions? Religion in an Age of Globalisation* (pp. 218–229). Sydney: Department of Studies in Religion, University of Sydney.

Geertz, C. (1973). *The Interpretation of Cultures: Selected Essays*. New York: Basic Books.

Gilchrist, P., & Wheaton, B. (2011). Lifestyle Sport, Public Policy and Youth Engagement: Examining the Emergence of Parkour. *International Journal of Sport Policy and Politics, 3*(1), 109–131.

Heelas, P., Woodhead, L., Seal, B., Szerszynski, B., & Tusting, K. (2005). *The Spiritual Revolution: Why Religion Is Giving Way to Spirituality*. Oxford: Blackwell.

Howell, O. (2008). Skatepark as Neoliberal Playground: Urban Governance, Recreation Space, and the Cultivation of Personal Responsibility. *Space and Culture, 11*(4), 475–496. https://doi.org/10.1177/1206331208320488

Lombard, K.-J. (2010). Skate and Create/Skate and Destroy: The Commercial and Governmental Incorporation of Skateboarding. *Continuum, 24*(4), 475–488. https://doi.org/10.1080/10304310903294713

MacKay, S., & Dallaire, C. (2014). Skateboarding Women: Building Collective Identity in Cyberspace. *Journal of Sport & Social Issues, 38*(6), 548–566. https://doi.org/10.1177/0193723512467357

Ostwalt, C. (2012). *Secular Steeples: Popular Culture and the Religious Imagination* (2nd ed.). London: Bloomsbury.

Scholes, J. (2012). The Coca-Cola Brand and Religion. In T. R. Clark & D. W. Clanton Jr. (Eds.), *Understanding Religion and Popular Culture: Theories, Themes, Products and Practices* (pp. 139–156). London: Routledge.

Taylor, B. (2007). Surfing into Spirituality and a New, Aquatic Nature Religion. *Journal of the American Academy of Religion, 75*(4), 923–951. https://doi.org/10.1093/jaarel/lfm067

Thorpe, H. (2014a). Action Sports for Youth Development: Critical Insights for the SDP Community. *International Journal of Sport Policy and Politics, 8*(1), 91–116. https://doi.org/10.1080/19406940.2014.925952

Thorpe, H. (2014b). *Transnational Mobilities in Action Sport Cultures*. New York: Palgrave Macmillan.

Thorpe, H., & Rinehart, R. (2013). Action Sport NGOs in a Neo-Liberal Context: The Cases of Skateistan and Surf Aid International. *Journal of Sport & Social Issues, 37*(2), 115–141. https://doi.org/10.1177/0193723512455923

Transworld Skateboarding. (2015). 20 Questions: Manny Santiago. *Transworld Skateboarding*.

Turner, E. (2012). *Communitas: The Anthropology of Collective Joy*. New York: Palgrave Macmillan.

Wheaton, B. (2013). *The Cultural Politics of Lifestyle Sports*. New York: Routledge.

Wheaton, B. (2015). Assessing the Sociology of Sport: On Action Sport and the Politics of Identity. *International Review for the Sociology of Sport, 50*(4–5), 634–639. https://doi.org/10.1177/1012690214539160

Wilder, C., & Rehwaldt, J. (2012). What Makes Music Christian? Hipsters, Contemporary Christian Music and Secularization. In T. R. Clark & D. W. Clanton Jr. (Eds.), *Understanding Religion and Popular Culture: Theories, Themes, Products and Practices* (pp. 157–171). London: Routledge.

Index

© The Author(s) 2020
P. O'Connor, *Skateboarding and Religion*,
https://doi.org/10.1007/978-3-030-24857-4